E-discovery: An Introduction to Digital Evidence

Amelia Phillips

Ronald Godfrey

Christopher Steuart

Christine Brown

CENGAGE
Learning·

Australia · Brazil · Japan · Korea · Mexico · Singapore · Spain · United Kingdom · United States

**E-discovery: An Introduction
to Digital Evidence**

**Authors: Amelia Phillips, Ronald Godfrey,
Christopher Steuart, Christine Brown**

Vice President, General Manager:
Dawn Gerrain

Product Manager: Nick Lombardi

Senior Director, Development:
Marah Bellegarde

Senior Content Developer:
Michelle Ruelos Cannistraci

Developmental Editor: Lisa M. Lord

Marketing Director: Lisa Lysne

Senior Market Development Manager:
Mark Linton

Marketing Coordinator: Elizabeth Murphy

Production Director: Wendy Troeger

Production Manager: Andrew Crouth

Content Project Manager: Allyson Bozeth

Art Director: GEX

Technology Project Manager:
Jonathan White

Media Editor: Bill Overocker

Chapter Image: ©Photosani/Shutterstock

For product information and technology assistance, contact us at
Cengage Learning Customer & Sales Support, 1-800-354-9706

For permission to use material from this text or product,
submit all requests online at **cengage.com/permissions**
Further permissions questions can be emailed to
permissionrequest@cengage.com

Library of Congress Control Number: 2012953691

ISBN-13: 978-1-111-31064-6

ISBN-10: 1-111-31064-5

Course Technology
20 Channel Center Street
Boston, MA 02210
USA

Cengage Learning is a leading provider of customized learning solutions
with office locations around the globe, including Singapore, the United
Kingdom, Australia, Mexico, Brazil, and Japan. Locate your local office at:
international.cengage.com/region

Cengage Learning products are represented in Canada by
Nelson Education, Ltd.

For your lifelong learning solutions, visit **www.cengage.com/coursetechnology**

Purchase any of our products at your local college store or at our
preferred online store **www.cengagebrain.com**.

Visit our corporate website at **cengage.com**.

Printed in the United States of America
1 2 3 4 5 6 7 16 15 14 13

Brief Contents

Table of Contents

CHAPTER 3
E-discovery Planning and Tools 53

CHAPTER 4
Experts: The Right Person for the Right Job 81

Introduction

Welcome to *E-discovery: An Introduction to Digital Evidence*. E-discovery is the process of applying the traditional legal discovery process to digital evidence, which can include documents, e-mails, pictures, Web pages, and databases and can be found on hard drives, cell phones, DVDs, CDs, and laptops. It's a fast-growing field, as 90% of all office documents are electronic. Therefore, the amount of evidence consisting of electronically stored information (ESI) that must be gathered for investigations and legal proceedings can be staggering, as is the task of converting paper documents to digital format. A major challenge in this field is that it involves both the legal field and the highly specialized IT field, and those in both fields have to learn new terms and familiarize themselves with new issues and procedures.

This hands-on, how-to training guide gives you an overview of the technology used in e-discovery in civil and criminal cases. From discovery identification and preservation to collection, processing, review, production, and trial presentation, this practical book covers what you need to know about e-discovery. Throughout the book, you have the opportunity to work with e-discovery tools, computer forensics tools, processing and review platforms, and trial presentation software.

This book draws on the Sedona Principles, which are helpful guidelines for handling electronic evidence. It's also organized to reflect the phases of the Electronic Discovery Reference Model, a useful collection of guidelines for shrinking huge amounts of data down to a manageable level. Real-life examples and case law are woven throughout the book, revealing potential pitfalls and offering suggestions on best practices and cost management. Finally, the Enron bankruptcy scandal and resulting charges are used as the basis for several projects in this book that have you apply what you've learned to a real-life—and complex—case.

Intended Audience

This book is intended to reach a wide range of students. One of its main objectives is to emphasize the need for better communication and cooperation between legal and IT personnel. It's useful for a variety of professionals, including paralegals, attorneys, forensics experts, judges, policy makers, and business owners. The advent of mobile devices and cloud storage has forced people who didn't have to worry about technology to take a close look at their effects on the way business is conducted. Regulations such as the Freedom of Information Act and the Sarbanes-Oxley Act affect e-mail, social media content, and many other types of information. As more content is available via the cloud, the more important it is to be aware of the potential hazards.

This book can be used as just a reference, or it can be a guide to learning about the new territory of e-discovery. More technically minded students will want to explore the software used in Chapters 3 through 6, and others will be more interested in seeing state, federal, and international laws work together by using the database introduced in Chapter 8. The examples used in this book are very real and give you a good idea of how a simple e-mail or text message can affect a company.

Chapter Descriptions

Here's a summary of the topics covered in each chapter of this book:

- **Chapter 1**, "Introduction to E-discovery and Digital Evidence," defines e-discovery and digital forensics and explains factors affecting the collection of digital evidence. This chapter also summarizes the U.S. Federal Rules of Civil Procedure, Federal Rules of Criminal Procedure, and Federal Rules of Evidence. The chapter also describes other laws and regulations related to digital evidence and e-discovery.

- **Chapter 2**, "A Brief History of E-discovery," gives you an overview of the origin of e-discovery and the laws and language surrounding it. You learn about the types of metadata and see e-discovery from both civil and criminal perspectives. This chapter also explains how to use the FIRAC method to read and analyze a case and how to use the Electronic Discovery Reference Model to process electronic evidence. Finally, you get an overview of the case study used in several chapters of this book—the Enron scandal.

- **Chapter 3**, "E-discovery Planning and Tools," introduces the tools used for e-discovery. You examine how to select a scope for gathering e-discovery and review important planning factors, including cost and time considerations. You get a useful overview of a variety of software tools that can be used for e-discovery and a chance to practice using one tool to conduct a search for e-mail data.

- In **Chapter 4**, "Experts: The Right Person for the Right Job," you learn about the skills needed for e-discovery and digital forensics, how to learn these skills, and when they're used during civil and criminal litigation. You explore some certification programs and free tool-centered training options. Best practices in e-discovery team staffing are also reviewed, including outsourcing and using court-appointed neutrals, such as special masters and forensics mediators.

- **Chapter 5**, "Digital Evidence Case Flow," gives you an overview of the litigation process from the perspective of a defendant responding to a discovery request. You learn procedures for preserving and producing e-discovery data in accordance with the Electronic Discovery Reference Model as well as best practices for the model's different phases. Finally, you learn about using Web-based repositories to process data and have a chance to use iCONECT to identify and review e-discovery data.

- In **Chapter 6**, "Case Study: From Beginning to Trial," you learn the technical and legal aspects of initiating civil and criminal litigation from the plaintiff's perspective, including prelitigation investigation practices. Next, you learn about common e-discovery legal documents and review project management tasks, including sampling for quality control and metrics for cost management. You also learn about fact-finding procedures and pretrial motions. Last, technical and nontechnical trial presentation factors are reviewed, and you have a chance to explore a virtual courtroom.

- **Chapter 7**, "Information Governance and Litigation Preparedness," explains how to be prepared for litigation. You examine current acts and laws and their impact on both organizations and people and revisit the Information Governance Reference Model as a way to approach the requirements of these acts and laws. You also learn how to plan for multiple litigations and evaluate an organization's readiness to respond to a litigation hold.

- **Chapter 8**, "Researching E-discovery Case Law," examines case law—state, federal, and international—related to e-discovery issues. Laws such as the FRE might not specifically address what can be done with new technology. So when technology outpaces existing court rulings, case law is the main source of information, although not always the most reliable or accurate. This chapter describes resources for researching case law and describes some issues in multijurisdictional and international cases.

- **Chapter 9**, "The Future of E-discovery," gives you an overview of what lies ahead for e-discovery. With technological advances such as the cloud, social networking, tweets, and blogs, what will e-discovery encompass? What will its global impact be? What do legal and technical professions need to do to be ready for the challenges ahead? This chapter also describes privacy laws and how new technology is affecting them and gives you an overview of anti-forensics methods.

- **Appendix A**, "Resources," summarizes some useful resources for exploring the field of e-discovery in more depth.

Features

To help you understand e-discovery, this book includes many features designed to enhance your learning experience:

- *Chapter objectives*—Each chapter begins with a comprehensive list of the concepts to be mastered. This list gives you a quick reference to the chapter's contents and serves as a useful study aid.

- *Figures and tables*—Numerous screenshots show you how to use several e-discovery tools and help you understand searching and organizing procedures. In addition, a variety of diagrams aid you in visualizing important concepts. Tables are also used in the book to organize information in an easy-to-grasp manner.

- *Chapter summary*—Each chapter ends with a summary of the concepts introduced in it. These summaries give you a helpful way to review the material covered in each chapter.

- *Key terms*—All terms introduced in a chapter with bold text are gathered in a key terms list with definitions at the end of the chapter as another way to review key concepts.

- *Review questions*—The end-of-chapter assessment begins with review questions that reinforce the main concepts in each chapter. Answering these questions helps ensure that you have mastered the chapter's objectives.

- *Hands-on projects*—Although understanding the theory behind e-discovery is important, nothing can improve on real-world experience. To this end, each chapter has hands-on projects aimed at giving you experience with e-discovery tools. These projects use Windows 7 and software supplied on the book's DVD or downloaded from the Internet.

- *Case projects*—At the end of each chapter are case projects that give you the opportunity to apply the skills and knowledge you gained in the chapter to real-world settings.

- *Software and student data files*—This book includes a DVD containing student data files, examples of standard legal documents, and free software demo packages for use with activities and projects in the chapters. (Additional software demos or freeware can be downloaded to use in some projects.) The following software companies have graciously agreed to include their products with this book: Sherpa Software (Discovery Attender) and IPRO (eScan-IT). To check for newer versions or additional information, visit their Web sites at *www.sherpasoftware.com* (Sherpa Software) and *http://iprotech.com* (IPRO).

Additional Materials

Additional materials designed especially for you might be available online for your course. At the *CengageBrain.com* home page, search for the ISBN of your title (from the book's back cover) using the search box at the top of the page. This will take you to the product page where these resources can be found.

Text and Graphic Conventions

Additional information has been added to this book to help you understand what's being discussed in the chapter. Icons throughout the book alert you to these additional materials:

The Note icon draws your attention to additional helpful material related to the subject being covered.

Tips offer extra information on resources and how to solve problems.

Caution icons warn you about potential mistakes or problems and explain how to avoid them.

The Hands-On Projects icon indicates a chapter's hands-on projects.

Case Projects icons mark end-of-chapter case projects, which are scenario-based or research assignments that ask you to apply what you have learned.

Instructor's Materials

A wide array of instructor's materials is available with this book. The following supplemental materials are available for use in a classroom setting. All these supplements are provided to instructors online and can be downloaded by going to *login.cengage.com*. After you have logged in to your Cengage faculty account, you can find instructor resources by searching for the ISBN of your title (on the book's back cover).

- *Electronic Instructor's Manual*—The instructor's manual that accompanies this book includes additional instructional material to assist in class preparation, including suggestions for discussion topics, information for setting up for hands-on projects, and solutions to all end-of-chapter material, including review questions, hands-on activities, and case projects.

- *ExamView Test Bank*—This Windows-based testing software helps instructors design and administer tests. In addition to generating tests that can be printed and administered, this full-featured program has an online testing component that allows students to take tests at the computer and have their exams graded automatically.

- *PowerPoint presentations*—This book comes with Microsoft PowerPoint slides for each chapter. They're included as a teaching aid for classroom presentation, to make available to students on the network for chapter review, or to be printed for classroom distribution. Instructors, please feel free to add your own slides for additional topics you introduce to the class.

- *Figure and table files*—All figures and tables in the book are available in the Instructor Companion Site. Similar to the PowerPoint presentations, they're included as a teaching aid for classroom presentation, to make available to students for review, or to be printed for classroom distribution.

E-discovery Software Tools

A few software tools, listed previously under "Features," are supplied with this book. Software used in other projects (as well as useful programs you might want to investigate) can be downloaded from the Internet as freeware, shareware, or free demo versions:

Because Web site addresses change frequently, use a search engine to find the following software online if URLs are no longer valid. Efforts have been made to provide information that's current at the time of writing, but things change constantly on the Web. Learning how to use search tools to find what you need is a valuable skill for any career.

- Concordance: Download from *www.lexisnexis.com/concordance-downloads/*.
- FTK Imager: Download from *www.accessdata.com*.
- iCONECT: Connect and use this tool at *www.ferc.gov/industries/electric/indus-act/wec/enron/info-release.asp*.
- OpenOffice: Download from *www.openoffice.org*.
- TrialDirector: Download a demo version from *www.indatacorp.com/trialdirectoreval*.

Hardware and Software Requirements

Following are the hardware and software requirements for hands-on projects:

- 2 GB RAM recommended
- Microsoft Windows 7 or later
- Microsoft Office, Open Office, or Libre Office
- An Internet connection and a Web browser

About Ipro Tech, Inc.

Founded in 1989, Ipro is a global leader in the development of advanced software solutions used by legal professionals to streamline the discovery process. Ipro's worldwide network of corporations, law firms, government agencies, and legal service providers rely on Ipro's Enterprise platform to organize, review, process, and produce litigation data of vast sizes and complexity levels more efficiently and cost effectively than ever before. For more information on Ipro, visit *www.iprotech.com*.

About Sherpa Software

Sherpa Software is a leading provider of cloud and on-premises information management and e-discovery solutions. Sherpa's award-winning software, services, and support have helped more than 3000 companies worldwide to address e-mail and file management challenges. Attender Online, Sherpa's new SaaS platform, extends information governance capabilities across a wide variety of electronically stored information (ESI), including files, e-mail, and SharePoint. Sherpa solutions for archiving, e-discovery, PST management, compliance, and policy enforcement are designed to be practical, reliable, and affordable. Sherpa Software, headquartered in Pittsburgh, PA, is an IBM Business Partner and a Microsoft Certified Partner. For more information, please visit *www.sherpasoftware.com*.

About the Authors

Amelia Phillips graduated from Massachusetts Institute of Technology with B.S. degrees in astronautical engineering and archaeology and an MBA in technology management. She's working on her PhD in computer security. After working as an engineer at the Jet

Propulsion Lab, she worked with e-commerce sites to prevent the theft of credit card numbers. She designed certificate and AAS programs for community colleges in e-commerce, network security, digital forensics, and data recovery. Amelia is a Fulbright Scholar who taught at Polytechnic of Namibia in 2005 and 2006 and is currently Chair of the Pure and Applied Science Division at Highline Community College in Seattle.

Ronald Godfrey is the secretary of the Computer Technology Investigators Network and an adjunct computer forensics instructor at Highline Community College in Seattle. He holds a Computer Forensic Examiner/Data Recovery certificate from Highline Community College and has training in MCSE networking, Department of Defense computer security, and other computer forensics courses. He's employed by a Fortune 50 company as a computer forensics examiner. His e-discovery work on a class-action lawsuit has been noted in national law journals. In addition, as a NASA employee and a U.S. government contractor, he was responsible for ensuring compliance with computer security requirements. He is also a Marine Corps veteran who served with the military police in Yuma, Arizona.

Christine Brown is a Certified Fraud Examiner and president of Essen Resources, Inc., an e-discovery consulting firm. She has more than 10 years' experience in civil and high-profile criminal litigation and provides training in case management, using forensics, litigation, and trial presentation software. In addition, she has more than 10 years' experience in commercial lending as a senior credit officer for a Fortune 50 company. Christine is a board member of the Computer Technology Investigators Network and serves on advisory boards of the University of Washington School of Law and UW Department of Computer Science and Engineering continuing education programs.

Christopher Steuart is vice president and general counsel of ITForensics, Inc. in Seattle. He has worked as a computer forensics examiner and an information systems security specialist for a Fortune 50 company and the U.S. Army. He is also general counsel for Computer Investigators Northwest. He has presented digital forensics seminars in regional and national forums, including the American Society for Industrial Security, Agora, and Northwest Computer Technology Crime Analysis Seminar.

Acknowledgements

Amelia Phillips: Thank you to my co-authors for dealing with my ups and downs. Special thanks go to our development editor, Lisa Lord, for patiently guiding us through the perils of topic sentences and paragraph flow. Thanks to Steve Helba, who has moved on to a new job. To all my dear friends for supporting me through this—listening to me moan and complain while trying to put together a first edition of a hot new topic—*thank you*. And last but not least, to my dear aunties—Bernice McRae, who will be 100 this year, and Dr. Eunice Grisby—who were both teachers and encouraged me to become one.

Ron Godfrey: Thank you to my wonderful wife, Polly, for sacrificing a lot of lost time while I spent countless evenings behind the keyboard. To my grandma-in-law, Carline Green from Kellogg, Idaho: You've been my biggest fan, always asking me about the book and patiently waiting for your autographed copy. You'll be getting my first copy for your 92nd birthday this year. All my love and thanks to you both!

Christine Brown: My sincere gratitude goes to my coauthors and especially our editor, Lisa Lord. I would also like to thank Bill Nelson, Brett Shavers, Dave Matthews, and the other digital forensic mentors who share their knowledge through the Computer Technology Investigator's Network

(CTIN). It was through CTIN that I gained a thorough understanding of metadata and, therefore, more insight into managing e-discovery. I would also like to thank the judges, prosecutors, and defense attorneys who work with the often taxing and complex federal criminal cases that come through the Western Washington Federal Courts. They have given me great appreciation for the work they do. Last, I would like to thank Larry Bunn and the many paralegals I have met throughout the years who shared their knowledge, patience, and grace.

The authors and publisher would like to extend their thanks to the following reviewers, who reviewed the manuscript during different stages of development: Richard Austin, Kennesaw State University; James Bode, State College of Florida; Jan Fuller, Computer Forensics Investigator, Redmond Police Department; Robert Holtfreter, Central Washington University; Herbert Mattord, Kennesaw State University; Anne Peterson, Duquesne University School of Law; David Pope, Ozarks Technical Community College; and Mike Whitman, Kennesaw State University.

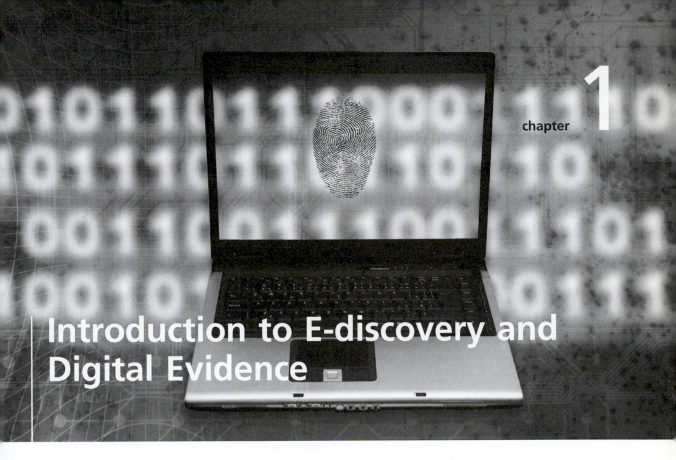

chapter 1

Introduction to E-discovery and Digital Evidence

After reading this chapter and completing the exercises, you will be able to:

- Define e-discovery and digital forensics
- Describe types of digital evidence
- Explain factors affecting digital evidence collection
- Summarize U.S. federal rules on digital evidence
- Describe other laws related to digital evidence and ESI discovery

In this chapter, you learn what's meant by the terms e-discovery, digital forensics, and digital evidence. It also gives you an overview of types of digital evidence, describes methods to acquire this evidence (including concepts such as chain of custody), and explains some tools you use in this book. You're introduced to the U.S. Federal Rules of Civil Procedure (FRCP), the Federal Rules of Evidence, and the Federal Rules of Criminal Procedure, and then learn about other rules and policies for digital evidence, including the Sedona Principles, the 2006 amendments to the FRCP, state amendments, United Nations law, and Canadian law.

An Overview of E-discovery

E-discovery is the process of applying the traditional legal discovery process to electronic evidence. The discovery process is the compulsory disclosure of data, facts, and documents in civil and criminal cases. Electronic evidence encompasses any **electronically stored information (ESI)**, which can include documents, e-mails, pictures, Web pages, and databases. ESI can be found on hard drives, cell phones, DVDs, CDs, and laptops. One way to look at e-discovery is as a form of **data mining**, a method companies use to gather information about customers or vendors. E-discovery can be thought of as data mining to gather information for use in legal proceedings.

Digital forensics—formerly known as computer forensics—is a scientific method for extracting data or evidence from a digital device, including an active network. Following this process ensures that the information will stand up to scrutiny in court. Digital forensics is carried out by people with expertise in a variety of devices, hardware, computer operating systems (OSs), and network OSs. The field of digital forensics is divided into two specialties: device forensics and network forensics. In device forensics, the expert retrieves items such as existing files, deleted files, hidden files, encrypted data, and more. Network forensics deals with network intrusion and hackers. In these cases, the focus is on finding out how intruders got into the network and making sure they're locked out so that business can continue. In addition, network forensics investigators might want to re-create the attack and analyze the "digital footprints" as part of the forensics process. As shown in Figure 1-1, digital forensics can be considered to overlap with e-discovery or viewed as a subset of e-discovery, depending on your perspective. Those who specialize in network forensics don't consider e-discovery, to be related to their jobs. On the other hand, e-discovery experts might often have to call on device forensics experts to retrieve data and, therefore, view this task as a subset of their jobs.

A key difference between e-discovery and digital forensics is that in digital forensics, investigators are typically looking for incriminating or exculpatory evidence in a criminal case or an investigation of a corporate policy violation. One type of evidence they examine is OS information, such as **MAC times**. MAC stands for "modified, accessed, and created" dates and times. In a Linux OS, investigators might be able to retrieve the time files were deleted and who deleted them. Although Linux is just beginning to become popular in the United States, it's widely used in other parts of the world because it's open-source software and, therefore, more economical. Finding information such as file access times and network logins is part of the forensics process. These tasks vary from e-discovery's focus on identifying and preserving ESI.

In e-discovery, Company A asks Company B for data pertaining to a litigation matter. A large percentage of digital forensics examiners come from law enforcement or similar backgrounds,

E-discovery perspective   **Digital forensics perspective**

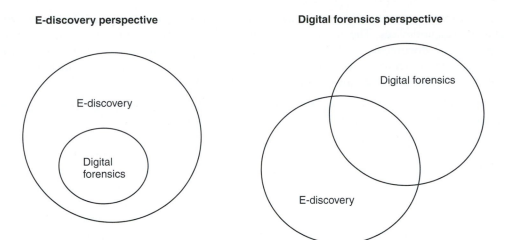

Figure 1-1 The relationship between e-discovery and digital forensics
© Cengage Learning 2014

so the idea of asking the opposing side for the information isn't considered part of the digital forensics process. In a digital forensics case, investigators might not know ahead of time what they're looking for; an e-discovery case, such as a trademark or contract dispute, is well defined, and investigators know exactly what information they need. In digital forensics cases, they might also be conducting the investigation without the knowledge of the parties being investigated but have the necessary warrants and subpoenas.

As recently as 30 years ago, a company sued by another would have to turn over boxes full of documents that an investigator had to examine one by one. Today, most documents are in digital form, whether generated by software or scanned.

Although e-discovery emerged from the corporate world, it spans civil, criminal, and bankruptcy cases. This book discusses several cases covering these three areas. A major challenge of e-discovery is that it involves both the legal field and the highly specialized IT field. Those on either side have to learn new terms and familiarize themselves with new issues and procedures. Cases have been thrown out because the judge or attorney didn't have a background in digital terminology, although more people in the legal profession are becoming adept in technology-related fields. Similarly, an IT person might not understand the law and legal proceedings. Therefore, bridging the gap between the legal and IT fields is a primary goal of this book.

What Is Digital Evidence?

Digital evidence is data or files in digital format that pertain to a civil or criminal complaint. ESI and electronically transmitted information fall under this definition. Both can be used in court as evidence in much the same manner as gunshot residue or DNA gathered from a bloodstain. In any home or office, many common items contain digital evidence. Toaster ovens, cameras, watches, fax machines, copiers, and phones—all contain processors or electronic storage devices. The storage device in a standard office copier, for example, can contain critical documents with sensitive information. How many companies have sold or donated old copiers with that sensitive information still stored on them? In a legal case, a copier's storage device might be considered digital evidence.

Taking this example a step farther, many employees can now access companies' copiers from remote locations. In fact, anyone on a network might be able to send a print job to both a printer and a copier, and storage devices on both machines can contain an immense amount of information. Also, think about the number of e-mails a company sends and receives every day. A decade ago, e-mail was still a mere convenience. Today, it's a major means of communication. All sorts of corporate, legal, and privacy issues are negotiated via e-mail, text messages, blogs, instant messages, and other digital forms of communication. Today, even traffic tickets can be issued by using only the digital evidence from cameras set up at intersections. Likewise, toll road fees are collected by scanning digital passes on windshields. Digital evidence is everywhere. However, to stand up in court, the evidence must be acquired by following procedures; there must be accountability.

Types of Digital Evidence

Digital evidence comes in a variety of types: DVDs, audiotapes, phone SIM cards, memory sticks, and a host of other forms. As mentioned, almost anything—even a refrigerator—can contain digital evidence. In examining digital evidence, a distinction must be made between data and metadata. **Data** is the actual information being retrieved, such as a letter or document. **Metadata** is information about that data—that is, data about data. For example, when people use social media sites to post photos, the metadata in a picture file can tell investigators the type of camera used, the date the photo was taken, and the GPS coordinates where the photo was taken (as shown in Figure 1-2), assuming the GPS locator was turned on.

Data

Metadata from the photo

Camera: Canon Powershot A1100 JS
Date Taken: January 13, 2013 11:55 am
Type: JPEG
Size: 2.51 MB
GPS: Lat + 19.769 Long-156.021

Figure 1-2 Data and metadata
© Cengage Learning 2014

Imagine what could be done with this information. If it's deemed authentic in a court of law, a person could have difficulty denying he or she was in a particular location at a particular time. The GPS information is embedded in the photo in the Exchangeable Image Format (EXIF) header. To access a photo's metadata, do the following:

1. Open Windows Explorer.

2. Right-click the photo file and click Properties.

3. Click the Details tab. Figure 1-3 shows the typical details that are displayed.

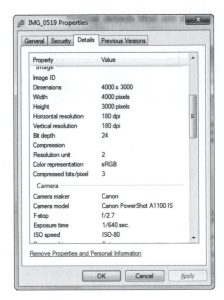

Figure 1-3 Photo metadata in the Properties dialog box
Source: Microsoft, Inc.

Metadata is also available for documents. Figure 1-4 shows a Word document, `Olmec Artifact Purchase Agreement.docx`, open in AccessData Forensic Toolkit. Notice the files associated with this document in the lower pane. Selecting the `app.xml` file displays what's shown in Figure 1-5. The investigator can see how long the person had the document open, how many words and characters are in the document, and so forth.

As you'll see in upcoming chapters, metadata has to be handled carefully. Recent court cases have cited or fined companies for deleting metadata. In addition, an investigator should be aware that including metadata showing who worked on a particular file might violate other standards, such as privacy regulations and copyright infringement.

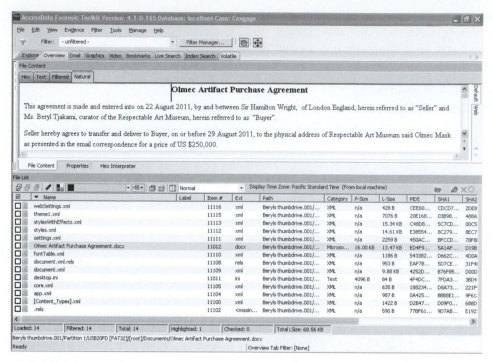

Figure 1-4 Olmec Artifact Purchase Agreement viewed in AccessData Forensic Toolkit
Source: AccessData, Inc.

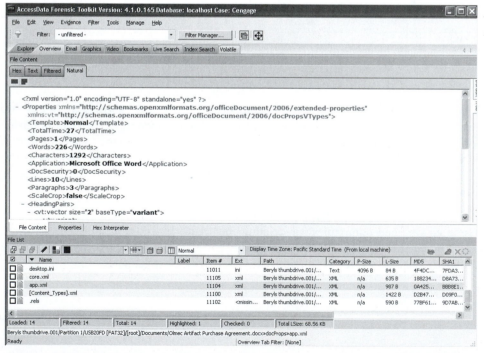

Figure 1-5 Metadata about the `app.xml` file
Source: AccessData, Inc.

Cloud Computing and Digital Evidence

Cloud computing is on-demand access to remote servers, software, applications, and other computing resources. Traditional computing models consist of client computers with servers hosting software applications and storing data. The cloud offers a new model in which client software, data, and computing resources are hosted remotely, so client computers and servers don't need to support as many on-site resources.

The National Institute of Standards and Technology (NIST) defines the cloud in terms of three service models and four deployment methods. The service models are software as a service (SaaS), platform as a service (PaaS), and infrastructure as a service (IaaS). The deployment methods are private, community, public, and hybrid (National Institute of Standards, 2011). Newer methods and terms are being introduced at a steady pace, so the terms are updated constantly.

Although NIST uses the term "models" for both service and deployment, this book uses the terms "service models" and "deployment methods."

SaaS refers to applications provided for customers. Typically, these applications are for users who want the convenience of accessing their files from any location and sharing them with any location. For example, businesspeople traveling from one country to another might create a security risk caused by storing confidential files on their laptops or portable devices, which are vulnerable to theft or intrusions. In addition, carrying encrypted devices across international borders can cause delays in crossing. If files are stored in the cloud instead of on a device, however, these potential problems aren't an issue. People can access their files via the cloud and make changes with SaaS applications. Two common SaaS providers are Dropbox and Google Docs.

PaaS is more of a company or business model. Users select a platform (the OS installed by the cloud provider) and then install their own applications or software. As for the IaaS model, users get what's commonly referred to as a "bare metal" environment (using the cloud provider's equipment but having no physical access to the equipment), where they install their own OSs, applications, tools, and so forth.

As for deployment methods, the most secure is the private cloud, assuming it's implemented correctly. The client—usually a large multinational corporation—owns the hardware and has physical access to it. Depending on the service level agreement, a cloud provider might even ensure that no other customers or clients use the same physical hardware.

A community cloud is for people or organizations with similar interests, of similar business types, or in nearby geographic areas. With a public cloud, a person's files are on the same physical machine as another person's or organization's files. Finally, in a hybrid cloud, users keep some files in the cloud and the rest on their own servers for data security reasons. Some organizations further divide cloud computing with a public/private distinction. NASA, for example, might put pictures taken from outer space on the public cloud so that anyone can view them but put the specifics of a shuttle launch on a private cloud. Figure 1-6 shows the cloud models and deployment methods.

How does the cloud affect e-discovery? If an employee is in Los Angeles but the data she's accessing is stored in London, New York City, Bangkok, and Cape Town, which location's laws apply when collecting e-discovery evidence? Does it depend on where the employee is located or where the evidence is located?

Cloud service models   **Deployment methods**

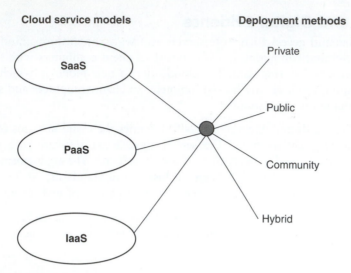

Figure 1-6 Cloud service models and deployment methods
© Cengage Learning 2014

Factors Affecting Evidence Acquisition

How digital evidence is acquired affects the way it's presented and accepted in court. In civil cases, in which one company is suing another, evidence is acquired by issuing a request for production, meaning one company requests physical or electronic documents or other information, and the second company produces them. In criminal cases, the procedure is different. It requires strict adherence to **chain of custody**, use of search warrants, subpoenas, and so forth. The objective of a strict chain of custody is to make sure evidence hasn't been tampered with or altered in the process. Civil cases generally don't require search warrants. Because the companies are facing the prospect of a lawsuit and have most likely received a document retention order, it's their responsibility to store and produce documents or files. The police or the FBI, who need a search warrant, aren't involved. However, be aware that a civil case can develop into a criminal case, and vice versa.

Chain of custody is the path evidence takes from the time the case opens until it goes to court or is dismissed.

A well-known example of a case type changing is the O.J. Simpson case. When the prosecution couldn't convict him of murder, the victim's families filed a civil suit.

In digital forensics cases, an investigator requests or obtains a hard drive or other digital media device, transports it to a forensics lab, creates a forensic image of the device, and begins to analyze the image. A forensic image copies a device down to the smallest component. (For a magnetic device, such as a hard drive, the copy includes the disk sector level.) Using this copy, an investigator can retrieve deleted files, deleted e-mails, file fragments, and other information that isn't included in a simple file copy. As you see later in the discussion of e-discovery, unless a team is investigating a criminal case, it's typically not looking for deleted files or e-mails.

Until recently, forensic analysis was rarely done on a physical device unless a write blocker was used for the initial examination to determine whether the device should be analyzed more thoroughly. In some cases, the volume of digital evidence retrieved requires an evaluation to see whether a full forensic image is needed. Write blockers prevent data from being copied back to the evidence item inadvertently. Data on digital devices can be corrupted easily, so care must be exercised at every step. Because hard drives are increasing in size and can contain huge amounts of data, live acquisitions are common now. In the past, forensic copies were made on machines that were powered down or "dead"; live acquisitions are done while machines are running. The question before the courts now is that the results of a live acquisition might not be reproducible, which violates forensics standards. A final determination on this method hasn't been clarified yet.

Overview of E-discovery Tools

Deduplication of files is common in civil cases. It's explained in more detail in Chapter 2, but simply put, it means that if the same e-mail is sent to 20 people in an e-discovery case, typically only one copy is retained. Keeping only one copy in a criminal case, however, could destroy or alter the case timeline. As a result, forensic tools and e-discovery tools differ in the scope of what they do. One goal of this book is to introduce you to a variety of tools so that you can choose the one that's best suited to the task.

Demonstrating all the e-discovery tools on the market is impossible, but you learn about the major ones in Chapter 3. E-discovery is growing rapidly, so the number of available products is expanding. AccessData and Guidance Software, for example, have e-discovery tools that work independently or with their digital forensics tools. If a company has its own digital forensics team and legal team, their efforts can be correlated easily with these tools. The legal team can view results at the e-discovery level, and if it determines that more analysis is needed, the technical forensics team can search deeper, retrieving deleted files and examining metadata in more detail.

In this book, you use several e-discovery tools, including Sherpa Software Discovery Attender (a tool for analyzing e-mail; demo version included on the DVD), IPRO, eScan-IT, Eclipse, Trial Director by InData Corporation (a helpful tool in preparing for court presentations), and iCONECT by iCONECT Development, LLC, which is useful for cases involving multinational corporations.

Cost and Time Considerations

In selecting software, a company involved in e-discovery has to consider cost and time. Large multinational corporations can afford expensive packages to handle e-discovery tasks, but small and medium firms that have the same need for e-discovery tools might not have the budget. Freeware and shareware products can be used reliably, but they might be difficult to learn, and technical support might not be readily available. As with any software selection, weighing cost against the time required to learn and maintain a product can be difficult.

The time needed to process and produce documents and other information is also important. In the past, a typical stalling tactic was responding to a request for production by sending a truckload of boxes filled with paperwork, making the task of processing it daunting and time consuming. Today's document storage, however, gives "volume of information" a new meaning. Files might not take up as much space physically as a truckload of boxes, but an overwhelming amount of information can be stored on a terabyte hard drive in the cloud. Going through all the information could take a legal team several years.

One way to reduce the cost and time of an investigation substantially is to ask "Which information is needed to prove a case?" Is it in an e-mail from a particular two-month period? Is it in documents containing a certain word or phrase? Instead of requesting "everything," strive to be more specific and narrow the focus of what you're searching for.

Federal Rules in U.S. Courts

In the United States, three sets of rules govern the conduct of federal court cases:

- Federal Rules of Civil Procedure (FRCP)
- Federal Rules of Criminal Procedure (FRCrP)
- Federal Rules of Evidence (FRE)

In addition, each state has its own interpretation of these rules, discussed later in this chapter. Attorneys and paralegals can quote these three sets of rules by heart the same way IT personnel can tell you the range of nonroutable IP addresses. The following sections give you an overview of each set of rules.

The Federal Rules of Civil Procedure

The U.S. Supreme Court established the **Federal Rules of Civil Procedure (FRCP)** in 1938 for resolving issues or legal matters in civil cases at the federal level. Early U.S. laws were based largely on British Common Law as well as several other sources. As a result, before the FRCP, courts were formal and detailed in their approaches to procedure. FRCP Rule 1 states, "These rules ... should be construed and administered to secure the just, speedy, and inexpensive determination of every action and proceeding" (U.S. Supreme Court, 2010). Notice the terms "speedy" and "inexpensive," a marked contrast to the lengthy formal proceedings that had been the norm.

As of this writing, the FRCP consists of 86 rules and several supplemental rules. The rules are updated periodically, with the next major update projected for 2013.

Those involved in e-discovery or digital evidence need to be aware of the following rules:

- FRCP Rule 16. Pretrial Conferences; Scheduling; Management
- FRCP Rule 26. Duty to Disclose; General Provisions Governing Discovery
- FRCP Rule 33. Interrogatories to Parties
- FRCP Rule 34. Producing Documents, Electronically Stored Information, and Tangible Things, or Entering onto Land, for Inspection and Other Purposes
- FRCP Rule 37. Failure to Make or to Cooperate in Discovery; Sanctions

For more information on the FRCP, see *www.uscourts.gov/uscourts/ RulesAndPolicies/rules/2010%20Rules/Civil%20Procedure.pdf*.

The Federal Rules of Criminal Procedure

The U.S. Supreme Court also established the **Federal Rules of Criminal Procedure (FRCrP)** in 1944 (which took effect in 1946) to make criminal law in the United States more consistent from state to state. These rules specify that when dealing with someone charged in a criminal case, the rights of the individual take precedence. The main rule that addresses digital evidence is Rule 41, Search and Seizure, which states how evidence can be obtained in a criminal investigation. In addition, with the rise of digital evidence in criminal proceedings, the Department of Justice created the document "Searching and Seizing Computers and Obtaining Electronic Evidence in Criminal Investigations" in 2002. It outlines in thorough detail how to deal with search warrants, what can be seized at what point in time, what procedures to use, and other pertinent details when dealing with electronic evidence.

The Federal Rules of Evidence

The **Federal Rules of Evidence (FRE)**, drafted by the U.S. Supreme Court, became law in 1975 and applies to all evidence presented in court for both civil and criminal cases. The FRE contains 11 articles; however, like the FRCP and the FRCrP, only certain ones have a major impact on how e-discovery is performed:

- Article I, Rule 103. Rulings on Evidence
- Article I, Rule 105. Limited Admissibility
- Article I, Rule 106. Remainder of Related Writings or Recorded Statements
- Article IV. Relevancy and Its Limits—This article is certainly important, given the large amounts of digital information that must be sifted through during e-discovery.
- Article VII. Opinions and Expert Testimony—This article is crucial in cases involving digital evidence. Technical experts are the ones who extract and verify the data. Without them, much of digital evidence is useless.
- Article VIII. Hearsay—This article is relevant to the admissibility of e-mail messages.
- Article X. Contents of Writings, Recordings, and Photographs—This article applies even in the digital world.

The introduction of digital evidence hasn't changed the FRE extensively. It does, however, add many new interpretations of old rules. The hearsay rule is one example. Text messages and e-mails might prove the recipient had been told something; however, these messages can't prove the information's veracity.

For more information on the FRE, see *www.uscourts.gov/ RulesAndPolicies/rules/2010%20Rules/Evidence.pdf*.

Rules and Policies Governing Digital Evidence

In the context of e-discovery, digital evidence is called ESI. Distinctions between ESI and conventional information are based not only on the sophistication of the technology used to create, present, or understand information, but also on the ways computers create, modify, communicate, store, and dispose of digital information. There are also key differences in the ways computers have evolved and continue to evolve. Computers are faster, smaller, and more mobile than 10 or even 5 years ago.

Perhaps the most important aspect of ESI—and the most obvious one to those who deal with it—is its overwhelming volume. A major cause is that digital information isn't simply moved from one place to another; more typically, it's stored in several physical locations or, with the emergence of the cloud, moved to indeterminate locations as a result of load balancing. As mentioned, location can affect which country's laws are in effect for e-discovery purposes. Sending an e-mail, for example, initiates an electronic process that replicates data from one computer on other computer systems—potentially anywhere in the world—until it reaches the destination and is rendered as an image on the recipient's screen. The e-mail is likely to be replicated on several locations on the sender's and recipient's systems as well as on network e-mail servers and their backup media.

Load balancing is done to ensure that one server or CPU isn't handling all computational needs. In the cloud, this process might involve moving data from one server to another throughout the world, depending on the cloud provider.

Sedona Principles

The Sedona Principles were created by a group of lawyers and other professionals as guidelines for handling electronic documents. As you'll see throughout this book, the amount of data involved in litigation can be unmanageable. Having a method for dealing with it can save time and money. Although the Sedona Principles aren't specifically referenced in state and federal laws about the conduct of discovery relating to ESI, they're the basis for guidelines on handling e-discovery. Many states and Canadian provinces are in the process of amending their rules or adopting the Sedona Principles as their guide for court decisions.

For more information on the Sedona Principles, see *www.thesedonaconference.org*.

The Sedona Principles, which emerged from a conference held in 2007, are designed to ease the burden of e-discovery and speed the process along. The document lists 14 principles that link to the FRCP. For example, the first principle states that organizations are obligated to preserve ESI that's relevant to anticipated litigation (The Sedona Conference Working Group, 2011).

In today's business world, it's not a question of whether a company will end up in litigation; it's a question of when. The Sedona Principles lay the framework for what a company must do to prepare for possible litigation. A major motivating factor can be found in the document's opening statement:

> *In Spring 2002, many of us who would later form the Sedona Conference Working Group on Electronic Document Production began discussing ways to develop "best practices" for lawyers to follow in addressing electronic document production. The collapse of Enron and Arthur Andersen, and the legislative response to these events, including the Sarbanes-Oxley Act of 2002, confirmed the importance of handling electronic document production in a defensible manner. Litigants, particularly entities that generated large volumes of electronic information, did not know what obligations might apply to the preservation and production of electronic data and files* (The Sedona Conference Working Group on Electronic Document Retention and Production, 2010).

FRCP Amendments

In April 2006, the U.S. Supreme Court ordered that the FRCP be amended to address e-discovery. These amendments require companies to protect data that might be subject to discovery in anticipated litigation. Although the Sedona Principles aren't referenced in the FRCP, the Advisory Committee on Civil Rules incorporated them into the 2006 amendments, and the Sedona Principles have been referenced in at least 13 federal court cases since 2007. The FRCP amendments pertaining to ESI are directed at several aspects of e-discovery, thereby recognizing the unique nature of ESI.

Although the 2006 amendments are called "e-discovery amendments," the actual wording in the rules refers to ESI.

For examples of court cases referencing the Sedona Principles, use a search engine for commentary on *Cache La Poudre Feeds, LLC v. Land O'Lakes, Inc.* (D. Colo. 2007), and *Calixto v. Watson Bowman Acme Corp.* (S.D. Fla. 2009).

Rule 26(b)(2) permits parties to avoid discovery of ESI that isn't reasonably accessible because of "undue burden or cost," meaning the time and money involved might be unfair to parties involved in the litigation. Although the FRCP doesn't define the phrase "reasonably accessible," case law has offered some guidance. For instance, information in readily usable formats, such as Microsoft Word or Excel documents, has been deemed "reasonably accessible." It includes information on active hard drives, servers, and disks as well as systematically organized and easily retrievable backup tapes or disks. Data deemed not reasonably accessible includes electronic information that has to be converted or recovered to be usable. This typically includes data backup tapes that aren't systematically organized or indexed as well as data that's deleted, damaged, or fragmented.

For example, the responding party in a lawsuit might claim that the request for information isn't reasonable and would entail prohibitive costs. Say that Company A requests the ESI, and Company B claims the information isn't reasonably accessible. Company A can demand that Company B prove that producing the ESI would cause undue hardship in time and money. If challenged by Company A in a motion to produce the evidence, Company B bears the burden of establishing that the data isn't reasonably accessible. Courts have generally found that the burden rests with the party objecting to the production of metadata or ESI to show undue hardship or expense. If Company B proves hardship, the court might nonetheless order discovery if Company A shows good cause and is willing, among other things, to bear the cost of accessing the data.

For information on a case involving undue hardship, see *Romero, Camesi v. Univ. of Pittsburgh Med. Ctr.* (W.D. Pa. 2010).

TIP

From a responding party's standpoint, having data readily accessible lowers litigation costs. The simple fact is that if a company's data is readily accessible for analysis, time and money are saved. Later chapters introduce the concept of information governance, which is advocated in the Sedona Principles. In short, it means that ESI management contributes to cost management. When seeking information, a company should consider having computer forensics capabilities available to counter the producing party's claims that the data is inaccessible and, therefore, not subject to discovery.

FRCP Rule 34(b) dictates that ESI be provided in the form in which it's ordinarily maintained or a form that is readily usable. If the requesting party specifies another form in which the ESI should be produced, the producing party has the option of objecting to the form and proposing its own form. The FRCP rule provides dispute-resolution procedures if the parties can't agree.

Good ESI management requires keeping information in a readily usable form or at least in the form in which it's usually maintained. Organizations that image or scan paper documents and replace them with electronic documents in PDF and TIFF formats not only improve information-management capabilities, but also are better positioned to handle litigation. For example, imaging allows advanced indexing and searching capabilities. Keep in mind, however, that an image can't be indexed, given that it's only a picture. In this context, indexing means all words in a document are put into alphabetical order so that paralegals, investigators, and so forth can search on specific keywords.

To index the text, **optical character recognition (OCR)** software must be used. This software examines scanned pictures of documents and "recognizes" the letters and numbers in them. Converted documents—ones that have been scanned from hard copy to electronic format—contain layers. One layer is the "image"—the PDF or TIFF that's produced. The second layer is the OCR text. What often happens is that a paralegal accidentally produces an electronic document that has been redacted, but the OCR text of redacted material is still readable in certain software. This problem happens often and is discussed more in Chapter 5. Similarly, in criminal cases, the prosecution might generate digital forensic reports with PDF files included and argue that everything is "searchable" when, in fact, PDF files can't be searched without further processing.

The term "redact" means excluding parts of a document because of confidentiality, trade secrets, or other reasons related to disclosure.

NOTE

Not all PDF files have searchable text. For this feature to be available, the text feature has to be turned on when the document is converted to PDF.

The use of PDF-scanned copies instead of a **native file** is a point of major dispute in the legal industry. A native file has the file structure defined by the application used to create it (The Sedona Conference Working Group on Electronic Document Retention and Production, 2010). Some people advocate native files as being more efficient because the contents of a native Word document or Outlook e-mail, for example, can be searched without further processing, and the metadata still exists. If you convert these documents or e-mails into PDF or TIFF files, however, the text is stripped away when the image is created and then added back with OCR. Many in the industry think this process is wasteful in terms of time and needlessly expensive. The resulting images, if ordinarily maintained, comply with Rule 34(b) because they're in a usable format. However, turning word-processing files or e-mails into imaged documents also removes metadata, which can contain the creation date, deletion date, originating IP address, and other vital information. Recent court rulings have established the requirement to maintain both searchability and metadata.

Requesting parties should know their systems' capabilities and the ESI formats that can be used. This information should be gathered as early as possible in the discovery process. Lawyers have a duty to preserve evidence that's relevant to actual or potential litigation. Courts have often imposed sanctions for spoliation—a party wrongfully destroying evidence. Amended FRCP Rule 37(f) states that the court can't impose sanctions when a party destroys ESI as part of its "routine, good faith" operations. This "safe harbor" provision is perhaps the strongest reason to include ESI retention and destruction procedures in an ESI management program.

As a result of the "safe harbor" provision, companies should put their ESI retention policies in writing and be able to prove that the policies are followed routinely. Because the safe harbor provision doesn't protect a party if ESI was destroyed in anticipation of litigation, procedures should also be drafted to place a "litigation hold" on all potentially relevant ESI. An effective litigation hold procedure notifies all relevant people in an organization about what must be retained and for how long. Reminders and updates about the litigation holds should be circulated periodically.

A litigation hold, discussed in more detail in Chapter 6, restricts a company from deleting, changing, or purging data or backups.

The FRCP clarifies how ESI is handled during discovery, which affects how organizations manage creating, storing, using, and retrieving ESI. Businesses can prepare for litigation by identifying the information that's most relevant and taking steps to manage ESI, such as categorizing, indexing, and storing it in a way that makes it searchable and readily accessible.

ESI should be destroyed routinely in accordance with published policies when it's no longer legally or operationally required. ESI retention might be affected by IRS rules, corporate policy, or ongoing projects, and policies and procedures need to be in place to handle these requirements. Finally, all other policies and procedures—such as those related to e-mail, privilege protection, security, and privacy—should be reviewed and updated as needed.

State Amendments Related to ESI

In the United States, many states have adopted provisions to address some procedural issues in e-discovery. Texas led the way by developing rules for ESI discovery, even before the FRCP amendments were passed. In several other states, courts have used local rules, and rules have been enacted by counties or townships based on their authority to control litigation in their courtrooms. By general principle, states' rules can be more stringent than federal rules but not more lenient.

As of this writing, 30 states have adopted e-discovery procedural rules reflecting the 2006 FRCP amendments. Eight other states have some form of e-discovery legislation pending. In June 2009, for example, California adopted comprehensive e-discovery legislation. Although largely based on the FRCP amendments, these rules include features specific to the California legal system. This doesn't mean states don't have existing case law in which verdicts were handed down. Existing case law sets the precedents for e-discovery in states such as Georgia or Nevada, for example.

For more information on state rules of civil procedure, see *www.discoveryresources.org/library/case-law-and-rules/state-rules/annotated-list-of-state-rules-of-civil-procedure*.

United Nations Model Law

With multinational corporations, cases can span several continents and jurisdictions. When dealing with war tribunals and settling conflicts, the United Nations must process thousands of documents to determine what happened and who was responsible. The UN Model Law was developed as a result of burgeoning e-commerce in the late 1990s. Its focus was on civil procedures, and it has been used as a basis for both digital forensics law and e-discovery worldwide.

At *www.uncitral.org/uncitral/en/uncitral_texts.html*, you can find information on e-commerce law, international payments, international transport of goods, and other topics of interest to any company doing business on a multinational scale.

European Corporate Laws

Most European companies that conduct business in the United States feel compelled to improve their internal controls in response to U.S. demands, and retaining e-mail records is part of that internal control process. The European Union's 8th Company Law Directive, sometimes described as the European Sarbanes-Oxley Act, is slightly different from the U.S. Sarbanes-Oxley Act. For example, a "material weakness" under the Sarbanes-Oxley Act is reported to the market at large. A "material weakness" in a company indicates that a financial mistake or misrepresentation wouldn't be detected with current procedures. Under the EU law, the weakness would be reported to the auditing committee and approved by the corresponding government, and the company would have the opportunity to correct the issue. However, foreign corporations that want to be listed on U.S. stock exchanges generally have to comply with the Sarbanes-Oxley provisions.

For years, European government authorities have sought more accountability and transparency among European companies and more uniformity in their financial reporting. The EU has amended the following directives:

- 4th directive 78/660/EEC (annual accounts of specific type of companies)
- 7th directive 83/349/EEC (consolidated accounts)
- 8th directive 84/253/EEC (auditor and audit committee requirements)

In accordance with the amendments, EU member countries are now enacting new laws. Informally known as "EuroSox," these laws reflect modern expectations that companies should open themselves to more scrutiny through disclosure and third-party review. The implementation details vary by country, but the broad message is clear: Publicly held companies and government-run larger public enterprises are expected to use strict internal controls.

E-mail is a critical component of internal controls. (Keep in mind that the term "e-mail" can now include instant messaging, text messages, and other forms not yet developed.) E-mail records can show who was delegated responsibility for what and when. They can also show the terms of a business deal or deter a company from engaging in fraudulent accounting practices. Therefore, e-mail records need to be maintained in a format that facilitates searching so that third parties can review transactions and relationships after the fact. As internal controls become more important in Europe, processes for archiving, deleting, and tracking business e-mails and text messages need to be improved.

Canadian Rules of Civil Procedure

Canada recognized the need for rules on e-discovery in 2006, when a subcommittee of the Canadian Discovery Task Force was created to deal with e-discovery issues in the Canadian courts. The result was a list of best practices or guidelines for e-discovery (E-Discovery Canada, 2011). The group went on to create additional guidelines under the Sedona Canada Working Group. In 2010, Ontario amended its rules of civil procedure to address ESI discovery. In many litigation categories—especially finance, intellectual property, and energy policy—actions (in which one party sues another for monetary damages) in U.S. federal courts have parallel actions in Canadian courts, particularly the Superior Court of Justice in Ontario.

No other Canadian jurisdiction, to date, has actually mentioned the Sedona Principles or the Sedona Conference by name in its rules. Although Ontario's amended rule mentions "electronic discovery" only once, what it has done is mandate that the legal profession be well informed about e-discovery and accept responsibility for retrieving and producing ESI. One of the biggest challenges in this field is the legal profession's lack of knowledge in dealing with e-discovery, so Ontario's amendment is a good start in addressing this problem.

When creating the Canadian Sedona Principles, the Sedona Canada Working Group considered the Ontario Rules of Civil Procedure and the Quebec Civil Code rules for "paper discovery" and found them useful. The Canadian principles recognize the differences between electronic and paper document production and the relevance of case law that has been applied. How can courts and parties use case law guiding the discovery of paper documents in the context of electronic documents? Appreciating the differences between electronic and paper documents allows courts and parties to break from past practice, when appropriate, yet achieve the fundamental objective of securing the "just, most expeditious and least expensive" (Ontario Government, 2011) resolution of litigation.

In 2010, Ontario created a rule that formalizes the requirement for a discovery plan (Sedona Canada Working Group, 2011), mandating that parties in a lawsuit agree on and file with the court a written discovery plan within 60 days after the close of pleadings. The Ontario E-Discovery Implementation Committee (2010) created the following checklist for preparing a discovery plan:

(3) The discovery plan shall be in writing and shall include,

(a) the intended scope of documentary discovery under rule 30.02, taking into account relevance, costs and the importance and complexity of the issues in the particular action;

(b) dates for the service of each party's affidavit of documents (Form 30A or 30B) under rule 30.03;

(c) information respecting the timing, costs and manner of the production of documents [under Rule 30.01(1) "documents" includes electronic data] by the parties and any other persons …

(d) any other information intended to result in the expeditious and cost-effective completion of the discovery process in a manner that is proportionate to the importance and complexity of the action.

The subrule after this passage recommends consulting the Sedona Canada Working Group principles (2011) and making sure written discovery plans take into account all the Sedona Canada Principles. Therefore, lawyers must be knowledgeable about rules related to ESI. Important principles include the following:

- *Principle 1*—Electronically Stored Information is discoverable.
- *Principle 3*—Parties must consider their obligation to take reasonable and good faith steps to preserve potentially relevant Electronically Stored Information as soon as litigation is reasonably anticipated.
- *Principle 4*—Parties and counsel should meet and confer soon and on an ongoing basis.
- *Principle 5*—Parties should be prepared to produce relevant Electronically Stored Information that is reasonably accessible in terms of cost and burden.
- *Principle 8*—Parties should agree early on the format in which Electronically Stored Information will be produced.
- *Principle 9*—Parties should agree on or seek judicial direction to protect privilege and confidentiality.

The Sedona Canada principles and the Ontario checklist for preparing a discovery plan are now part of Canadian procedural law. These documents don't explicitly discuss metadata, but Principle 8 mentions agreeing on a method of production that preserves metadata. It also defines metadata along with other terms pertaining to electronic discovery.

In comparison, the amendments to the U.S. FRCP specify that parties discuss ESI preservation, forms of production, and procedures for dealing with its disclosure and outline a procedure for requesting a specific format of electronic production, a procedure for objecting to the requested form, and a default minimum standard for a form of production, under Rule 34(b). Despite all the details, there are still disputes and misunderstandings about the implications of these amendments. Nothing in the U.S. FRCP tells lawyers to refer to the Sedona Principles. In fact, most U.S. litigators haven't even read the Sedona Principles, even though the document is only 102 pages. One objective of this book is to explore how following these principles can save companies both time and money.

Rule 29.1.05 of the Ontario Rules of Civil Procedure states that the court can refuse to award any costs if parties haven't agreed on a discovery plan and can impose cost penalties and other sanctions. In the Ontario legal system, "costs" generally means more than it does in the United States, as the losing party must pay a sizeable portion of the winning party's legal fees.

As another example of ESI-related law in Canada, Nova Scotia has amended its rules of civil procedure to address ESI without expressly mentioning the Sedona Principles; these amendments are more similar to the amendments to the U.S. FRCP.

Chapter Summary

- E-discovery is the accumulation of digital information for use in litigation. It can be considered data mining for legal purposes. Digital forensics is a specialized subset of e-discovery that has had a focus in criminal cases; however, it's also used in civil and bankruptcy cases.

- Digital evidence can be found in a variety of forms and on a wide range of devices, including cars, cameras, cell phones, printers, copiers, computers, and PDAs.

- The methods used to acquire digital evidence can determine its effectiveness and admissibility in court. Policies and procedures should be in place to address this issue.

- A number of software tools are designed for e-discovery. They include digital forensics tools with e-discovery overlays, such as AccessData and Guidance Software, and tools specifically designed for e-discovery, such as iCONECT and eScan-IT.

- Cost and time considerations affect what tools a company selects for e-discovery and ESI retention. Commercial products offer technical support and are well documented, but they're expensive. Freeware and shareware tools might not be worth the reduced cost because of the time required to learn them and the lack of technical support.

- In the United States, the Federal Rules of Civil Procedure, along with laws such as the Sarbanes-Oxley Act, govern the ways in which corporations preserve data and data is presented or exchanged during legal proceedings.

- The Federal Rules of Evidence in the United States have a direct bearing on how evidence is collected and maintained in both civil and criminal cases.

- The Federal Rules of Criminal Procedure take into account the U.S. Constitution and defendants' rights under the Bill of Rights.

- The UN Model Law was created to address e-commerce investigations. Although it's specific to civil procedures, it lays a foundation for digital forensics and e-discovery worldwide.

- Other countries, such as Canada and members of the European Union, have similar rules and procedures for governing e-discovery.

- The Sedona Principles are 14 rules that can be used to help mitigate costs and preserve evidence in e-discovery cases.

Key Terms

chain of custody   The path evidence takes from the time the investigator obtains it until the case goes to court or is dismissed.

cloud computing   On-demand access to remote servers, software, applications, and other computing resources; generally categorized as software as a service (SaaS), platform as a service (PaaS), and infrastructure as a service (IaaS).

data   Numbers, documents, files, and other information (such as e-mail) stored on digital devices.

data mining   A method used to gather information about customers or vendors by monitoring what they purchase, examining where they go on a Web site, and culling other ESI. *See also* electronically stored information (ESI).

digital evidence   Any evidence that's stored or transmitted electronically or in a digital format.

digital forensics   The application of traditional forensics procedures to acquiring computer evidence; used to retrieve existing files, deleted files, hidden data, and metadata on digital devices. *See also* metadata.

e-discovery   Gathering ESI for use in litigation. *See also* electronically stored information (ESI).

electronically stored information (ESI)   Any information stored electronically or in a digital format.

Federal Rules of Civil Procedure (FRCP)   Rules created by the U.S. Supreme Court that govern the way evidence and procedures are applied in civil cases.

Federal Rules of Criminal Procedure (FRCrP)   Rules created by the U.S. Supreme Court to ensure that defendants' constitutionally guaranteed rights are protected in federal court cases.

Federal Rules of Evidence (FRE)   Rules that spell out how evidence can be gathered and used in both civil and criminal cases in U.S. federal courts. Created by the U.S. Supreme Court and signed into law in 1975, the FRE have been updated and amended by both Congress and the Supreme Court.

MAC times   Metadata that specifies dates and times that a file was modified, accessed, and created. *See also* metadata.

metadata   Information about data that can be used to determine when a file was created, modified, accessed, or destroyed.

native file   A file in the originating application's format, such as a Microsoft Word document in .doc or .docx format.

optical character recognition (OCR)   A software method of scanning a picture (or a scanned picture of a document) and converting the characters to text.

Review Questions

1. The Sarbanes-Oxley Act was enacted to protect investors and preserve corporate data. True or False?

2. The Sedona Principles link closely to which of the following?
    a. Amendments to the U.S. Constitution
    b. FRCP
    c. Bill of Rights
    d. U.S. Constitution

3. If the responding party in a lawsuit considers the retrieval of requested information to be excessive, the requesting party can do which of the following?
    a. File an additional lawsuit
    b. File an injunction
    c. File a petition to have the responding party prove that producing the requested information would be costly and unreasonable
    d. File for cause

4. The European Union's 8th Company Law Directive is sometimes called what?

5. In Canada, all ESI is considered "discoverable." True or False?

6. Metadata can help in determining which of the following?
    a. Type of camera used to take a picture
    b. Contents of a letter
    c. Relationship between parties
    d. Position held by parties to a lawsuit

7. If a party to a lawsuit destroys ESI, it's guilty of which of the following?

    a. Deduplication

    b. Spoliation

    c. Causation

    d. Conversion

8. In Canada, what must parties to a litigation have within 60 days of a filing?

    a. A formal meeting

    b. A written discovery plan

    c. Results of the e-discovery

    d. Nothing is required.

9. In e-discovery, indexing refers to what?

    a. Putting documents in Bates numbering order

    b. Putting documents in order by date

    c. Listing all terms in a document alphabetically

    d. Listing documents by author

10. In many jurisdictions, text messages, instant messages, and similar information are treated as which of the following?

    a. Metadata

    b. Data

    c. E-mail

    d. Documents

11. Files in the originating software's format are called which of the following?

    a. Original files

    b. Native files

    c. Edit files

    d. Converted documents

12. The FRE apply only to civil cases. True or False?

13. The Canadian Sedona Principles state that all electronic evidence is discoverable. True or False?

14. In the IaaS cloud computing model, customers can do which of the following? (Choose all that apply.)

    a. Install their own OSs.

    b. Install their own applications.

    c. Have physical access to machines.

    d. Remove unneeded applications.

15. OCR is typically used after a file is scanned to allow indexing terms or words in the document. True or False?

16. The Sarbanes-Oxley Act pertains to data and information that must be maintained for publicly traded companies. True or False?

17. In the United States, when law for a new technology doesn't yet exist, which of the following is used?

    a. Statutory law

    b. Case law

    c. Supposition

    d. The case is dismissed.

18. The Sedona Principles lay out best practices for ESI. True or False?

19. A file's MAC times can be used to do which of the following? (Choose all that apply.)

    a. Determine when a file was last accessed.

    b. Determine whether a file was modified.

    c. Access all a file's metadata.

    d. Specify the file's owner.

Hands-On Projects

The hands-on projects in this chapter are meant to encourage you to begin looking at different tools for working with e-discovery. Data files for this chapter are on the DVD in the Chapter01\Projects folder. If necessary, be sure to copy them to your working directory on your machine before starting the projects.

Hands-On Project 1-1

In this project, you use a standard digital forensics tool, AccessData FTK Imager, to learn about its basic functions and features.

Check with your instructor to see whether FTK Imager has been loaded on your lab machine. If not, follow Step 1 of this project.

1. If necessary, start a Web browser, and go to **www.accessdata.com**. Click **Support, Product Downloads**, and then **FTK IMAGER**. Download FTK Imager version 3.1.2. When it's finished, double-click the downloaded file, and follow the installation instructions, using the default settings.

2. Start FTK Imager, and click **File, Add Evidence Item** from the menu.

3. Click **Image File**, and then click **Next**.

4. In the Select File dialog box, click **Browse**, and then find and click the **Beryls thumbdrive.001** file. (*Tip:* Be sure to select the file with the .001 extension.) Click **Finish**.

5. Expand the directory listing in the Evidence Tree pane at the upper left (see Figure 1-7).

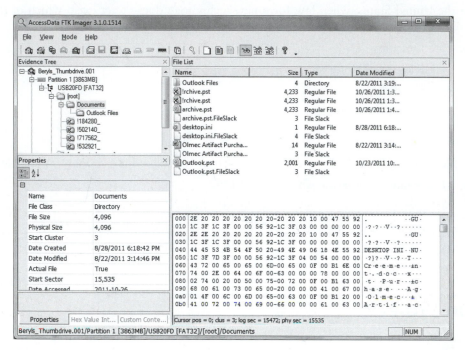

Figure 1-7 FTK Imager with Beryls thumbdrive.001 open
Source: AccessData, Inc.

6. Click items in each of the four panes of this application to get an idea of what kind of information is available.

7. Write a one- to two-page paper summarizing what information can be gleaned from the data shown for this file.

Hands-On Project 1-2

Using a search engine or other source, such as *www.download.com*, find an e-discovery product that can be used for photo files, and then download and install it. Take a picture with your cell phone or digital camera and download it to your machine. Open the photo in the software you downloaded. What do you see? What information are you supposed to be able to retrieve? In what ways does the software meet or exceed your expectations? Write a one- to two-page evaluation of the results.

MetadataTouch has a free download available at *www.download.com*.
Use the search term "ediscovery tool."

TIP

Hands-On Project 1-3

Using a search engine, find an e-discovery tool designed to work with e-mail. Download and install it on your machine. Copy a `.pst` or similar e-mail file from your computer. Open the file in the software you downloaded. What do you see? What information are you supposed to be able to retrieve? In what ways does the software meet or exceed your expectations? Write a one- to two-page evaluation of the results.

Try Emailchemy, which you can find at *www.download.com* with the search term "email ediscovery."

TIP

Case Projects

CASE PROJECTS

Case Project 1-1

Using your library, a standard search engine, or Westlaw (the online legal library, if you have access to it), find a case that applies the Sarbanes-Oxley Act. In what ways was this act useful to the parties involved? Would the case have gone to trial if the act didn't exist? Justify your answer and be sure to cite your sources in your conclusions.

Case Project 1-2

Using your library (or Westlaw, if you have access to it), find an article that discusses the Sedona Principles. Which of the 14 principles do you find practical, and which do you have concerns about? Write a one- to two-page paper summarizing your thoughts.

Case Project 1-3

Compare two or three items from the Canadian Rules of Civil Procedure and the U.S. FRCP. In what ways are they similar, and in what ways do they differ? How would e-discovery be affected if one party were in the United States and one were in Canada? Which rules do you think would apply?

References

E-Discovery Canada. Canadian e-Discovery Portal - Background. Lexum—Canadian e-Discovery Working Group, June 2011, *www.lexum.com/e-discovery/*.

National Institute of Standards. "NIST Definition of Cloud Computing." Gaithersburg, MD, 2011: U.S. Department of Commerce.

Ontario Government. Rules of Civil Procedure, RRO 1990, Reg 194. Ontario, Canada, 2011.

Sedona Canada Working Group. Canadian e-Discovery Portal, April 2011, *www.lexum.com/e-discovery/*.

Ontario E-Discovery Implementation Committee. Ontario Bar Association, 2010, *www.oba.org/en/publicaffairs_en/e-discovery/default.aspx*.

Rothstein, B. J., R. J. Hedges, and E. C. Wiggins. *Managing Discovery of Electronic Information: A Pocket Guide for Judges*. Washington, DC, 2007.

The Sedona Conference Working Group on Electronic Document Retention and Production. The Sedona Conference, September 2010, *www.thesedonaconference.org*.

U.S. Supreme Court. Rules and Forms in Effect. United States Courts, 2010, *www.uscourts.gov/RulesAndPolicies/rules.aspx*.

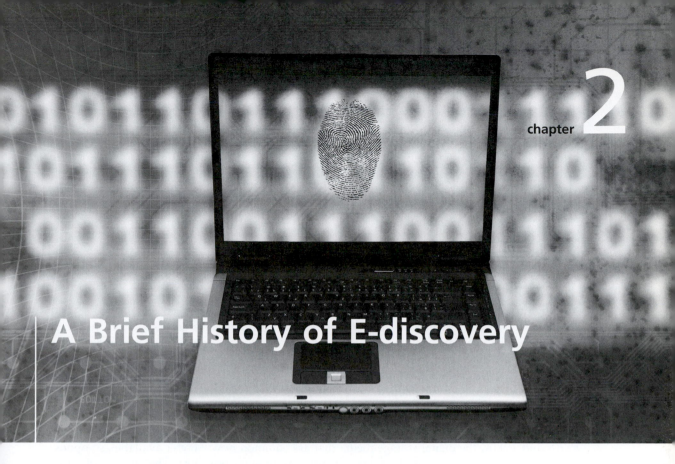

chapter 2

A Brief History of E-discovery

After reading this chapter and completing the exercises, you will be able to:

- Describe the origins of e-discovery as well as the laws and language surrounding it
- Define types of metadata
- Describe e-discovery from a civil and a criminal perspective
- Use the FIRAC legal analysis method to read a case
- Use the Electronic Discovery Reference Model

This chapter examines the roots of e-discovery and laws enacted in the past four decades to deal with the mounting challenge of electronically stored information (ESI). Next, you learn about the different types of metadata and how it's used in e-discovery and legal cases. Because e-discovery is used in both criminal and civil cases, this chapter also explores these two perspectives and how they affect the way a case is approached. In addition, because many cases go to trial or are determined based on case law, you need to know how to read and analyze legal cases, so you learn about the FIRAC method to help you with these tasks. Another tool, the EDRM model, is introduced as a method for reducing huge amounts of data and culling what's relevant. Finally, you get an overview of the case studies used in hands-on projects and case projects throughout this book.

When Did E-discovery Begin?

Although the term "e-discovery" is new, the field it represents has been around for several decades. Companies began using computers, in the form of mainframes, to store financial records, purchase orders, and other files in the 1950s. By the late 1960s, universities and the government were the first to make use of the ARPANET, the precursor to the Internet. During the 1970s, computers' use and popularity expanded, and by the mid-1980s, the Internet backbone was developed, and companies around the world began using the Internet.

Computers had an effect on the legal world, too. For example, when lawsuits were filed in the 1970s and 1980s, the digital storage media that are common now weren't available, so opposing sides presented evidence in the form of reams of computer printouts. The amount of information might have been far less than what's produced today, but the stacks of paper were high enough to intimidate opponents. To explain what has led to contemporary e-discovery, the following sections summarize applicable laws that have been enacted.

The Computer Fraud and Abuse Act

The **Computer Fraud and Abuse Act (CFAA)** came into effect to address the growing problem of computers being hacked. Before this act, the Counterfeit Access Device and Abuse Act of 1984 targeted fraud and similar criminal activities involving computers. Until that time, prosecutors had no specific laws addressing **computer abuse**, which is the illegal use of computers or related services to steal or modify data. The U.S. Congress adopted the CFAA in 1986 as an amendment to the 1984 act, which had been deemed too vague in wording and limited in scope.

The CFAA was created as a criminal statute and is referenced as 18 U.S.C. § 1030 (read as "U.S. Code Title 18 Section 1030"). Amendments in 1996 included changing the term "Federal interest computer" to "protected computer" (defined later in this section). As part of the National Information Infrastructure Protection Act of 1996, wording was added to the CFAA to cover extortion that threatens harm to a protected computer. Additional changes were made to the CFAA in 2001 and 2006 with the passage of the U.S. PATRIOT Act. A more recent amendment made as part of the Identity Theft Enforcement and Restitution Act of 2008 allows prosecution if the victim and perpetrator are in the same state (before this act, data had to cross state lines to warrant prosecution) and allows victims of identity theft to seek restitution.

In the 1970s and 1980s, most computers were large mainframes used by the government, banks, insurance firms, and large corporations. (PCs didn't begin to make inroads until the mid-1980s and early 1990s.) These organizations varied in how they managed physical access to mainframes. Some had strict security; others, such as the Massachusetts Institute of Technology (MIT), placed mainframes in open labs. Whatever the setup, most employees and students could access mainframes remotely via Telnet or FTP services. These services weren't designed to be secure, so they did little to prevent hacking. (Most network administrators now disable these services or use secure versions.)

Many data security breaches during this time didn't make it to the front page of the *New York Times* or the *Wall Street Journal*; you could read about them only in technology trade magazines. In the mid-1990s, for example, the story of more than $10 million stolen from accounts at Citibank (PCWorld.com staff, 2001) wasn't aired on major news channels because it might have created a panic along with a rush on banks. Despite data security breaches not being the stuff of network news stories, information from other sources showed the increasing severity of the problem. The accounting firm Ernst & Whinney's 1987 report, for example, stated that U.S. firms were losing from $3 to $5 billion annually to computer abuse (Farlex, 2011). In addition, CERT (the Computer Emergency and Response Team at Carnegie-Mellon University) estimated that computer intrusions increased almost 500% between 1991 and 1994 (Farlex, 2011).

In the 21st century, internal threats are no longer the main source of data breaches. Criminal hackers and online gangs have automated strategies for launching thousands of network attacks a day. A detailed discussion of this problem is beyond the scope of this book, however.

In the early days of the Internet, hackers often broke into networks just to show that they could or to snoop around for information. Their defense attorneys often argued that the data was only "copied," so it wasn't actually stolen. These arguments and counterarguments led to passing the CFAA, which introduced terms such as **protected computer**. A protected computer, according to the CFAA, is one that meets the following guidelines (U.S. Congress, 1996):

> *(A) exclusively for the use of a financial institution or the United States Government, or, in the case of a computer not exclusively for such use, used by or for a financial institution or the United States Government and the conduct constituting the offense affects that use by or for the financial institution or the Government*

> *(B) used in or affecting interstate or foreign commerce or communication, including a computer located outside the United States that is used in a manner that affects interstate or foreign commerce or communication of the United States*

In short, a protected computer is one used by a financial institution or government agency or used for commerce or communication, whether foreign or domestic. In addition, the CFAA covers seven types of computer offenses under Title 18 Section 1030(a):

- Accessing a computer or network without authorization or by exceeding authorization
- Accessing a computer or network to collect financial information, credit information, or other information from a government computer or any protected computer

- Making a computer or network unavailable for its intended use by a department of the U.S. government or another entity

- Transmitting programs, information, codes, or commands to intentionally cause harm or damage to networks or computers

- Accessing information on a computer or network to commit fraud or cause damage, whether intentionally or as a result of reckless actions

- Intentionally obtaining and trafficking in passwords

- Threatening harm to a computer or network for use in extortion or a similar practice

Before the explosion of the Internet in the late 1990s, more than 70% of hackers were members of the organizations they hacked into—hence the CFAA's reference to "exceeding authorization." In other words, an employee might have access to the network to do his or her job, but collecting other employees' login profiles and passwords, for example, exceeds his or her authorization.

 The CFAA assigns fines and prison terms for offenses that include international or government espionage, fraud, identity theft, credit card fraud, and other crimes. To see a table of these offenses and punishments, go to *www.infragard-mo.net/Computer_Crimes_Statute _Summary.htm*.

The timeline in Figure 2-1 gives you an idea of how e-discovery laws have progressed. Although the CFAA took effect in 1986, the first mention of e-discovery didn't occur until 1997, and its first use in the legal field wasn't until 2006.

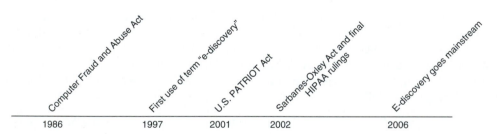

Figure 2-1 Timeline of e-discovery law
© Cengage Learning 2014

One fascinating criminal case in which the CFAA was applied (along with other laws) is described in the book *The Lure* (Schroeder, 2012). It's about two Russian cybercriminals who hacked into companies, schools, and ISPs across the country. The FBI came up with a plan to catch them by setting up a fake start-up security company called Invita in Seattle. Schroeder, a retired Department of Justice Assistant States Attorney who prosecuted the case along with his colleagues, had to follow the law precisely to avoid a charge of entrapment. Therefore, the FBI filed a sealed complaint in Connecticut that charged one of the hackers under U.S. Code Title 18, Section 1951, which deals with commerce and extortion threats, and Title 18, Section 1030 of the CFAA—specifically, items 2, 3, and 7 listed previously. In addition, Rule 15 of the Federal Rules for Criminal Procedure (FRCrP) was applied because it pertains to a detained witness's deposition.

The 1928 case *Olmstead v. United States* (277 U.S. 438) is cited in *The Lure*, too, because it was the first case involving wiretapping, long before the Wire Tap Act of 1968. No search warrants had been obtained before the taps, but because the law at that time addressed only eavesdropping, the wiretapping was deemed legal. Yet again, technology was ahead of the law—a rule of thumb that's evident when examining the history of e-discovery.

EDI, ESI, and E-discovery

To understand the full scope of e-discovery, it's helpful to examine the amount of information companies generate in the course of doing business. When business processes, such as payroll and billing, became automated and large companies began communicating electronically more often, **electronic data interchange (EDI)** was created in the mid-1970s to make exchanging information electronically easier. At that time, an EDI system cost hundreds of thousands of dollars and took six months or more to set up. Documents transmitted via EDI went through a translation program that resulted in a standardized format, so except for situations involving errors or quality review, transmissions between machines could take place without human intervention. EDI's purpose was to automate business transactions, such as purchase orders, request for proposals, invoices, and packing slips. **Value-added networks (VANs)**, which are third-party service providers (similar to ISPs), were also created for transferring EDI documents between companies.

Automating transactions in this way resulted in most business records being in computerized form. EDI became the model for doing business on a global scale. Over the past 40 years, ANSI X12 has been developed as the EDI format. In addition, the United Nations/Electronic Data Interchange for Administration, Commerce and Transport (UN/EDIFACT) is a collection of international guidelines for exchanging electronic information between information systems (UNECE, 2011).

Guidelines for ESI have also become important in the way businesses store and handle information. For example, laws such as the **Sarbanes-Oxley Act** and the **Health Insurance Portability and Accountability Act (HIPAA)** require companies to keep accurate track of electronic documents. Sarbanes-Oxley requires publicly held corporations to hold on to e-mail for five years and be able to turn over data, such as financial records, e-mail, and other documents, when requested by the courts. HIPAA, which was passed in 2001, protects a patient's medical history and specifies other privacy rights (U.S. Department of Health and Human Services, 2011). Before HIPAA, information such as a patient's prescriptions wasn't protected under doctor-patient privilege. Now patients must be notified when their medical records are shared with third parties. Because these records are often placed online or in the cloud these days, HIPAA takes on a more critical role.

The first discussion in a major law journal of e-discovery being used in civil litigation appeared in 1997. In those days, e-discovery was defined as converting paper discovery to digital format so that it could be included in litigation databases. It wasn't until 2001 that e-discovery became a popular topic in civil litigation discussions and articles. (Until recently, most criminal cases focused on digital forensics, but the term "e-discovery" has started being used in criminal cases, too.) The Enron bankruptcy in 2001 and subsequent notable cases involved huge amounts of digital documents (including e-mail), which further spread the use of the term "e-discovery." "Introduction to the Case Study," later in this chapter, gives you an overview of the Enron case. You'll be examining actual files from the case in hands-on projects at the end of this chapter and throughout the book.

The term "Enron bankruptcy" is used in this book to refer to the many cases resulting from the scandal.

Overview of Metadata in E-discovery

As explained in Chapter 1, the term "metadata" means "data about data." It has a variety of definitions, depending on whether the term is used in discussing digital libraries, operating systems, or documents. Although this book focuses on the latter two, you need to know about its use in digital libraries as well because as the industry expands, people who are more familiar with library metadata will be involved in the process. In addition, because e-discovery requires cataloging and organizing information in a manner that allows it to be retrieved easily, ESI can be considered a digital library of sorts. **Metadata Encoding and Transmission Standard (METS)** is the standard used for objects in a digital library. It was developed by the Digital Library Association and is maintained by the Library of Congress. METS profiles are found in a variety of digital records, including PDF files, photographs, and CDs. Corporations can choose to store their digital records in this format, so its role in e-discovery will continue to be important. METS has five categories for metadata in digital documents or books:

- *Descriptive metadata*—This section lists metadata embedded in the document or external descriptive metadata stored on an Internet server.

- *Administrative metadata*—This section describes how a document was created and stored, the original source object, and intellectual property rights.

- *File groups*—This section groups electronic versions of a file, such as TIF versions, PDF versions, and so forth.

- *Structural map*—This section shows users how to navigate all the files.

- *Behavior*—This section deals with any executable portions of documents.

The terms "descriptive," "administrative," and "structural" are associated with ways of storing and retrieving electronic documents, files, and books.

For more details on METS, go to the Library of Congress Web site (*www.loc.gov/standards/mets/METSOverview.html*).

OS metadata is what's stored by computer and network operating systems. As mentioned in Chapter 1, a typical OS keeps track of a file's MAC times, which show when data was modified, accessed, and created. Both an OS and NOS can show investigators the last time a file was accessed and whose login was used to modify a file, for example.

Native digital files and paper documents converted to digital format are considered part of the data that must be examined during e-discovery. However, in civil cases, only the metadata embedded in documents is captured, not the OS or NOS metadata. In these cases, the content of documents and e-mails is more important than the metadata. Metadata is used mainly for organizing the discovery process (such as sorting by chronology, by document author, by document custodian, and so forth). In civil cases, OS metadata is rarely gathered because there's usually no dispute over who has the information (the custodian) or who created it (the author). Therefore, reviewing OS metadata to verify user activity isn't necessary.

Although younger attorneys tend to be computer literate and might have taken courses in e-discovery, many civil attorneys don't know that deleted documents can be retrieved. Even if they do, deleted information might be deemed "not readily accessible" or too costly to retrieve, so it isn't produced. In addition, attorneys might have limited knowledge of MAC times and other OS metadata details. Typically, what's used in e-discovery is metadata embedded in documents, which stores information such as the document's author and the application used to create it.

E-discovery Perspectives

At least four perspectives affect how people approach e-discovery projects:

- The legal professional, who is an attorney or a paralegal who understands the law but might not have knowledge of e-discovery or digital forensics
- The e-discovery professional, who comes from a corporate background
- The digital forensics professional, who understands forensics standards, software, and procedures
- The IT professional, who knows where information and files are stored on OSs and NOSs but might have limited legal knowledge

These widely varying perspectives can often hinder the e-discovery process. For example, here's a typical conversation between a criminal attorney and a civil attorney about a pending case:

Civil Attorney: Hey, John, I hear you just got a big criminal case with a terabyte of evidence. How comfortable are you managing the e-discovery?

Criminal Attorney: E-discovery? Oh, you mean computer forensics? We usually bring in a computer forensics expert with all the special software to go through that for us.

Civil Attorney: Well, yeah, but isn't prosecution providing the other seized discovery in digital format as well?

Criminal Attorney: Sure, they usually give us all the seized documents and photos of other seized evidence in PDF format for review.

Civil Attorney: Yep, that's what we call "e-discovery" on the civil side.

Criminal Attorney: Oh, yeah, I haven't kept up with all the civil discussion on that topic. I've just been too busy with my criminal caseload. Besides, it's only been recently that judges have been applying the civil rules on—oh, what's it called?—ESI to criminal cases. So I guess I'll be brushing up on the Federal Rules of Civil Procedure so I know what the score is on ESI.

Understanding some basic differences between civil and criminal litigation can help guide how you manage digital forensics and e-discovery. What underlies these differences is the type of punishment that can be administered. In criminal cases, guilty defendants are likely to face loss of their liberty or life; in civil cases, no one is incarcerated or sentenced to death. Furthermore, the legal fees in civil cases are usually higher than in criminal cases. As a result, most large civil law firms don't have a criminal law practice, as it's usually less profitable and less socially esteemed. As one attorney exclaimed, "I don't want my good-paying corporate clients sitting in the waiting room with a criminal." Therefore, a civil law firm usually dedicates substantial resources to litigation in service of its clients as well as its profits. Conversely, high criminal caseloads result in publicly funded resources being stretched thin in law enforcement, prosecution, and public defense, which leads to a more focused use of limited resources.

Many law firms work "pro bono" to help those who can't afford an attorney or who rely on public defenders.

E-discovery from a Criminal Perspective

As the previous conversation between the criminal and civil attorneys shows, e-discovery in criminal cases tends to focus on digital forensics (also known as computer forensics). Historically, digital forensics has played a role mostly in criminal cases. OS metadata is analyzed to identify evidence, alterations to evidence, and user activity, and embedded document metadata is used to organize case materials, similar to how discovery is organized in civil cases. Establishing a timeline is crucial in a criminal case because of the need to corroborate people's locations at particular times and determine who had access to what information. Timelines are less important in civil cases.

In criminal cases, the FRCrP comes into play, especially Rule 41: Search and Seizure. This rule specifies how to get and carry out a search warrant and explains motions to suppress evidence and how evidence must be returned. Rule 41 ties directly to the Fourth Amendment, which protects residents from unreasonable search and seizure. The influence of Rule 41 can also be seen in application of the Fourteenth Amendment. The U.S. Supreme Court has interpreted the Equal Protection Clause of the Fourteenth Amendment to mean that states can give citizens more protection under their laws and statutes than is guaranteed by the U.S. Constitution, but not less. Therefore, when working on a case, keep the federal standards for search and seizure in mind, but realize that you might need to meet additional requirements under state law. Because of the expanding nature of electronic evidence, case law has to be used if specific laws don't yet exist.

As mentioned in Chapter 1, the Department of Justice created the document "Searching and Seizing Computers and Obtaining Electronic Evidence in Criminal Investigations" to explain procedures to follow with search warrants. To read this document, go to *www.justice.gov/criminal/cybercrime/docs/ssmanual2009.pdf*.

In the past few years, most practitioners of corporate digital forensics have seen their caseloads expand with an ever-increasing number of e-discovery requests. There are two perspectives on the relationship between e-discovery and digital forensics. E-discovery professionals see digital forensics as a subset of what they do, whereas digital forensics practitioners see the two fields as overlapping. As an example of how the fields are closely linked, suppose Company A steals Company B's intellectual property (IP). It seems to be a simple e-discovery case, with Company A filing a lawsuit against Company B. However, what if evidence comes to light that a Company B employee broke into Company A's network and downloaded confidential information?

This case is now a criminal one, but it's also still part of a civil proceeding. Along with the FRE, which apply in both civil and criminal cases, Rule 41 of the FRCrP plays a key role in determining this case's outcome. Search and seizure law is critical in making sure volatile electronic evidence isn't compromised. Investigators must work with network administrators to view network logs so that they can determine who was logged in at the time of the incident. They might also have to talk to physical staff to find out whose keycard was used to get into a restricted area.

Digital forensics and e-discovery have their own paths to securing evidence. In digital forensics, focusing on hardware, OSs, and network devices (such as routers, servers, and switches) is critical. In addition to data mining, forensics technicians look for deleted files, deleted e-mails, hidden partitions, and hidden files and examine devices' RAM and other places data could be stored in an effort to find clues. In e-discovery, typically investigators already know where data is located.

Some have argued that e-discovery in criminal cases doesn't differ from e-discovery in civil cases. A deciding case in this debate is *U.S. v. O'Keefe* (2008). The argument was that the government is obligated to produce evidence in a criminal proceeding in much the same way that litigants are obligated to produce evidence in a civil proceeding (under the FRCP). The court regarded this argument as reinventing the wheel to take a different tack in handling a criminal matter, citing Rule 34(b) of the FRCP. As discussed by Andrew Goldsmith, National Criminal Discovery Coordinator for the Department of Justice, the Sixth Circuit rejected the reasoning that FRCP 34(b)2(E)(i), which requires producing documents in a specific format, is applicable to criminal cases. The Sixth Circuit noted that federal discovery rules are governed by FRCrP 16, which contains no guidance on producing documents in criminal cases (Goldsmith, 2011). As a result of the Sixth Circuit's action, the O'Keefe case is no longer used as a reference for criminal proceedings, so the distinction between civil and criminal cases to e-discovery remains.

E-discovery from a Civil Perspective

As shown in the conversation between the civil and criminal attorneys, e-discovery and well-established procedures for culling documents are more common on the civil side. Civil attorneys also tend to be more aware of the FRCP, naturally. As discussed in Chapter 1, the FRCP has adapted to the burgeoning use of e-discovery. Most states follow federal law or have adopted their own equivalents. As of this writing, the following states don't have specific rules for e-discovery in civil cases: Alabama, Colorado, Delaware, Florida, Georgia, Hawaii, Kentucky, Missouri, New Mexico, Nevada, Oklahoma, Oregon, Pennsylvania, Rhode Island, South Carolina, South Dakota, Vermont, Washington, Wisconsin, and West Virginia. Several do have existing case law, however. The remaining states have their own rules that map to the FRCP.

Before the dominance of ESI, managing the discovery process involved organizing thousands of paper documents in manila folders. Indexes and master logs were created, which have since been changed to electronic versions. Although hard-copy files still exist, documents are more likely to be in electronic format. However, civil attorneys still use paper as a frame of reference, even though data is usually converted into electronic format for storage. They rarely focus on digital forensics, and they tend to rely on metadata embedded in documents, not OS metadata. However, this focus is changing as the field expands and matures.

Although internal corporate investigations are more of an administrative or policy violation, they usually fall into the civil category instead of criminal. A search warrant isn't needed for these corporate investigations, but an employee can't simply begin investigating a colleague. Most companies have policies specifying that when a complaint is filed, an internal investigation is done to determine whether the situation involves just a policy violation, such as using a company machine to run a personal business, or a more serious act, such as corporate espionage. If criminal activity is discovered during the investigation, the internal investigator stops all work and notifies the corporate legal counsel, who notifies the authorities. At this point, a search warrant is needed.

In the United States, corporate investigations put corporate interests ahead of personal privacy, but this approach isn't always used in other countries or regions, such as the European Union.

As discussed in the previous section, criminal cases require a search warrant and protection of individual rights. Civil e-discovery bypasses many of the search warrant procedures required in criminal cases because lawyers on both sides are involved from the beginning.

Two cases that affected the way corporations handle document retention are the *WorldCom Bankruptcy* (2002) and *Zubulake v. UBS Warburg LLC* (2003). WorldCom, the world's second largest telecommunications company, filed for bankruptcy for $107 billion. The WorldCom CEO was involved in securities fraud, including millions of dollars of personal loans to himself and friends, so the investigation focused on how corporate assets were handled, among other issues. Sarbanes-Oxley was passed as a result of this case and the Enron bankruptcy (discussed later in "Introduction to the Case Study").

The Zubulake case, which was heard before the 2006 FRCP amendments, dealt with gender discrimination. Ms. Zubulake filed an Equal Employment Opportunity Commission (EEOC) case and produced more than 400 pages of e-mail evidence to prove she hadn't been promoted because of her gender, and the company retaliated by firing her two weeks after she filed the case under Title VII (New York State Human Rights Law). The company failed to save some electronic evidence, such as e-mail, on backup tapes. Ms. Zubulake asked that UBS be required to carry the cost burden of the discovery process, but UBS claimed the cost was excessive. In the end, UBS was found at fault for failing to retain the backup tapes and had to bear 75% of the cost of discovery, which totaled almost $300,000. The ruling was groundbreaking in creating requirements for retention that would later become law. The Zubulake case is an excellent example of how case law can lead to actual laws being created to deal with changes in technology as well as the unexpected consequences that develop.

Another case that caused the court system to take a closer look at the cost burden was *Rowe Entertainment v. The William Morris Agency*, 205 F.R.D. 421 (S.D.N.Y. 2002). As a result of this case and the Zubulake case, the courts developed a test consisting of the following seven factors to determine cost shifting:

"Cost sharing" is discussed in Chapter 6. "Cost shifting" means that courts are allowed to shift the financial burden to the party able to afford it.

- The extent to which a request is tailored to discover relevant information
- The availability of information from other sources
- The total cost of production, compared with the amount in controversy
- The total cost of production, compared with the resources available to each party
- Each party's ability and incentive to control costs
- The importance of issues at stake in the litigation
- The benefits to both parties of obtaining the information

How to Read a Case

One challenge for IT personnel involved in e-discovery is reading case law. Because so much of the law pertaining to e-discovery and digital forensics is new or in the process of being interpreted and developed, the only way to determine how to proceed is referring to recent case law. There's the notion that IT people like to do things and legal types like to read. However, IT personnel need to understand how to read a case and determine what issues are relevant.

Law students learn how to use a basic tool called IRAC for reading, analyzing, and writing legal cases. In this book, you use a modification of IRAC called **FIRAC**, which stands for facts, issues, rules and references, analysis, and conclusions. Figure 2-2 shows the FIRAC method. When reading a case, facts refer to who, what, when, where, and how something happened. The issues in the case are why the plaintiff has filed the lawsuit. The rules and references are any laws, acts, or case law that might apply. The analysis is the court's reasoning and any considerations it uses in rendering its decision. The conclusion is the final ruling on a case.

Many people use a word processor's highlight feature as they read or review a case so that finding important items is easier later. For example, facts could be highlighted in green (indicating where to start), and conclusions could be highlighted in red (indicating a stoplight to represent the "end" of a case). To see how this method works, try Activity 2-1, where you take a look at the case *U.S. v. Trotter* (478 F.3d 918).

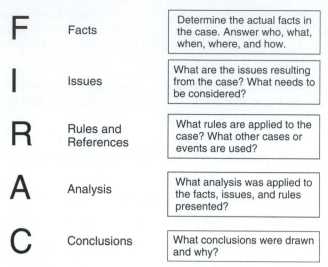

F	Facts	Determine the actual facts in the case. Answer who, what, when, where, and how.
I	Issues	What are the issues resulting from the case? What needs to be considered?
R	Rules and References	What rules are applied to the case? What other cases or events are used?
A	Analysis	What analysis was applied to the facts, issues, and rules presented?
C	Conclusions	What conclusions were drawn and why?

Figure 2-2 The FIRAC method
© Cengage Learning 2014

Activity 2-1: Using the FIRAC Method

Time Required: 45 minutes

Objective: Analyze a case by using the FIRAC method.

Description: In the case *U.S. v. Trotter*, a Salvation Army IT supervisor damaged the organization's network and sent obscene e-mails from the mail server. Repairing this system cost the Salvation Army more than $19,000. In this activity, you download the case description and use the FIRAC method to analyze the case.

1. Go to the **Chapter02\Projects** folder on this book's DVD, and open the **Highlighting Guide.doc** file. Review the colors assigned to Facts, Issues, Rules and references, Analysis, and Conclusions. Although you can choose your own colors, follow this guide for this activity.

2. Next, open the **FIRAC Analysis Example.doc** file, and examine how highlighting is applied, following the guide you reviewed in Step 1.

3. Open the **US v. Trotter.doc** file, and examine it, referring to the Highlighting Guide if needed. As shown in Figure 2-3's excerpt, the issue is Trotter challenging the constitutionality of applying the CFAA to his actions.

4. When you're finished, submit the highlighted Trotter case document along with a one- to two-paragraph summary outlining the issues, rules, and conclusions that were drawn.

For more practice, you can try using the FIRAC method on two other straightforward cases; both are available on the book's DVD in the Chapter02\Projects folder. The first is *U.S. v. Middleton* (231 F.3d 1207; on the DVD as **US v. Middleton.doc**), which was decided in the U.S. Ninth Circuit Court of Appeals in 2000. In this case, the defendant worked for an ISP that allowed him to retain a customer account after he left the company. Shortly

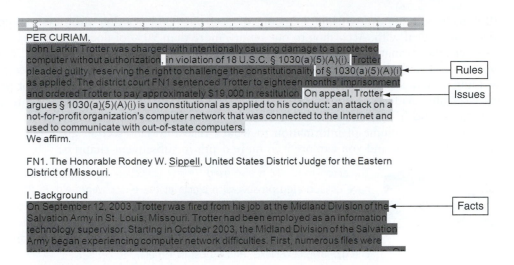

Figure 2-3 FIRAC analysis
© Cengage Learning 2014

thereafter, he accessed the ISP's network without authorization and damaged the company's computer systems. He was charged under Item a) 5 of the CFAA. His defense was that an ISP isn't a person.

The second case is *U.S. v. Phillips,* 477 F.3d 215, available on the DVD as U.S. v. Phillips.doc. Christopher Phillips, a student at the University of Texas at Austin, signed the traditional code of conduct agreement required of all incoming students. This agreement forbids hacking and using another person's password. However, he used port scans, in violation of this agreement, to access user accounts of other UT students, private businesses, U.S. government agencies, and the British Armed Services Web server. Phillips stole personal data from these accounts, including credit card numbers and sensitive government information. This case also refers to the CFAA as the rule to apply, which should make it easy to analyze.

Applying FIRAC to these cases takes around 20 minutes to an hour, depending on the number of pages. Use these two cases to establish your own highlighting code and create a file with a coding key listed for easy reference. When reading cases, keep in mind that case elements falling into the rules and regulations category might also fit into the analysis category. You can find most cases cited in this book by doing a Google search, although access to Westlaw, if available, makes searching easier.

Overview of the Electronic Discovery Reference Model

One objective of this book is to help you understand culling data—using a strategy that starts with a focused approach to searching data and adds relevant data as needed. Although the Electronic Discovery Reference Model takes a slightly different approach, the objective is the same: Shrink huge amounts of data down to a manageable scale. George Socha and Tom Gelbmann created the **Electronic Discovery Reference Model (EDRM)** in

2005 to handle the overwhelming amount of electronic evidence that attorneys and companies have to deal with. According to one report, more than 90% of documentation is now in
an electronic format, and that percentage is still rising (The Sedona Conference Working
Group on Electronic Document Retention and Production, 2010). For most companies,
winding up in a situation requiring e-discovery is inevitable, so having a method for producing electronic evidence is crucial. The EDRM serves as a roadmap for handling this task in
civil cases, and it's widely used in the business and legal communities. It's especially useful
in reducing the volume of information to what's relevant. This section gives you an overview of the model, and you explore it in more depth in subsequent chapters.

NOTE The acronym EDRM is also used for the collection of companies that
have collaborated on several projects in the e-discovery field. EDRM
has an advisory committee and a public relations committee along
with several ongoing projects. Participating companies include
AccessData, Guidance Software, Deloitte, Avantstar, Chesapeake
Energy, IBM, LexisNexis, and a host of others.

The EDRM has nine stages: information management, identification, preservation, collection,
processing, review, analysis, production, and presentation. As shown in Figure 2-4, some
stages overlap or take place simultaneously. For example, collection and preservation are
done in a loop, meaning these two tasks are a repetitive process. Processing, review, and analysis are also done in a loop.

TIP For a detailed description of the EDRM stages, go to *www.edrm.net*
and click each stage to see more information.

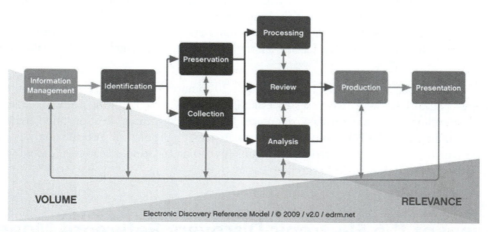

Figure 2-4 The Electronic Discovery Reference Model
Source: *EDRM.net*

Information management is how a company organizes and manages the data it stores. Laws
such as Sarbanes-Oxley require that publicly held and traded companies maintain accurate
records and report issues that affect a company's assets and debts. **Information governance** is

a way of ensuring that data is managed correctly from the top down (Grobler and Dlamini, 2010). During the development of the EDRM model, participating companies decided that information management needed its own model and created the **Information Governance Reference Model (IGRM)**, shown in Figure 2-5.

Information Governance Reference Model (IGRM)

Linking duty + value to information asset = efficient, effective management

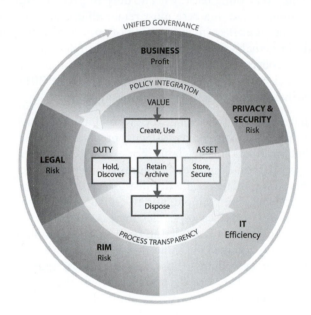

Duty: Legal obligation for specific information

Value: Utility or business purpose of specific information

Asset: Specific container of information

RIM = records information management

Figure 2-5 The Information Governance Reference Model
Source: *EDRM.net*

The IGRM model reflects the common lack of communication and collaboration in dealing with information management, so it shows each group's effect on the process. The three main groups are business users; legal, regulatory, and risk-management departments; and IT support staff. Privacy and security have recently been added as part of the model. The processes include value, duty, and asset. As shown in the figure, "value" refers to the business purpose of the information, "duty" refers to the legal obligation to retain and store information, and "asset" refers to the information's actual container. The inner ring represents the actual workflow. Each group has skills needed to maintain or dispose of information: The regulatory group understands applicable laws or regulations, the IT group deals with security and storage, and the business group knows which documents contain which information. Clear communication between groups requires preserving data in a way that makes it easy to access and easy to send to a third party or legal counsel.

In the EDRM, the identification stage starts with assigning a team responsibility for identifying potential sources of relevant data. It might involve interviewing IT staff, business units, and others. The information might consist of e-mails, text messages, and even posts on Twitter or other social-networking sites used to attract customers. During this stage, the team sets up the requirements for what to collect.

The preservation and collection stages are intertwined; after all, data must be preserved before it can be collected. After a company has received notification of the duty to preserve, it must suspend routine tasks, such as overwriting backups. The **duty to preserve** is a provision of the FRCP, stating that a company involved in a case must retain all documents and data pertaining to the case. This duty might take effect in anticipation of an order from legal counsel, or it might not take effect until an actual suit is filed. Because only relevant data should be collected, care must be taken to collect ESI and its associated metadata in a way that's "legally defensible, proportionate, efficient, auditable, and targeted" (EDRM, 2011). The collection stage relies on the requirements developed in the identification stage.

As shown previously in Figure 2-4, the processing, review, and analysis stages take place in a loop. The processing stage has four subtasks: assessment, preparation, selection, and output. You begin by assessing what information is available. For example, in a company with 50,000 employees, data might be stored on employees' computers, servers, backup tapes, CDs/DVDs, and other media, resulting in large-scale duplication of information. Although most e-mails are stored in .pst archives, for example, not all e-mails in these archives will be relevant to the case. To reduce costs in civil cases, irrelevant e-mails aren't produced to opposing counsel. Furthermore, deduplication (or "deduping") might be undertaken. Deduping occurs when multiple people have received the same e-mail, and software is used to compare e-mail identifiers across multiple **custodians** (those responsible for granting access to files and e-mail) or a single custodian. The case details dictate whether only one copy of an e-mail is enough to address the legal issues or whether multiple copies from multiple people or places (such as several managers receiving and reading the same e-mail on the same day) are necessary to prove a legal position.

After the assessment task is finished, the preparation task includes restoring backups, converting file types, full-text indexing, and other procedures. Next, the selection task reduces the amount of data that will be sent to opposing counsel, and then the output task converts data into the required formats.

During the review stage, investigators not only take into account what's relevant, but also consider whether to exclude proprietary information, such as trade secrets in a civil case or confidential government information (such as informants' names) in a criminal case. During the analysis stage, investigators examine the files for relevant information—patterns, key terms, people's names, and so forth.

The production stage packages data and puts it into the format both sides have agreed on. This stage often generates debates over whether files should be left in their native format or converted to PDF, what information might be added or lost if files are converted or processed in any way, and other issues. If a conflict goes before a court or an arbiter, the presentation stage comes into play. Depending on the objectives of the trial, arbitration, or mediation, you select what ESI should be included and decide whether to present it onscreen, in paper format, or another format. Chapter 6 explores this topic in more detail.

Criminal Cases and the EDRM

The EDRM cycle and culling data are applicable to most corporate civil cases. The process differs in criminal cases, especially during the early investigative stages. Unlike civil cases, in which the opposing side is openly notified of pending litigation, criminal cases usually rely on surveillance and other secretive tactics at various stages. Unless a criminal investigation is taking place in a company, there probably won't be records managers or IT staff to identify, preserve, and collect discovery. Law enforcement, usually with special training, performs these tasks with a wide variety of devices and sources.

Furthermore, civil litigation, in its simplest form, leaves the burden of finding evidence of wrongdoing on the requesting party, who must identify precisely through discovery requests or depositions what it wants to review. Criminal cases might also follow this approach partially, but after a complaint or an indictment is filed, enough evidence of wrongdoing has been obtained (at least in law enforcement's opinion). In most situations, after a criminal case has been filed, the law requires the prosecution team to disclose case evidence to the defendant, even if the defendant hasn't requested this evidence.

In addition to the FRCrP and constantly changing case law, three main legal directives influence the disclosure of criminal discovery: the Brady doctrine (*Brady v. Maryland*), the Jencks Act, and *Giglio v. United States*. Briefly, what's important to understand about these cases is that the prosecution team is required to disclose all exculpatory evidence (based on Brady) and all witness impeachment information (based on Jencks and Giglio) to the defense team. In most cases, the prosecution also requests a review of the defense team's evidence and expert or witness information. If the prosecution team violates these directives, the case might be dismissed or a mistrial could be declared, and other court action might be taken against the prosecutor. For example, in the criminal case against Senator Ted Stevens of Alaska (*United States v. Stevens*, Cr. No. 08-231, D.D.C. Apr. 7, 2009), the prosecution's failure to hand over important exculpatory evidence to the defense resulted in the guilty verdict being reversed.

Introduction to the Case Study

To understand the tools and methods introduced in this book, you need to know how to access the electronic data generated by cases to determine its relevance. To help you learn this skill, the case study used throughout this book allows you to practice techniques in real-world settings. The case study focuses on the landmark case surrounding the Enron bankruptcy.

The Enron Case

When most people hear the word "Enron," corporate greed comes to mind, but they aren't familiar with the case's facts. Before the scandal emerged in October 2001, Enron, with employees in 40 countries, was the largest seller of natural gas in the United States. After government deregulation was granted, Enron executives were allowed to "maintain agency" over the earnings reports sent to investors and employees (Laws.com, 2011). In other words, executives didn't have to report losses or their own financial statements, so they were able to present a profitable public image while pocketing the profits. Investors, however, lost more than $70 billion. The company filed for Chapter 11 bankruptcy in December 2001 after a series of events, including investigation by the Securities and Exchange Commission (SEC) in November 2001.

Falsified earnings, hidden losses, and embezzlement caused the collapse of a powerful firm. In addition, the accounting and auditing firm Arthur Andersen was charged with obstruction of justice after destroying documents related to its audit of Enron (Kadlec et al, 2002). As mentioned, the Sarbanes-Oxley Act was passed as a result of corporate scandals such as Enron.

To prepare you for searching Enron files in later chapters' case projects, review this list of some major players in the scandal (BBC News, 2002):

- *Andrew Fastow*—Former Enron chief financial officer and alleged creator of the deceptive accounting practices; fired when the scandal unfolded
- *Kenneth Lay*—Enron's former chief executive and chairman since 1986; refused to testify at the last moment after saying he had been prejudged
- *David Duncan*—Andersen's chief auditor, who was responsible for checking Enron's accounts; shredded key documents related to the case
- *Joseph Berardino*—Andersen's chief executive; vigorously defended his firm's role in the affair
- *Jeffrey Skilling*—Enron's chief executive in the first half of 2001; denied knowing anything was wrong at the company
- *Sherron Watkins*—Enron employee who was the whistleblower of the scandal; claimed Ken Lay was "duped" and placed the blame on Jeffrey Skilling and Andrew Fastow

Fastow, Lay, and Duncan were forced to appear and pled the Fifth Amendment, citing self-incrimination, but Berardino, Skilling, and Watkins did testify. More than 300,000 e-mails were part of the evidence used in court. Imagine sifting through that much data. One of the truly challenging aspects in e-discovery is narrowing search parameters so that you don't have to sift through terabytes of data. Many attorneys are reluctant to use this approach for fear that opposing counsel will find something they missed. As you see in later chapters, however, there are techniques to safeguard against this problem.

Enron's bankruptcy ruined many people's lives. The company's top executives inflated the stock prices to pad their own pockets and then used golden parachutes, leaving the company's employees (and others) in the lurch. It was a major case of securities fraud, and the e-mail messages are available now on several Web sites. Most sites post a warning that the e-mails might contain malware or viruses, which can be expected in a large corporation.

On both the civil and criminal sides of e-discovery, foreign data sets (those not from the corporation's own system) should be examined on computers that aren't critical to a company's production or that can be restored easily.

In this book's hands-on and case projects, you examine Kenneth Lay's e-mails primarily, but in Chapter 8, you examine e-mails of others involved in the Enron scandal. The purpose of using this well-known case is to make you aware of a few important points:

- The volume of e-mails involved in a corporate investigation
- What steps are involved in the search process

- How deduping works
- What's relevant and what's not in investigations

The e-mails from all Enron employees are available at *www.edrm .net*. When downloading them, be sure your computer has an up-to-date antivirus program and isn't a system you use for work because the e-mails might contain malware.

Chapter Summary

- Although the term "e-discovery" is new, it's been around for a few decades, ever since digital documents and e-mail became a regular part of doing business. The first discussion in a major law journal of e-discovery used in civil litigation appeared in 1997.

- The Computer Fraud and Abuse Act was created as a criminal statute to address people who exceeded their privileges on a computer or network or caused damage to these systems. Other legislation important in e-discovery law includes the Sarbanes-Oxley Act and HIPAA.

- With the development of automated business processes and electronic means of storing and transmitting documents, EDI was created to give companies an easier way to exchange information electronically and have a standardized format for electronic documents. EDI guidelines played a role in how companies store and handle information.

- Metadata is data about data. E-discovery tends to focus on metadata associated with a particular file, such as the date a file was created, who viewed it last, and so forth. Digital forensics examines metadata from the OS, which might include who deleted the file and other information.

- The four main e-discovery perspectives are from the point of view of legal professionals, e-discovery professionals, digital forensics professionals, and IT professionals.

- Because technology moves so rapidly, the law rarely keeps pace with it. As a result, case law is crucial in making determinations in trials. For example, as a result of *Rowe Entertainment v. The William Morris Agency* and the Zubulake case, the courts developed a test consisting of seven factors to determine cost shifting.

- FIRAC, which stands for facts, issues, rules and references, analysis, and conclusions, is a common method of reading and analyzing case files.

- The EDRM is a widely accepted approach to culling massive amounts of digital data. It has nine stages: information management, identification, preservation, collection, processing, review, analysis, production, and presentation. The EDRM organization also offers the IGRM, a separate model for information governance.

- The duty to preserve requires data custodians to take all precautionary measures to make sure information pertaining to an upcoming case isn't destroyed or deleted.

Key Terms

computer abuse   Gaining illegal access to a computer or the information stored on it.

Computer Fraud and Abuse Act (CFAA)   A federal law passed in 1986 to address the ongoing problem of computer abuse, fraud, and illegal access to government and financial computers.

custodians   People in an organization with the responsibility of granting access to data or e-mail and protecting the organization's assets.

duty to preserve   A provision of the FRCP that states a company involved in a case must retain all documents and data pertaining to the case.

electronic data interchange (EDI)   A system for automating business transactions and transmitting documents electronically; widely used before the Internet was available.

Electronic Discovery Reference Model (EDRM)   A model developed as a guideline for handling electronic evidence and culling what's relevant. It includes these stages: information management, identification, preservation, collection, processing, review, analysis, production, and presentation.

FIRAC   A method used to analyze cases; stands for facts, issues, rules and references, analysis, and conclusions.

Health Insurance Portability and Accountability Act (HIPAA)   A federal law that protects patients' privacy and requires notifying them when third parties are given access to their medical records.

information governance   A method for ensuring that data is managed correctly from the top down.

Information Governance Reference Model (IGRM)   A model created during development of the EDRM that targets information management. It illustrates the processes of information management and the effects on these processes of communication and collaboration between three groups: legal, risk-management, and regulatory departments; business users; and IT support staff. *See also* Electronic Discovery Reference Model (EDRM).

Metadata Encoding and Transmission Standard (METS)   The standard used for objects in a digital library; developed by the Digital Library Association and maintained by the Library of Congress.

protected computer   A computer used exclusively by a financial institution or government entity or used in interstate or foreign commerce.

Sarbanes-Oxley Act   A law passed in the wake of the bankruptcies of Enron and WorldCom that requires retaining documentation for up to seven years.

value-added networks (VANs)   Third-party service providers for transferring EDI documents. *See also* electronic data interchange (EDI).

Review Questions

1. Which of these cases caused a reversal of decision when using the FRCP in a criminal case?

   a. *U.S. v. Phillips*

   b. *U.S. v. Trotter*

   c. *U.S. v. O'Keefe*

   d. *U.S. v. Zukula*

2. Which FRCrP rule deals with search and seizure?

3. In which stage of the EDRM does a practitioner interview IT staff or speak with business units?

   a. Preservation

   b. Identification

   c. Processing

   d. Review

4. Explain why the *Zubulake v. UBS Warburg* case is considered groundbreaking.

5. Criminal attorneys often use OS metadata. True or False?

6. The CFAA was created as a criminal statute. True or False?

7. Why isn't deduping used in criminal cases?

8. Under the FRCP, what are some penalties for failing to preserve information?

9. Which of the following means backup tapes can't be overwritten?

   a. The IGRM is being followed.

   b. A duty to preserve exists.

   c. Data is being culled.

   d. The chain of custody has been broken.

10. In the processing stage of the EDRM, a practitioner must do which of the following? (Choose all that apply.)

    a. Identification

    b. Assessment

    c. Analysis

    d. Selection

11. The Zubulake case established requirements for which of the following?

    a. The custodial care of data

    b. The 2006 FRCP amendments

    c. Cost shifting

    d. The burden of proof

12. The CFAA addresses which types of offenses? (Choose all that apply.)

    a. Exceeding authorization

    b. Performing tasks in the normal course of your job

    c. Making an online threat

    d. Transmitting harmful code

13. What was the first case in the United States to deal with wiretapping?

14. Which of the following ensures that information is managed correctly from the top down in a company?

    a. Information management

    b. Information governance

    c. Information retention

    d. Information organization

15. A protected computer is defined as one that's which of the following?

    a. Behind a firewall

    b. Used by a private company

    c. Used by the government or a financial institution for interstate communication

    d. Used by anyone for interstate communication

16. Which of the following requires publicly held companies to publish financial records and any major changes promptly?

    a. The Sarbanes-Oxley Act

    b. The Gramm-Leach-Bliley Act

    c. FIRAC

    d. CFAA

17. A person's medical records are protected under which of the following?

    a. CFAA

    b. HIPAA

    c. The Gramm-Leach-Bliley Act

    d. IDRM

18. In dealing with metadata, which of the following items might be found in OS metadata? (Choose all that apply.)

    a. Structural map

    b. Creation date

    c. User behavior

    d. Login history

19. Proprietary information is excluded in which EDRM stage?

    a. Assessment

    b. Review

    c. Presentation

    d. Output

20. The Enron bankruptcy case was a major force in creating the Sarbanes-Oxley Act. True or False?

Hands-On Projects

You can find data files for this chapter on the DVD in the Chapter02\Projects folder. If necessary, copy them to your working directory before starting the projects.

Hands-On Project 2-1

Ms. Beryl Tjakami is a museum curator. As a museum employee, she entered into a contract with Sir Hamilton Wright to purchase an Olmec jade mask. The museum sent the down payment; however, the wrong item was sent. Sir Wright is now demanding the rest of the payment. Shirley Johnson is the legal counsel for the museum. Using the EDRM, write a one- to two-page paper describing the identification stage tasks Shirley Johnson needs to follow, and include a discussion of what kind of information about the transaction (conducted mainly by e-mail) might be on Ms. Tjakami's computer.

Hands-On Project 2-2

Make sure you completed the in-chapter activity before starting this project.

Search for and download the case file for *Olmstead v United States*, 277 U.S. 438 (1928). Using the FIRAC method, examine the case and highlight portions of the file. Write a one- to two-page paper on how a case dealing with new technology during Prohibition can be used to determine rulings on new technology today.

Hands-On Project 2-3

In this chapter, you were introduced to the EDRM method. Several tools have been created to make it easier to use the EDRM in a company. Search for and download a tool developed for use with the EDRM, using the search terms "EDRM tools" or "EDRM toolkit." Write a one- to two-page paper describing how the tool works, summarizing its strengths and short-comings, and explaining what you might do to improve it or what has been suggested by online comments.

Case Projects

CASE PROJECTS

Case Project 2-1

Using a search engine, look for information on the Enron bankruptcy and the involvement of the accounting firm, Arthur Andersen. How much data was destroyed, and how much was actually preserved for the court case? What existing laws were violated? If this case were taking place today, what laws would Enron have violated? Write a one- to two-page paper answering these questions.

Case Project 2-2

Using a search engine, download the case proceedings for *Zubulake v. UBS Warburg LLC, 2003* as well as some commentaries on the case. Note how much information Ms. Zubulake had to produce on her own. In what ways did the 2006 FRCP amendments help in cases such as hers? Write a one- to two-page paper about the case and its implications.

References

BBC News Business. "Enron scandal at-a-glance," August 22, 2002, *http://news.bbc.co.uk/2/hi/business/1780075.stm*.

EDRM, LLC. "Collection Guide - The EDRM," 2011, *www.edrm.net/resources/guides/edrm-framework-guides/collection*.

EDRM, LLC. "Information Governance Reference Model (IGRM) Guide," 2011, *www.edrm.net/resources/guides/igrm*.

EDRM, LLC. "Processing - The EDRM," 2011, *www.edrm.net/resources/guides/edrm-framework-guides/processing*.

Farlex. "Computer abuse - Legal definition," 2011, *http://legal-dictionary.thefreedictionary.com/Computer+abuse*.

George, Molly. "Electronic Discovery: Litigation's Newest Challenge to Corporate Records." The Metropolitan Corporate Counsel, January 1997, pp. 45–54.

Grobler, M. and I. Dlamini "Managing Digital Evidence: The Governance of Digital Forensics," *Journal of Contemporary Management* 7: 1–21, 2010.

Kadlec, D. et al. "Enron: Who's Accountable?," January 13, 2002, *www.time.com/time/printout/0,8816,1001636,00.html*.

Krebs, B. "New Federal Law Targets ID Theft, Cybercrime," *Washington Post*, October 1, 2008, *http://voices.washingtonpost.com/securityfix/2008/10/new_federal_law_targets_id_the.html*.

Laws.com. "Enron Scandal Summary," 2011, *http://finance.laws.com/enron-scandal-summary*.

Library of Congress. "METS overview and tutorial," METS Official Website, May 9, 2003, *www.loc.gov/standards/mets/METSOverview.html*.

Nelson, B., A. Phillips, and C. Steuart. *Guide to Computer Forensics and Investigations*. Boston, MA: Course Technology, 2010.

PCWorld.com. "Hacking's History," April 10, 2001, *www.pcworld.com/article/45764/hackings_history.html*.

Schroeder, S. *The Lure*. Boston, MA: Course Technology, 2011.

The Sedona Conference Working Group on Electronic Document Retention and Production. The Sedona Conference, September 2010, *www.thesedonaconference.org*.

UNECE. "Introducing UN/EDIFACT Trade - UNECE," July 2010, *www.unece.org/cefact/edifact/welcome.html*.

U.S. Congress Computer Fraud and Abuse Act, Washington, DC, 1996.

U.S. Department of Commerce, National Institute of Standards. FIPS 161-1 - EDI, April 9, 1996, *www.itl.nist.gov/fipspubs/fip161-2.htm*.

U.S. Department of Health and Human Services. "Understanding Health Information Privacy," 2011, *www.hhs.gov/ocr/privacy/hipaa/understanding/index.html*.

Zubulake v. UBS Warburg LLC, 220 F.R.D. 212, U.S. District. LEXIS 18771, U.S. District Court for the Southern District of New York, October 22, 2003.

chapter 3

E-discovery Planning and Tools

After reading this chapter and completing the exercises, you will be able to:

- Describe e-discovery tools and their uses
- Explain how e-discovery and forensic tools are used in the e-discovery process
- Summarize e-discovery planning considerations
- Describe what types of e-discovery data are useful in court

As technology has developed, software has become a powerful, essential tool in the e-discovery process. Software is typically designed to make computing tasks easier and increase productivity. Choosing the right software for the job depends on several factors, such as the software's capability to log and validate data integrity and whether the software is designed to work with small or large data sets. Digital forensic and e-discovery tools have many of the same capabilities; however, they're designed to focus on different data sets and investigative depth levels.

This chapter introduces you to tools used in the e-discovery process and explains how to choose the right tool for the job. Reducing large amounts of irrelevant data and honing in on responsive data is a cost effective discovery tactic that can be successful with prediscovery planning and targeted scoping.

Selecting the E-discovery Scope

E-discovery costs can inflate rapidly when investigators haven't planned the discovery's scope carefully, and acquiring data can be costly. The e-discovery scope helps determine the amount of data to be collected or searched and plays a key role in controlling costs. In this section, you examine the **reverse funnel method** as a way to reduce costs and save time. It's not a formal term used in the field; it's simply an analogy to help you understand a **targeted e-discovery scope** versus a **broad e-discovery scope**. A targeted e-discovery scope begins with small, focused data collections and expands based on parsing and reviewing data during the initial collection. By contrast, broad e-discovery scopes target large data collections and analyze the data to find what's relevant. Figure 3-1 compares these two e-discovery scopes.

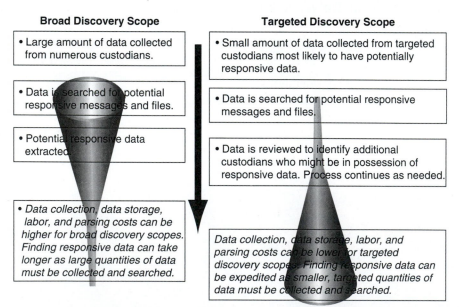

Example of the Reverse Funnel Method

Broad Discovery Scope

- Large amount of data collected from numerous custodians.

- Data is searched for potential responsive messages and files.

- Potential responsive data extracted.

- *Data collection, data storage, labor, and parsing costs can be higher for broad discovery scopes. Finding responsive data can take longer as large quantities of data must be collected and searched.*

Targeted Discovery Scope

- Small amount of data collected from targeted custodians most likely to have potentially responsive data.

- Data is searched for potential responsive messages and files.

- Data is reviewed to identify additional custodians who might be in possession of responsive data. Process continues as needed.

- *Data collection, data storage, labor, and parsing costs can be lower for targeted discovery scopes. Finding responsive data can be expedited as smaller, targeted quantities of data must be collected and searched.*

Figure 3-1 The reverse funnel method
© Cengage Learning 2014

Broad E-discovery Scopes

E-discovery requests often ask for all available data, including all data and metadata from all electronic media, backups, servers, computers, users, and sources. This request is a broad approach to capturing data—hence the term "broad e-discovery scope." This approach typically doesn't focus on specific types of data or information; it's designed to capture as much data as possible, on the premise that relevant data will be found.

Placing yourself in the position of the plaintiff's counsel can help you understand why a broad e-discovery approach is used. In this situation, you don't usually know details about the opponent's network, such as how data is stored, the size of the network, software components, and retention policies. Using a broad e-discovery scope can give you information about the opponent's network.

You might also use the concern that failing to collect all available data might result in relevant data being overlooked or destroyed to justify a broad e-discovery scope. For example, an auto manufacturer is in litigation for an accident in which the vehicle's owner and occupants were injured. The cause of the accident is unknown; however, the plaintiff's counsel knows of previous, similar accidents involving several vehicle models from the manufacturer. The plaintiff's counsel doesn't know whether each model has its own business or engineering unit in the company and doesn't know the manufacturer's network configuration or retention policies. In this example, the plaintiff's counsel might submit an e-discovery request seeking multiple data backups, all e-mail messages from all business units, design data for all vehicle models, crash safety test results, and so forth. If the company's networks span a global enterprise, the amount of data being requested could be very large.

Being uncertain what data on the system actually *is* evidence can also be a reason to use a broad e-discovery scope. Communication can be an important factor in reducing costly and time-consuming e-discovery processes. Attorney-to-attorney communication at the onset of litigation proceedings and during e-discovery helps narrow the discovery focus to identify systems and data that might reveal relevant information to support the opposing counsel's case. Communication between litigants also reveals information about the opposing client's network retention policies and system operations, thus reducing the need to generate e-discovery requests that most likely won't produce relevant data.

Communication between attorneys and information technology (IT) personnel is critical, too. IT personnel work with networks, computing systems, and digital storage devices daily, so they know where data is most likely to be found. In addition, they know about retention policies, OSs, e-mail servers, backup systems, and other network components that might pose unique problems during the discovery process. More useful information is gathered when attorneys consult with IT professionals who are familiar with the system or network. If an attorney is representing a client who's received a discovery request, consulting with an IT employee from the client's company to get information about the network, computing systems, and retention policies is a good investment of time. The following questions posed to IT professionals can elicit valuable insights:

- Do retention policies exist and apply for the data or information you need?
- What are the account deletion and data retention policies for former employees of the company?

- Does the backup policy indicate whether the data you're seeking is or isn't available for the time period you're interested in?

- How long do e-mail servers retain deleted messages? Does an existing policy specify the retention period or dictate server settings?

- Do IT personnel have the training, skills, and tools for acquiring data in a manner that preserves its integrity?

- If a third-party vendor is used to collect data, what steps must be taken to grant access to the company's systems? Will the vendor have access to the data and system tools needed to carry out the data collection? Is the vendor likely to be an asset or an impediment?

Effective communication with IT professionals gives attorneys the knowledge that will help them respond to e-discovery requests and negotiate e-discovery terms and conditions.

The advantage of using a broad e-discovery scope is that it increases the prospect of acquiring data that could be useful. However, there are multiple disadvantages to consider, discussed later in "Data Collections."

Targeted E-discovery Scopes

A targeted e-discovery scope usually specifies the types of information, data, people, and components to use when searching for and collecting data. In addition, keywords and date ranges help narrow the focus to relevant data. This approach starts by collecting and searching smaller amounts of data and gradually expands the focus as data is reviewed and relevant data is identified.

Discovery requests aren't limited to just one. A request with a targeted e-discovery scope is more likely to generate additional discovery requests because the narrower scope is more likely to produce less data than a request with a broad e-discovery scope does. As data is reviewed, additional information of interest could be identified, which results in additional discovery requests.

For example, an auto manufacturer is in litigation for defective brakes on its vehicles, which are believed to be responsible for multiple accidents resulting in fatalities. The plaintiff's attorney has targeted the engineering group for the e-discovery request and searches because it designed the brakes. E-mails from the engineering manager and lead engineer have been searched, and relevant data has been sent to the plaintiff's attorney. While reviewing these e-mails, the plaintiff's attorney finds several e-mail messages from a quality inspector on the assembly line, who expresses concerns about the quality of the brake line components. Because the quality inspector has indicated he might have additional information about the brake problems, the plaintiff's attorney could submit a second discovery request for the quality inspector's e-mail as well as quality assurance records from a server where quality control records for brakes on the specified vehicle model are stored. The second discovery request would broaden the e-discovery scope because of the need to collect and review the additional custodian's data.

Factors in Planning Discovery

Before using a broad e-discovery focus, you should take the following into consideration during the planning stage:

- Look at the size or projected size of the opponent's network to help you determine whether to use a broad or targeted e-discovery scope. Specifics of network components, software, e-mail systems, and so forth often aren't fully understood in the beginning phases of e-discovery. Using a broad discovery scope on a large network can generate large amounts of irrelevant data, which must be stored and reviewed. Using a targeted discovery scope on a large network can reduce the amount of data to review but could require additional searches if new data locations are identified.

- Large, well-established companies typically have networks with system and file backups and different types of logs as well as an extensive IT department. Their systems are designed to enable business continuity after catastrophic events. As a result, large corporations usually retain backup files containing data from previous months or years. A targeted e-discovery request could focus on file backups for a specified period, thus eliminating the need to use a broad e-discovery scope that would probably capture data outside the period.

- Smaller companies often don't have as many IT resources at their disposal as large companies do, so retention policies might be in limited use, and there might be fewer data backups. In addition, recovering data from the time period you specify might be difficult or impossible. With smaller companies, a broad e-discovery scope might be more useful in finding relevant data.

Legal Considerations

Company's networks often span the globe, so you must also consider the data's physical location when planning the discovery scope. Physical location can add problems to the e-discovery process. If the data is stored in a foreign country, that country's laws might apply to the data. Privacy laws vary by country, and in many European Union (EU) countries, a person's privacy takes legal precedence over the data's owner. For example, if an employee is using a company e-mail system, the company might not have the right to copy the employee's e-mails just because the e-mail system is company owned.

Cloud computing also poses challenges for the e-discovery process. ISPs frequently offer Web hosting and data storage to their clients, who can upload data to their accounts, and then access the data from any computer. Legal implications include determining who has authority over the data. At the time of this writing, case law is in its infancy when determining whether the data's owner or the location of the server where data is stored has precedence. These legal considerations can affect the choice of scope based on how much data is stored and whether access is granted by courts in other countries.

Both U.S. and foreign courts are debating the jurisdictional authority over data owned by U.S. companies but stored on cloud and international systems.

Data Authentication

Both digital forensic software and e-discovery tools have the capability to collect, search, and produce data so that it can be validated and authenticated in court. Data must be collected in a manner that allows recovering file contents and metadata in an unaltered form. The forensics examiner or data collection specialist must be able to verify that the data hasn't changed and is as authentic in court as it was when it was collected.

When forensics examiners are collecting digital data, one method they use to validate that the file hasn't changed or been modified is a **digital hash**, which is a value created by using a mathematical formula (a hashing algorithm) that translates digital data into a unique hexadecimal code value. These hexadecimal values are called hash values, hash codes, hash sums, checksums, or simply hashes. Common hashing algorithms are Message Digest 5 (MD5) and Secure Hash Algorithm version 1 (SHA-1). If data in the file has been altered or changed in any way, the unique hexadecimal value also changes (Nelson, Phillips, and Steuart, 2010).

Another method of authenticating data is a chain-of-custody form, which is used when transferring data between people or between physical locations on removable media devices. This form documents the route the evidence takes from the time you obtain it until the case is closed or goes to court (Nelson, Phillips, and Steuart, 2010). It accompanies the media device and contains information about the device and the names of people who have retained custody of it. As a media device moves between physical locations or people, the form's chronological listing of people and the dates and times the device was in their possession is updated. The people listed on the form can attest to the data's integrity if its authenticity is challenged in court.

A digital hash authenticates digital evidence (such as a Word document or an Excel spreadsheet), and a chain-of-custody form authenticates physical evidence, such as what's stored on a laptop or digital camera. However, what about paper documents converted into electronic format? Despite the Digital Age reducing the amount of paper companies use, e-discovery professionals must still process paper documents and convert them to electronic format (usually PDF or TIF) for searching and review. Recording the origin of the paper document used to produce the scanned version is essential. It's often done by noting which custodian provided the paper document. If needed, the custodian can then verify that the scanned PDF or TIF file represents the original data in the paper document.

Data Collections

An important component of successful litigation is the data collection process. The Sedona Principles recommend that organizations choose a scope that addresses the issues in the case fairly and appropriately. When choosing a scope, organizations should consider the impact data collection will have on normal business activities and the cost of collecting data. Data collections should target repositories used by key people and follow reasonable selection criteria for identifying relevant data (Sedona Principles, Second Edition, June 2007). This task might seem fairly easy, but litigation personnel must consider several factors when drafting e-discovery requests for data collections. The following sections discuss these factors in relation to large- and small-scale collections to help determine whether a broad or targeted scope should be used.

Large Data Collections
Collecting large data sets can be quite complex and expensive because with improvements in data storage, vast amounts of data can now be stored on even small devices. Servers and computers are capable of using multiple hard drives as large as 2 terabytes (TB) each.

The size of the opponent's network doesn't always correlate to the amount of data on the system, but for the purpose of this chapter, large data collections imply a large organization with networks containing a multitude of computers, servers, backup servers, and software. Using a broad e-discovery scope in this situation can produce vast quantities of irrelevant data in addition to the data you're seeking.

The main disadvantage of using a broad e-discovery scope against a large organization is the cost. The probability that the opponent will challenge a broad discovery request in court increases, so searching large networks can become time consuming and expensive, and affect corporate operations.

In addition, the larger the network, the more likely it is that problems affecting the timing and cost of discovery will happen. For example, large networks typically contain file servers in different geographical locations, and searching and copying data across all these locations can be impeded by network latency, a slowdown caused by high volumes of network traffic.

A common problem when conducting e-discovery with large networks is identifying where relevant data might be located: file servers, employees' computers, removable media devices, e-mail servers, backup tapes and servers, and so forth. In addition, backup media isn't always on site. Many companies transfer backup files and media to off-site storage in other geographical locations, often as part of disaster recovery planning to help ensure that the business can continue operating. Having to retrieve and restore data before searching it can increase discovery costs dramatically in both time and labor.

Access permissions to devices and data can cause problems, especially if a third-party vendor is used to collect data. Company computers are usually members of a corporate domain, so access to data is restricted to domain users. A third-party employee would need to have an account created on the domain and have permissions assigned to the account to allow access to data and devices. When collecting data across multiple internal domains in a company, an administrator account is usually needed.

Password-protected files and encrypted data pose problems, too. If the data's owner or user is no longer with the company or forgets the password set for the data, you might need password-cracking software. If the employee used a strong password on the file, a password cracker could run for days or weeks attempting to guess the password. In many cases, the password might not be recovered. Dedicating a computer to crack files can also delay the discovery process and increase costs.

Storage and media costs can increase in correlation to the amount of data collected. Many third-party vendors who store and analyze data charge fees based on the amount of data stored on their systems. If in-house processing is used, the cost of hard drives for storing and transferring data is a factor.

Shipping and data-integrity costs must also be factored into the e-discovery process. Data that's collected and placed on removable media might need to be protected in case it's lost or to preserve its integrity. Encrypted removable hard drives can be used to secure data and help preserve its authenticity. Keep in mind, too, that data being shipped might contain personally identifiable information (PII), and its loss during shipment could constitute a breach of data security. These breaches can be inconvenient and costly because of legal reporting and response requirements. Therefore, the shipping mode you choose should take into account the consequences of losing data.

When storage media are transferred to other locations, shipping delays must be taken into consideration. To ensure that data reaches its destination in a timely manner, many law firms and companies use overnight or priority shipping. Although this method increases costs, delays of time-sensitive data or data needed to meet a court-ordered deadline can result in additional costs. Requiring the recipient to sign for a shipment is a good way to verify delivery and can be useful in retaining the chain of custody.

Another factor to consider is the cost of legal representation. Typically, attorneys are responsible for reviewing the collected data to determine what data is relevant and what data is covered by attorney-client or work-product privileges. With large data collections, multiple attorneys or paralegals might be needed to review data. To assist in reducing costs, a targeted e-discovery scope is helpful in reducing the amount of data to review and reducing the probability that the attorney has to review irrelevant data.

Medium to Small Data Collections   Generally, with e-discovery targeted at small companies or a single person, the scope of data collection is medium to small. Small companies might not have the financial or IT resources to retain data the way larger companies do. Lack of resources or knowledge of IT best practices can increase the risk that a smaller company might not be prepared for litigation. For example, a small sole proprietorship company could have a backup drive connected to the computer, but the backup drive might not be configured to retain data on a schedule that ensures data is available if a system failure occurs. This lack of preparedness could indicate to the plaintiff's attorney that relevant data might not be retained.

In many cases, smaller companies have fewer computer systems and smaller IT infrastructures, so there's usually less data to review. The risk of losing relevant data is also higher. In this situation, a broad e-discovery scope is more feasible; indeed, it might be necessary to ensure that as much data as possible is searched and collected.

Cost and Time Considerations

Many digital forensics tools have capabilities that are useful in e-discovery. If a discovery request calls for producing deleted data, for example, forensics tools are usually required. Discovery requests often seek data that hasn't been deleted, however. In this case, using forensics tools can delay discovery collection and increase costs because these tools are designed for in-depth review and analysis of digital evidence. For this reason, initial processing times can be lengthy. Forensics tools examine the entire hard drive or other sources for data in all forms, including undeleted files, deleted files, partial files, and file fragments. These tools also have logging and indexing features. As a result of all these features, processing time and costs can skyrocket.

Regardless of whether forensic or e-discovery tools are used, the size of the data collection also plays a crucial role in overall costs. Data must be collected, stored on external media (such as hard drives), and searched, which takes time and adds to the cost, particularly with large data collections. Extracting the results and shipping them to counsel for review adds to hardware and time costs. Finally, counsel's review of data adds to the time and cost.

A targeted e-discovery scope can decrease costs by reducing the areas in which relevant data is likely to be found. For example, in a dispute about a contractual agreement, does collecting all the data on an inventory server make sense? An inventory server probably doesn't contain relevant data. A contract dispute might involve a procurement employee and a file server. A targeted scope, therefore, would collect the procurement employee's e-mail and search for files on the server containing keywords unique to the contract. As the data is searched and reviewed, additional employees or data locations that could contain relevant data are likely to be identified and searched. Using a broad e-discovery scope in this example could result in a huge amount of irrelevant data to search and, therefore, increase time and costs considerably.

Using Digital Forensics Tools for E-discovery

E-discovery can be a complicated and overwhelming task. Data and evidence must not only be collected, but also be acquired in a manner that validates the data's authenticity in court. Specialized software tools are available that help with collecting, sorting, and producing relevant data. Although digital forensics tools and e-discovery tools have many common features, they're designed for different purposes. Digital forensics tools are designed to collect data in a manner that retains crucial file information so that data can be validated and used in court. They perform functions in these major categories: acquisition, validation and discrimination, extraction, reconstruction, and reporting (Nelson, Phillips, and Steuart, 2010). Not all these functions are needed for e-discovery. E-discovery tools are designed to analyze data that hasn't been deleted and search for files and other information that could be relevant in a case.

Digital forensics tools are used to capture hard drive images (sometimes called "image and hold") as part of the duty to preserve (refer back to Chapter 2). They can also be used to mount forensic images in read-only mode so that other tools can be used to extract or search for relevant data. In addition, they can identify deleted files, Registry entries, and partial files and carve through a hard drive's free space to find file and data fragments.

Although digital forensics tools are designed to collect data in a manner that retains crucial file information so that data can be validated and used in court, the process an examiner uses to extract relevant data is equally important. Many digital forensics and e-discovery tools offer activity logging to capture the examiner's actions when using the software. Activity logging creates a record of the examiner's actions as well as system activities and events. When evidence items are added or searches are created or modified, the activity log records these events and places timestamps in the log file. This log can be used to review search settings and summaries of search results.

E-discovery Software

E-discovery software is used to extract information from electronic data. Data is stored in multiple formats and consists of vast amounts of information that needs to be produced accurately. This data covers a huge scope, and recovering it is an enormous undertaking, as it includes documents, spreadsheets, databases, e-mails with attachments, presentations, and more. The information is stored in a multitude of places, including laptops, network servers, desktop PCs, backup media, e-mail systems, PDAs, smart phones, and removable storage devices, to name a few. Several processes for extracting information are common to all software packages: keyword searches, converting data to TIF or PDF format, using optical character recognition (OCR) software, Bates numbering for document tracking, and exporting results in a report or a native file format.

At least 29 suites of e-discovery software are available, ranging from services for small companies, such as ImageMAKER Discovery Assistant, to services for large companies, such as CasePoint @Legal Discovery. The scale of the litigation is an important factor when choosing an e-discovery software package. This section reviews some tools designed for small to medium businesses.

ImageMAKER Discovery Assistant

ImageMAKER Discovery Assistant (*www.discoveryassistant.com*) is designed to capture, search, and process Windows-based documents and Microsoft Outlook PST files. It is scalable and ideal for small businesses. The software uses the DT Search engine, which enables you to search a variety of scanned documents, e-mails, and attachments and export results in native file, TIF, and PDF formats. The exported data can be imported into legal review tools, such as Ringtail, Concordance, Summation, and Relativity. The e-mail thread identification and deduplication features help reduce review time and costs by eliminating redundant data.

Catalyst Repository Systems

Catalyst (*www.catalystsecure.com*) has multiple versions of its software package: Catalyst CR, Catalyst XE, and Catalyst Enterprise. Each version varies in cost and features to target e-discovery processing for small to large cases. The software is a Web-based platform, and Web browsers are used as the reviewing mechanism.

The main advantage of this software is the grid-based system for litigation support. The grid allows spreading searches over multiple servers for faster response times. The software is multilingual capable and uses both Unicode and non-Unicode pages to accommodate a variety of languages.

Catalyst provides tools for document review, analysis, and production. The program allows you to search by keyword, full text, date range, Bates number range, proximity, and key concepts. Catalyst XE is used mainly for e-discovery in litigation and business matters, such as managing insurance claims and financial transactions. It can send e-mail and documents directly to folders on the site in addition to many of the Catalyst CR basic features.

Catalyst Enterprise is designed to process e-discovery data for large litigation cases. It's typically used by corporations and law firms that require a platform for tracking users and content in addition to case status and schedules.

Access Data AD Summation

Access Data AD Summation (*http://accessdata.com/products/ediscovery-litigation-support/summation*) offers useful litigation support features. Its search, review, and production tools are comparable with the features available in e-discovery software. An interesting feature is its capability to manage transcripts, including real-time feed of a transcript from the court reporter. It has a Quick Search feature that allows broad searches, or you can conduct more complex searches with Boolean elements or fuzzy search criteria for OCR documents.

AD Summation's production capabilities are flexible and enable you to export data into multiple types of load files (explained in "Trial Presentation Tools" later in this chapter). You can also access the stamping and redacting tools needed for producing documents to opposing counsel.

Nextpoint Discovery Cloud Nextpoint Discovery Cloud (*www.discoverycloud.nextpoint.com/*) helps you manage and process a large volume of data. As the name suggests, it works completely in the cloud, so there's no local software to purchase. It's integrated with the company's Cloud Preservation and Trial Cloud products.

Discovery Cloud's search capabilities include a complete set of Boolean controls and results filtering. Search results can be viewed in order of relevance, and you can move directly to the page with the search term to view the search results. A built-in processing engine imports data into a review platform, where you can view documents in several formats, e-mail them to others, and sort them by date, issue, title, or other criteria. With advanced reviewer management features, project administrators can create custom access permissions for each reviewer. This tool supports native files and a variety of file types; can handle OCR, PDF, and TIF formats; and can process files up to 5 GB.

eDiscovery Toolbox eDiscovery Toolbox (*www.ediscoverytools.com/products.html*) is a software suite with three components: eDiscovery QuickPeek, eDiscovery Processor, and eDiscovery Reviewer. It's aimed at decreasing processing costs associated with large amounts of data.

eDiscovery QuickPeek is an early case assessment (ECA) tool with features for filtering and removing irrelevant documents before processing or review. It includes the Guestimator application used for estimating the costs of processing, printing, and conducting the review. A proportionality check is available to compare these costs with the litigation budget.

eDiscovery Processor is used to process electronic files so that they can be loaded into a review platform. Multiple load file formats are supported for a variety of reviewing applications, such as FTI Ringtail Legal, LexisNexis Concordance, and CT Summation, and contents of load files can be Bates stamped. Deduplication features are included for removing duplicate files and e-mails.

eDiscovery Reviewer is a Web browser viewer that enables a legal team to review processed documents. Search capabilities make it possible to create custom search queries using keywords, date ranges, and Boolean operators. The display screen and data contents can be customized to suit your preferences, and relevant data can be redacted and then exported in PDF and TIFF formats.

Sherpa Software Discovery Attender Discovery Attender (*www.sherpasoftware.com/microsoft-exchange-products/discovery-attender-2.shtml*) is one of the most cost-effective, powerful e-discovery tools on the market today. It's designed mainly for working with Microsoft Exchange and Lotus Notes e-mail collections. It can also be used with network drives, file shares, and SharePoint Web sites. You use this tool in many hands-on projects in this book, so a detailed description of its features isn't included in this chapter.

Enkive Enkive (*www.enkive.org*) is a Linux open-source e-mail archive and e-discovery tool used for document and records management. It's designed to be used with an e-mail system and retains and purges e-mail based on an organization's retention policies. A retention policy can also be configured so that e-mail and attachment copies are purged automatically.

With Enkive's Web browser interface, you can search messages based on sender, recipient, subject, content, date, and so forth. You can also search a variety of common file types found in e-mail attachments, including PDF, Microsoft Office formats, and text files. You can save the search queries and export the search results to the open-source Thunderbird e-mail client. Enkive also deduplicates e-mails and attachments to save on storage devices and generates reports of archive storage use and retrieval activity.

Access Data AD eDiscovery Access Data AD eDiscovery (*http://accessdata.com/products/ediscovery-litigation-support/ediscovery*) is a suite of tools tailored to support the entire e-discovery lifecycle, from litigation hold to final review and production. You can get real-time status for litigation holds and generate hold status reports. The collection tool enables you to gather data in a variety of formats from network resources, such as workstations, servers, and Web repositories. The processing tool has a handy feature that retains the chain of custody for data you collect. In addition, data is automatically categorized and deduplicated. The Early Case Assessment/First Pass Review feature analyzes collected data by using customized data filters; data can be filtered by custodian, data source, and document metadata and type. With the Final Review and Production features, you can use keyword searches, review scanned data (in addition to electronic data you've collected), use Bates stamping and document redaction filters, and keep a production history.

E-discovery and Trial

After discovery has been acquired and processed and key evidence has been identified for use at trial, information can be transferred from the litigation database to a format for use in the courtroom. This procedure involves narrowing the information further into case issues to present to a jury. Some cases are presented in court without a jury (known as a "bench trial"); the judge hears all evidence from both sides and determines the case outcome. Also, some cases go to a mediator or an arbitrator instead of to court or sometimes before court action. As mentioned in Chapter 4, using mediators and arbitrators is becoming a common requirement in many contracts to avoid the expense of jury trials, particularly contracts involving government projects. Narrowing the information to be presented is based on the issues the lead attorney wants to present to the jury, judge, mediator, or arbitrator. Case issues are key points of legal dispute identified in the complaint, indictment, and subsequent case motions.

 Most trial consultants advise legal counsel to limit the number of issues presented to a jury, mainly because most juries get lost and tune out if they're given too much material to absorb.

Each issue is supported or disputed by case facts, which are evidence to prove (or disprove) a particular viewpoint or belief. For example, the opposing party accuses your client of patent infringement by stealing software code developed for a new CAD program while your client was under contract as a programmer to help with code development. After the contract ended, your client went on to develop another CAD program independently and marketed it under a different name, using slightly different software code. Confidentiality could be a case issue, and the contract, with its confidentiality clause, could be a supporting fact document. If this document is a key evidence item, it's transferred to a trial presentation tool. The attorneys then argue whether applicable laws tie into the fact document and the issue in dispute. In a jury trial, the jury must follow instructions prepared by each attorney and approved by the judge to determine how to evaluate the evidence. The remaining discovery is kept in the litigation database for quick reference if needed, as case strategy could change during the trial.

In civil cases, the Federal Rules of Civil Procedure require evidence to be exchanged by all parties before trial. Criminal cases are a little different, and the Federal Rules of Criminal Procedure allow evidence to be admitted during trial.

Trial Presentation Tools

A number of trial presentation tools are available (discussed in more detail in Chapter 6), ranging from basic to high-end tools with enough bells and whistles to dazzle any jury. The tool you choose depends on the trial team's experience and background as well as the nature of the case and case strategies. For example, some attorneys like to present a "down-home" image to the jury to gain trust, and they might believe that a high-tech presentation detracts from their believability. They often stand at a podium and use only paper documents shown on an overhead projector, occasionally dropping paper and apologizing to the jury for their lack of sophistication compared with the opposing counsel's high-tech presentation tool.

The trial presentation tool and the trial team's courtroom setup also depend on what technology can be accommodated in the courtroom. For example, Internet access might not be available or might not be allowed by the judge for various reasons. The nature or sensitivity of the litigation matter can be an issue in some cases, including national security (the U.S. PATRIOT Act), organized crime, child sexual abuse or pornography, or highly sensitive trade secrets. In litigation cases of these types, the court could impose stringent security measures that control or restrict use of certain electronic devices, such as laptops, overhead projectors, and recording devices.

PowerPoint, a slightly more sophisticated tool, is often used as a trial presentation tool. Because it's a well-known tool in general office use, it's not described in this book. Just keep in mind that it's adequate for presenting documents, audio, and video in civil or criminal cases.

The top three tools for trial presentation are TrialDirector (*www.indatacorp.com/TrialDirector.html*), Sanction (*http://sanction.com*), and Visionary (*www.visionarylegaltechnologies.com*), but there are many others. Typically, these tools import and export documents by using load files from litigation databases. A **load file** is a set of scanned images or electronically processed files that might contain attachments to documents, e-mails, or files. Indicators in a load file show where each document begins and ends. A load file can also contain data related to documents it contains, such as selected metadata, coded data, and extracted text. Load files should be in standardized or agreed-on formats to ensure that accurate and usable images and data are transferred (Sedona Conference Glossary, 2010). Their main components include the following:

- A database component that's smaller and less powerful than litigation database software. With this component, exhibits and documents can be organized before trial or searched during trial. These tools are developed to present a limited amount of information to a jury and should be used as a litigation database substitute only in small cases.

- Audio and video presentation, with linking (synchronization) to a deposition transcript. Using video-recorded depositions has become more common; attorneys often play the video to a jury while scrolling the transcript along the side. This method allows the jury to see whether the deponent's body language reveals anything.

- Editing and animation tools for adding callouts, zooming, and other graphic features to emphasize certain sections of documents, audio, and video. Another popular feature is displaying different versions of a document side by side for comparison, which is especially useful for pointing out possible alterations.

- Bar-code features used with a bar-code scanner and a notebook of bar-coded exhibits. The scanner sends a signal to the presentation computer to display the scanned exhibit. This feature gives the attorney complete control over presentation from a podium.

Why not just use a litigation database for trial presentation? Litigation databases are developed to handle certain functions well, such as sophisticated searches, global coding, redaction, large-scale review and production, and simultaneous multiuser access. Trial presentation tools are developed for one user with a limited amount of preprocessed material and have features for producing more effective presentations of material to a jury.

Almost all trial presentation tools are developed for PCs running Microsoft OSs. Macintosh users should consider compatibility issues during all phases of case management.

Early in the case, it's important to consider document formats, naming conventions, and capacities of your trial presentation tool to avoid the needless costs associated with format changes or file renaming. For example, most trial presentation tools were developed to accept documents in TIF format with OCR and later adapted to accept PDF and native formats; however, not all tool features work equally well with all formats. Check to see whether document tear-outs are needed and whether they can be created in native files. A tear-out, also known as a call-out, is a software feature for emphasizing parts of a document, photo, video, and so forth. It's similar to and often used with a zoom feature. Often this type of tear-out can't be created in native files in trial presentation software. Many trial attorneys rely on this presentation feature, however, so native files often have to be converted to TIF with OCR to create tear-outs. You should check to see whether search features work equally well with PDFs and native files. At the beginning of a case, establishing naming conventions for files is advisable because most trial presentation tools limit the number and type of characters in filenames. In addition, the days and weeks just before trial are stressful, and last-minute changes might result in lost documents or poor quality control.

Finally, most courts respond favorably to digital trial presentation methods for "judicial economy." Judicial economy is anything that reduces the time the judge, court staff, and jury need to spend on the case yet still offers adequate service. Generally, if digital trial presentation tools are used correctly, they reduce the time spent on presenting evidence. In addition, some courts that are more proactive in courtroom technology have dedicated IT support and training classes that give an overview of the court's technology capacities; however, they don't offer actual trial support.

Chapter Summary

- A broad e-discovery scope is intended to capture as much data as possible, on the premise that relevant data will be found. Typically, this approach doesn't focus on collecting specific data types or narrowing a search to certain data locations.

- A targeted e-discovery scope begins with small, focused data collections and expands based on parsing and reviewing data during the initial collection. This approach focuses on collecting data types from specified data locations or custodians.

- When planning a discovery approach, consider factors such as network size, extent of IT resources, and use of backups. Legal considerations, such as the data's location, should also be taken into account.

- Data must be collected in a manner that allows recovering file contents and metadata in an unaltered form. To verify that data hasn't been changed, forensics examiners use methods such as digital hashes and chain-of-custody forms.

- The size of a data collection is determined by the scope of the discovery activity. When choosing a scope, organizations should consider the impact data collection has on normal business activities and the cost of collecting data. Data collections should target repositories used by key people and follow reasonable selection criteria.

- A broad e-discovery scope increases discovery costs because of storing, searching, and reviewing data that might not be relevant. A targeted e-discovery scope can decrease costs by reducing the areas in which relevant data is likely to be found.

- Digital forensics tools and e-discovery tools have many common features but are designed for different purposes. Digital forensics tools are designed to collect data in a manner that retains crucial file information so that data can be validated and used in court. E-discovery tools are designed to analyze data that hasn't been deleted and search for files and other information that could be relevant in a case.

- Trial presentation tools process key evidence for use at trial by transferring information from the litigation database to a format for use in the courtroom. This procedure involves narrowing the information further into case issues to present to a jury.

Key Terms

broad e-discovery scope   An e-discovery method that attempts to capture as much data as possible, on the premise that relevant data will be found.

digital hash   A value created by using a mathematical formula (a hashing algorithm) that translates a file into a unique hexadecimal code value; used to determine whether data in a file has changed or been altered.

load file   A set of scanned images or electronically processed files containing pages and attachments to documents, e-mails, or files. A load file can also contain data related to documents it contains, such as selected metadata, coded data, and extracted text.

reverse funnel method   An analogy describing how discovery can begin with small, targeted data collections and expand in scope based on parsing and reviewing data in the initial collection.

targeted e-discovery scope   An e-discovery method that focuses on small data collections, usually from specified data locations or custodians; typically, the data collection is expanded as relevant data is identified.

Review Questions

1. Which of the following is responsible for reviewing data and determining what's relevant?
   a. Forensics examiner
   b. Custodian
   c. Client
   d. Attorney

2. Effective communication between _____ and _____ can reduce the number of e-discovery requests that are unlikely to produce relevant results.
   a. Attorneys, courts
   b. Litigants, IT personnel
   c. Attorneys, software vendors
   d. Attorneys, arbitrators

3. A digital hash is created by using a mathematical formula that translates a file into a unique _____ code value.
   a. Binary
   b. Electronic
   c. Hexadecimal
   d. ASCII

4. A chain-of-custody form documents the route evidence takes from the time it's collected until the case is closed or goes to court. True or False?

5. Which of the following functions is one that digital forensics tools perform? (Choose all that apply.)
   a. Acquisition and searching
   b. Validation and discrimination
   c. Indexing and parsing
   d. Deleting and printing

6. Broad discovery scopes specify the types of information, data, persons, and components to be collected from or searched. True or False?

7. Explain one way in which cloud computing simplifies the e-discovery process.

8. Trial presentation tools are developed for large-scale review and multiuser access. True or False?

9. Which of the following can occur when data has to compete with other data in the network?

   a. Collisions

   b. Shutdowns

   c. Latency

   d. Catastrophic failures

10. In many European Union (EU) countries, a person's privacy takes legal precedence over the data's owner. True or False?

11. Broad e-discovery collections alleviate high costs and reduce the time involved. True or False?

12. Which of the following is a software feature used for emphasizing part of a document, photo, or video in a trial presentation?

   a. Cut-out

   b. Screenshot

   c. Tear-out

   d. Magnifier

Hands-On Projects

You can find data files for this chapter on the DVD in the Chapter03\Projects folder. If necessary, be sure to copy them to your working directory on your machine before starting the projects. In addition, the Discovery Attender demo software you use for projects in this chapter is available on the DVD. Make sure you install it before starting these projects.

Discovery Attender *can* run with a 64-bit OS. However, you need the 64-bit version of Discovery Attender to run with a 64-bit installation of Outlook 2010. The hands-on projects in this chapter use a 32-bit installation of Outlook 2010.

Hands-On Project 3-1

In this project, you use Discovery Attender for the first time. A Discovery Attender project stores the searches you create for a litigation case. You can use these searches to analyze the ESI you collect for the case and identify relevant data. This project is for the Enron litigation case.

You can create multiple projects in Discovery Attender, but only one project can be open at a time.

If you haven't installed Discovery Attender yet, follow the instructions in the `Configuring_Discovery_Attender_Settings.wmv` video on the DVD before beginning this project.

1. To start this program, right-click the **Discovery Attender** desktop icon and click **Run As administrator**. If necessary, click **Yes** in the User Account Control message box. In the welcome window, click **Create New Project**.

2. In the New Discovery Attender Project dialog box, type **Enron** in the Project Name text box. In the Description text box, enter a description similar to the one in Figure 3-2. Leave the default path directory C:\Projects, and click the **Create** button.

Figure 3-2 Starting a new project in Discovery Attender
Source: Sherpa Software, Inc.

3. When the Create a New Search dialog box opens, click **Cancel**. You have created your first Discovery Attender project to use when you search Enron files for relevant data. Exit Discovery Attender, closing all open windows.

Hands-On Project 3-2

In this project, you develop searches to use on the Enron project you created in Hands-On Project 3-1. A project can contain multiple searches and include search revision levels, so you need to learn how to choose descriptive search titles and enter search criteria. Discovery Attender logs every search and the options used in the search.

1. Start Discovery Attender, click **Open Existing Project**, and when prompted to open a project, click the **Enron** project you created in Hands-On Project 3-1, and then click **Open**. Click **OK** in the Create a New Search dialog box.

2. In the General Search Details window, enter **Kenneth Lay** in the Search Title text box, and enter a description of the search in the Description text box (see Figure 3-3). Click the **Next** button.

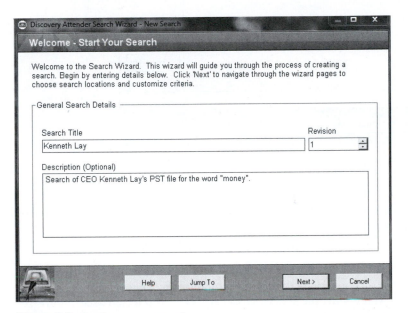

Figure 3-3 Starting a new search
Source: Sherpa Software, Inc.

3. In the Select Areas to Search window, you choose the areas to search. Common areas are PST files and network shares. Click **Outlook Personal File Folders (PSTs)**, and then click **Next**.

 Selecting the Exchange Server option enables you to search up to 500 mailboxes on the Exchange server, but you must have Exchange server administrator rights to access mailboxes.

4. In the Select PST Files window, you can use the Search button to display all PST files in a specified directory and subdirectories, and then select which files you want to include in the search. With the Add button, you can add PST files one at a time. Click the **Add** button, navigate to and click the `zl_lay-k_000.pst` file, and then click the **Open** button. The file is displayed as shown in Figure 3-4. Click **Next**.

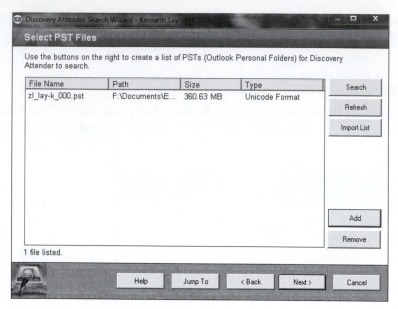

Figure 3-4 Selecting PST files
Source: Sherpa Software, Inc.

5. In the Specify Email Options window, click the **Search Both Messages** and **Attachments** options, and then click **Next**.

6. In the Select Email Folders window, click **Next**.

7. The Choose Search Criteria window specifies parameters for the search. Keywords, date ranges, file sizes, and filenames are common parameters used to identify relevant data. Make sure the **Keywords** check box is selected (see Figure 3-5), and then click **Next**.

8. You use the Choose Keywords window to conduct keyword searches with a word list or search expressions. When word lists are used, Discovery Attender returns a hit for each instance of a word in the list. You can use search expressions when counsel requests searching for specific combinations of words, such as "money AND (stocks OR investments)." Make sure the **Word List (Any)** option button is selected, type **money** in the list box (see Figure 3-6), and then click **Next**.

9. In the Keyword Search Options window, you set criteria for where Discovery Attender searches in the file. The Native Format option is used to search text, and the Raw Data option is used to search ASCII and Unicode binary data. In the Keyword Reporting Options section, the Simple option is selected to search a file for keywords. When a keyword is found, Discovery Attender stops searching the rest of the file and moves on to the next file, regardless of how many keywords are in the file. The hit stores the first keyword found but not other keywords in the file, if there are any. This option makes the overall search faster but not as accurate for reporting purposes.

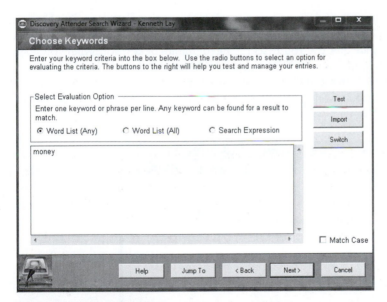

Figure 3-5 Specifying search criteria
Source: Sherpa Software, Inc.

Figure 3-6 Listing keywords
Source: Sherpa Software, Inc.

If you select the Complete option, Discovery Attender searches the file for keywords. When a keyword is found, Discovery Attender continues searching the file for additional keywords and storing all keyword hits. The Complete option gives you a more accurate listing of keywords found in the file; however, the search processing can be slower. Select the options shown in Figure 3-7, and then click **Next**.

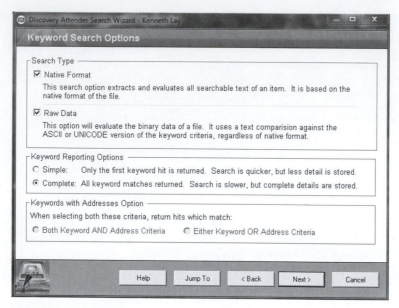

Figure 3-7 Setting options for keyword searches
Source: Sherpa Software, Inc.

10. In the Message Options window, you specify what areas of an e-mail message are searched for keywords. When keywords don't contain names, the Message Subject and Message Body options are usually adequate. If you're searching for names or keywords that you suspect might be found in an e-mail address or a Web page, select the Internet Headers and Message Addresses options. The Check Dates and Check Size options are available only if you selected the date range and file size options in the Choose Search Criteria window. Configure the message options shown in Figure 3-8, and then click **Next**.

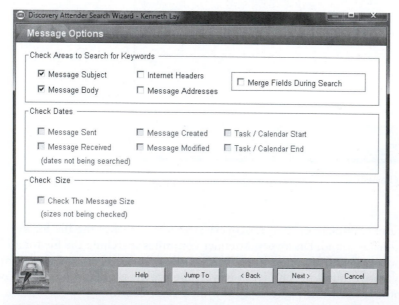

Figure 3-8 Selecting message options
Source: Sherpa Software, Inc.

11. In the Attachment Options window, you specify what areas of the message attachment are searched for keywords. By default, the Attachment Name, Attachment Body, and Nested Attachments options are selected. Again, the Check Dates and Check Size options are grayed out unless you selected the date range and file size options in the Choose Search Criteria window. Configure the attachment options shown in Figure 3-9, and then click **Next**.

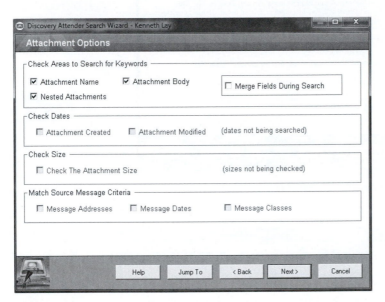

Figure 3-9 Selecting search options for attachments
Source: Sherpa Software, Inc.

12. In the Result Options window, you configure the search results. The default Hash Results option creates an MD5 hash value for every file, message, and attachment. When the search results are displayed, Discovery Attender can deduplicate the results based on identical hash values, among other criteria. (Deduplication removes identical files and messages and displays only one copy of the file or message.) Configure the result options shown in Figure 3-10, and then click **Next**.

13. In the Schedule Your Search window, you specify when the search should run, based on your needs. For example, if you're searching network shares or mailboxes on a server, you might want to schedule the search for a time when employees aren't at work to speed up processing. Click the **Save and start this search immediately** option button (see Figure 3-11), and then click the **Finish** button to start the search.

14. When the search processing is finished, leave Discovery Attender running, and proceed to Hands-On Project 3-3 to review the search results.

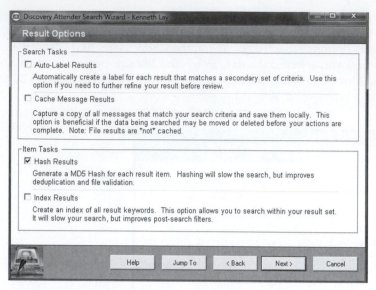

Figure 3-10 Selecting options for search results
Source: Sherpa Software, Inc.

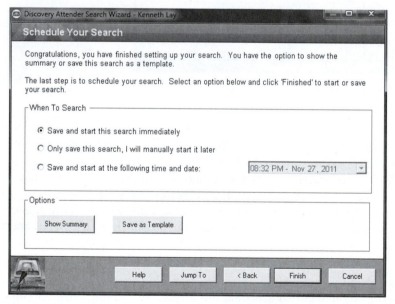

Figure 3-11 Scheduling a search
Source: Sherpa Software, Inc.

Hands-On Project 3-3

In this project, you review the results of the Enron search conducted in Hands-On Project 3-2. You must complete Hands-On Projects 3-1 and 3-2 to do this project.

1. If necessary, start Discovery Attender, click **Open Existing Project,** and click the **Enron** project when prompted to open a case. If the Create a New Search Wizard starts, click **Cancel.**

2. When the search processing is finished, Discovery Attender displays the Enron search results shown in Figure 3-12. This window contains some handy features that make your job easier. In the upper pane, the Hits column shows the number of times a search word was found. The Messages column identifies the number of messages in which the search word was found and the total number of messages in the PST file. The Attachments column shows the number of attachments containing the search word and the total number of attachments in the PST file. The lower pane lists the PST files and network file locations that were searched. The Hits column displays the number of hits found in *each* PST file or network location.

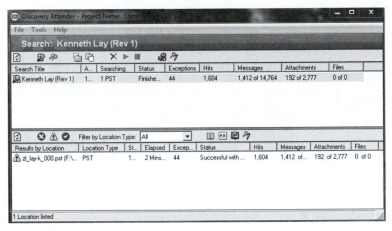

Figure 3-12 An overview of the search results

Source: Sherpa Software, Inc.

3. Click to select the **Kenneth Lay (Rev1)** search in the upper pane, and then right-click it to display a shortcut menu. All these options are useful, but the following are some you'll use often:

    *   *Search Again (Copy Search)*—A time-saving option that enables you to create an identical search with a revision number. You can also rename the search and assign a new revision number if the search criteria are identical, but the data sets and custodian names are different. For example, if you want to use the same search criteria as for the Lay search but search Enron President Jeffrey Skilling's PST files, you can select the Copy Search option, rename the search as "Jeffrey Skilling," change the revision number from 2 to 1, and select Skilling's PST files to search.

    *   *Open Results Management*—Displays detailed search results. You can also open this view by double-clicking a search revision in the upper pane.

    *   *Export List to CSV*—Exports a listing of results in the upper or lower pane to a comma-separated values (CSV) file. The list produces a useful summary that you can give to the attorney.

    *   *View Search Summary*—Creates a log of the search criteria and settings used for the search that's useful when you need to review this information later or when you've created multiple searches with variations.

4. To review detailed results for the search, double-click the **Kenneth Lay (Rev1)** search in the upper pane.

5. In the left pane of the Summary of Search Results window, click to expand the **By Location, By Result Type,** and **Keyword** folders (see Figure 3-13).

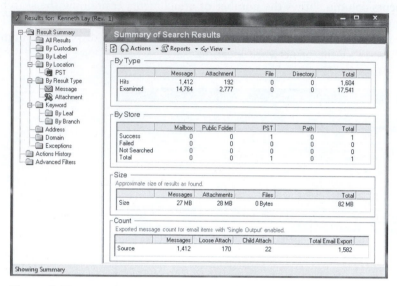

Figure 3-13 Viewing a detailed summary of search results
Source: Sherpa Software, Inc.

6. Click the **All Results** folder to display all the search hits in the List of All Results window. You can sort data in this window by clicking the field name at the top of each column. Click the **Keywords** column heading to sort the data based on keywords.

7. Notice that there are duplicate e-mail messages. Discovery Attender uses a deduplication tool to remove duplicate copies of data; typically, attorneys don't want to look at the same data several times. To remove duplicate e-mails, click the **Actions** list arrow on the menu bar, and then click **Deduplication**. In the Welcome - Start Deduplication window, click **Check All**, and then click **Next**.

8. In the Select Message Criteria window, Shift+click to select **Message Subject, Message Sender,** and **Message Sent Date** in the Available Criteria list box, click the **Add** button, and then click **Next**.

9. In the Select Attachment Criteria window, click the **Add Recommended Criteria** link. Notice that the Selected Criteria list box is filled in automatically. Click **Next**.

10. The Finish window displays a summary of the deduplication conditions used to remove duplicate files. Click **Finish**.

11. When the deduplication process has finished, Discovery Attender displays a summary window. Click the **Done** button to clear this window. In the List of 'Unique Items' Results window, "1351 Items Loaded" is displayed at the lower left. Before the deduplication process, 1604 results had been listed. A Unique Items folder has been added to the Result Summary list.

12. In many cases, search results produce data that's of no interest to the attorney. Before you export data to a PST file, the attorney might want to preview the search results summary. To do this, click the **Reports** list arrow on the menu bar, and then click **Export to CSV** to list all columns and rows of data in the List of 'Unique Items' Results window.

13. Create a new folder on your desktop named **Enron_Search_Results**. Name the CSV file **Kenneth_Lay_Rev1.csv** and save it to this folder. Click **OK** in the Successfully Exported list to CSV file message box.

The Configuring_Discovery_Attender_Settings.wmv video file (on this book's DVD) describes how the Export to PST options affect PST output formatting. For instance, internal PST folder structures can contain just the messages or a complete pathname to where the PST file was located when it was searched. The Export to PST settings can be changed while a project and search results are open, so you can make changes to the PST output formatting immediately. However, the Export to PST changes don't modify PST files that were created before the changes. The changes are applicable to PST files created with exported data after the Export to PST changes are made. In this project, the default Export to PST settings are used.

14. In the List of 'Unique Items' Results window, click the **Actions** list arrow on the menu bar, point to **Export,** and then click **Copy to PST.** Click **Yes** to confirm copying 1351 items.

15. Click **Create a new PST with user selected name,** and then click **OK.**

16. Navigate to and click the **Enron_Search_Results** folder on your desktop. Type **Kenneth_Lay_Rev1.pst** for the filename, and then click **Save.** Click **OK** when the export action is finished.

17. You can now send the Kenneth_Lay_Rev1.pst file to the attorney or another recipient. To view the contents of this file, you need to open it in Microsoft Outlook. Start Microsoft Outlook. Click **File** on the menu, point to **Open,** and click **Outlook Data File.** Navigate to the **Enron_Search_Results** folder on your desktop and click the **Kenneth_Lay_Rev1.pst** file. Click **Open** to review the file in Outlook. (*Note:* The steps required to open data files in Outlook 2003, 2007, and 2010 vary. Refer to the Help documentation for instructions specific to your Outlook version.)

18. When you're finished, exit Outlook and Discovery Attender.

Case Projects

Case Project 3-1

You're preparing an e-discovery request to collect information from a large company based in the United States. You need to collect company e-mail and financial files from six custodians. Three custodians live in the United States, one works in Spain, and two work in Australia. The company's computing systems use a logon banner. Write a one- to two-page paper describing computer and legal issues you should consider before serving a discovery request on this company.

Case Project 3-2

Use the Internet or a legal library to search for e-discovery rulings and laws pertaining to e-discovery and privacy rights. Choose a ruling from the U.S. courts in which a foreign plaintiff or defendant raised e-discovery privacy concerns or issues in the litigation. Write a two- to three-page paper summarizing the privacy concerns raised in the litigation and the U.S. court's ruling. Give your opinion of how the U.S. court's ruling will affect foreign privacy laws and future cases of this type.

References

Nelson, B., A. Phillips, and C. Steuart. *Guide to Computer Forensics and Investigations*, 4th Edition. Boston, MA: Course Technology, 2010.

The Sedona Conference Working Group Series. "The Sedona Conference Glossary: E-Discovery & Digital Information Management," September 2010, *www.thesedonaconference.org*.

chapter 4

Experts: The Right Person for the Right Job

**After reading this chapter and completing
the exercises, you will be able to:**

- Summarize the developments in managing discovery
- Explain the roles of digital forensics consultants and examiners in civil and criminal cases
- Describe when to use e-discovery consultants, including outsourcing factors
- Explain when to use special masters and forensics mediators
- Summarize best practices in e-discovery team management

In this chapter, you review the development, roles, and training of e-discovery consultants and experts as well as the roles and training of digital forensics consultants and experts used in civil and criminal litigation. You also learn about the use of special masters and forensics mediators in both civil and criminal cases. Understanding when and how to use these experts and consultants is important, as e-discovery case law and rules continue to develop and clients press to reduce litigation costs. Both law firms and IT professionals must keep improving processes and case management strategies to remain competitive, provide adequate client representation, and comply with changing court rules and agency directives.

Managing E-discovery

Managing e-discovery effectively involves understanding the process and tools as well as what skills staff members need, when to bring in the "experts," and how to select the right expert. It also involves merging the knowledge of two fields: law and information technology (IT). A case can't be managed effectively if the legal staff has limited technical skills. Similarly, problems can often be avoided if the IT staff has a reasonable grasp of litigation concepts and procedures.

In reality, law firms new to e-discovery often bring in an e-discovery attorney consultant, an attorney with special knowledge of e-discovery processes and procedures. However, these consultants often have limited "hands-on" technical skills, and many have their own IT staff or subcontract for IT support. An e-discovery attorney consultant might help the lead attorney with technical wording in court filings or interpreting e-discovery case law but doesn't add much practical support in processing the case discovery. A better alternative might be bringing in an IT consultant at a lower cost and turning to e-discovery attorney consultants for only law-related assistance.

In short, good case staffing involves an honest assessment of skill and knowledge levels. Does the e-discovery consultant know the pros and cons of the litigation database software used as the discovery review platform, and can he or she demonstrate these features (or lack of features)? Does the e-discovery attorney consultant have enough of an IT background to know whether a server backup tape is too old and expensive to restore, or will bringing in an IT subcontractor to make that determination be necessary, which would increase costs beyond the consultant's fees? For novice e-discovery practitioners, knowing *how* someone becomes an expert can be invaluable in forming a litigation team. In subsequent chapters, you see how legal professionals focus on case management and quality control, and IT professionals handle the remaining technical functions, such as database management and file conversions.

According to recent studies, litigation involving electronically stored information (ESI) typically costs between 17% and 48% more than cases without ESI (Lee III, Emery G. and Thomas E. Willging, 2010).

The Sedona Conference guide "Best Practices for the Selection of Electronic Discovery Vendors" (The Sedona Conference Working Group Series, 2005) addresses how to choose e-discovery vendors, including request for proposal (RFP) and request for information (RFI) processes. Similarly, the Electronic Discovery Reference Model (EDRM) has the "Project

Management Guide" (available at *www.edrm.net*) that covers how a law firm's e-discovery team, a corporate legal department, and vendors interact. These guides are a work in progress and are written mainly for corporate civil litigation teams; they don't address criminal litigation nuances or what training and certifications are available. Therefore, this chapter's discussion focuses on material not already covered by the Sedona Conference or EDRM, including a brief overview of e-discovery and digital forensics training options and certifications. This information, combined with the Sedona Conference and EDRM guides, give you a good foundation for making an informed e-discovery team selection.

You use the Sedona Conference and EDRM guides in Hands-On Project 4-2, and you can download them at *www.thesedonaconference. org/dltForm?did=RFP_Paper.pdf* and *www.edrm.net/resources/guides/ edrm-framework-guides/project-management*.

At the federal criminal level, in response to highly publicized discovery failings, former Deputy Attorney General David W. Ogden of the Department of Justice issued a memorandum for department prosecutors, "Guidance to Prosecutors Regarding Criminal Discovery" (Ogden, 2010). The memo restates prosecution's duty for discovery and identifies the role of a discovery coordinator in each U.S. Attorney's office. Similarly, federal public defenders have started using coordinating attorneys in complex criminal cases. The discovery coordinator (prosecution) or coordinating attorney (defense) function is a role similar to an e-discovery project manager in civil cases (see Figure 4-1).

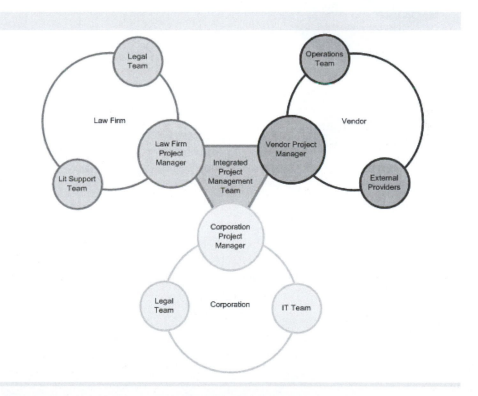

Figure 4-1 The EDRM project management team model

Source: *EDRM.net*

Deputy Attorney General Ogden's memo is available on this book's DVD in the Chapter04 folder (`DOJ_Memorandum.pdf`).

Figure 4-2 shows the relationships between roles in a complex multidefendant criminal case at the federal level. Most criminal cases have far fewer resources than in complex civil cases, so the use of a defense coordinating attorney is usually reserved for cases involving multiple defendants and substantial discovery. The coordinating attorney position is somewhat unique, in that one defendant often accuses another defendant of perpetrating the crime, which results in pitting defendant against defendant. The coordinating attorney is then a neutral resource facilitator between defendants but in opposition to the prosecution. In some circumstances, to save time and money, the coordinating attorney might act in a completely neutral position between all defendants as well as being a neutral resource facilitator for the prosecution.

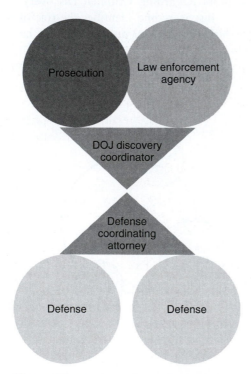

Figure 4-2 Members of a criminal case team
© Cengage Learning 2014

In federal criminal cases involving organized crime (racketeer influenced and corrupt organizations [RICO]), having 20 to 30 defendants per case isn't unusual, and each defendant is represented by an attorney. In capital cases (those that can result in the death penalty), two attorneys are assigned to each defendant. In addition, these investigations usually involve undercover work that can span years, with associated wiretaps, body wires, video surveillance, and seized computers and cell phones. Using a coordinating attorney to manage this kind of complex case structure and substantial discovery is becoming more common.

Before continuing, review the definitions of **expert** and **consultant**. Experts are those having special knowledge of a subject who can provide testimony. The courts state that this knowledge should consist of what's "not normally possessed by the average person." Their expertise can come from "study or education or from experience and observation." When an expert provides testimony, he or she becomes an expert witness. To testify in court or at depositions, expert witnesses "must be qualified by the court." They don't need to have formal training, but "the court must be satisfied that the testimony presented is of a kind which, in fact, requires special knowledge, skill, or experience" (Gifis, 1991).

Consultants are those who give professional advice or services and generally don't give testimony. In fact, a consultant doesn't need to have any special skills, knowledge, training, education, or experience. However, if consultants provide testimony, they become expert witnesses and are subject to the same qualifying standards as an expert. In short, the terms "consultant" and "expert" are often interchanged; however, to avoid confusion when working with legal professionals, try to use the term "expert" when denoting someone who is likely to give testimony.

This book sometimes uses the terms "expert" and "consultant" interchangeably; however, in practice, the two terms are often treated differently during litigation. In some circumstances, the work product of an expert or consultant might be subject to discovery by opposing counsel. For example, in criminal cases, notes taken during a forensics examination are likely discoverable if the examiner also testifies as a witness. Conversely, in a civil case, the notes and other work of a consultant who doesn't testify and is hired by a law firm are likely privileged and not accessible to the opposition. Each case is different, and roles can change throughout the case, so consult with the lead attorney if there's any doubt.

The developments of e-discovery and digital forensics technology influence the knowledge, experience, and technical skills of experts and consultants. Therefore, understanding the history of managing discovery is helpful because the same organization principles are applied to e-discovery today.

Discovery Management in the Past

After litigation formally started, usually by filing a complaint or an indictment, the case progressed in a variety of ways until discovery was exchanged between litigants. When a discovery request was received, the producing party gathered the necessary documents from all available sources (typically file cabinets and document storage facilities). Documents were then assigned a Bates number and reviewed to see whether they contained any privileged information; if so, that material was redacted. Next, document information was entered in discovery or privilege logs (discussed in Chapters 5 and 6), and the document was sent (produced) to the requesting party.

 These organizational processes are still used in civil and criminal cases, but now they're done digitally.

If the case was complex and involved a lot of documents, the lead attorney amassed groups of reviewers (often paralegals or junior attorneys) to go through the mounds of evidence, document by document and page by page, which was roughly organized in boxes. Document summaries were created to identify key information for each document, such as the date, title, source, author, recipient, and other important case issues determined by the lead attorney's case strategy or the discovery request from opposing counsel. This summary was often put on index cards (see Figure 4-3) or in word-processing documents.

CASE: Enron		
BegBates: Acct-000001	**EndBates:** Acct-000005	**Date:**
Production No.:	**Source:** Enron Accounting	**Location:** Box 13
Doc Type (circle): Letter Memo Report Contract Invoice Other _____		
Doc Title:		**Attached Doc Bates:**
Author:	**Recipient:**	**CC:**
Issues (circle all appropriate): Fraud Negligence Breach of Contract		
Privilege: Atty-Client Work Product Other _____		
Notes/Summary:		

Figure 4-3 Index card system for document summaries
© Cengage Learning 2014

Complex systems of cross-referencing were developed to assist paralegals and attorneys in locating documents, and notebooks were prepared to organize copies of core evidence. For example, witness notebooks often contained important documents used during depositions and again at trial. Similarly, issue notebooks contained documents related to specific case issues, trial notebooks contained exhibits to present in court, chronology notebooks with documents in date order were used to create a timeline of events, and expert witness notebooks were created for consultants and experts testifying in pretrial motions or at trial. The law firm handled creating most of these notebooks in-house, and only large projects were sent out for duplication, Bates numbering, and other organizational processes. At trial, selected documents were presented to the jury on an overhead projector.

E-discovery Management Today

As computer use became more common and the volume of discovery (particularly e-mail) grew, automated litigation software was developed to manage this increase in information. Paper documents were scanned into an image format (usually Tagged Image File Format [TIFF]) and processed through optical character recognition (OCR) software to convert word images into searchable text. These electronic documents were then loaded into the litigation software to be searched, reviewed, redacted, and organized. This process was the advent of the litigation database.

Gathering discovery is now more complex and might involve digital forensics experts or even Web-based services. Information previously entered on index cards or in word-processing documents is now captured digitally in a litigation database. Notebooks are still created but are in the form of folders or tags in litigation databases or trial presentation software. Depending on the nature of the case, having e-mail and other discovery in excess of 500,000 pages isn't unusual. Reviewing this much material in paper form would require large groups of reviewers working over a long time and could be quite costly. However, with litigation software and tech-savvy staff, far fewer people can manage the same amount of material more effectively and in a shorter time.

In 2005, Cisco migrated millions of documents into a new database, including e-mails, contracts, and other documents likely to be subject to discovery requests. The database was designed to eliminate duplicate copies and make finding documents easier. According to Cisco, one e-discovery firm bid $9 million to find evidence for a case. Cisco was able to handle the case for only $900,000 by using its in-house system (Krause, 2011).

However, as with most technology, litigation software is effective only if the user has been well trained in the software's basic and advanced functions. Unfortunately, time and cost constraints in law firms often limit staff training, which severely undermines using this technology efficiently. In fact, lack of training often creates problems in the form of errors as well as higher case costs. Instead of relying on the old-fashioned notion of going through stores of evidence page by page, searching for "the smoking gun" document, law firms should seek out experienced IT staff or legal staff trained in e-discovery processes and tools. IT staff can often search, organize, and process large volumes of electronic documents quite rapidly and effectively by using advanced litigation database features, programming, scripts, and other tools that are second nature to IT professionals.

IT professionals also know how to convert a wide variety of file formats into a form that can be viewed on a standard office computer. For example, an intellectual property case might involve CAD drawings, or a construction case might have geospatial maps. Most legal professionals don't have CAD or geospatial software; IT skills are needed so that legal professionals can view these digital drawings and maps. Criminal cases can be more complex, especially when law enforcement surveillance is done with proprietary software that's not accessible to non-law-enforcement users. These cases often involve thousands of wiretap recordings, and converting recordings one-by-one to a nonproprietary format for review isn't practical. IT skills are needed to find a compression/decompression algorithm (called a "codec") and do batch conversions to a usable format so that legal professionals can review these recordings.

Not all people are suited to all aspects of this work, and not all law firms should undertake the full spectrum of e-discovery processing. For example, someone who goes into law to help people or work with legal theory might not enjoy spending hours in front of a computer and learning new technology but might excel at case management and quality control. Conversely, IT professionals usually go into technology because they like computers and often find satisfaction in solving problems with technology and improving software systems, and these skills can reduce e-discovery costs. However, IT professionals might not be interested in the constantly changing subtleties of case law or case strategy nuances.

Digital Forensics Consultants and Examiners

Digital forensics consultants and **digital forensics examiners** are becoming crucial to the success of any litigation. They're the expert witnesses who identify an investigation's who, what, where, when, and how activities on a wide array of digital devices. In short, they find, preserve, collect, and analyze digital evidence. These experts typically have specialized, in-depth training on computers, cell phones, digital audio and video systems, and many other digital devices that can hold evidence.

Although digital forensics work is similar in both civil and criminal cases, there are some important differences in their roles. Before you continue, however, review two important terms. **Discovery** is "the process of identifying, locating, securing, and producing information and materials for the purpose of obtaining evidence for utilization in the legal process. The term is also used to describe the process of reviewing all materials that may be potentially relevant to the issues ... and/or that may need to be disclosed to other parties ... There are several ways to conduct discovery, the most common of which are interrogatories, requests for production of documents, and depositions" (The Sedona Conference Working Group Series, 2010). **Evidence** is the "testimony of witnesses, introduction of records, documents, exhibits, objects, or any other ... matter offered for the purpose of inducing belief in the party's contention ..." (Gifis, 1991).

In a civil case, discovery is generally done through interrogatories, requests for admission, requests for production, or depositions after a complaint is filed. **Interrogatories** are written questions submitted to another party for the purpose of gathering discovery; they're answered in writing and under oath. In essence, the requesting party asks the opposing side for the information, and the opposing side produces the material to the requesting party, unless it's privileged, work product, or not relevant. (Chapters 5 and 6 explain how to determine whether material is privileged, work product, or not relevant and discuss using protective orders in both civil and criminal cases.)

In criminal cases, the discovery exchange typically starts after the complaint or indictment and arrest; however, digital forensic examiners (often commissioned law enforcement officers) are often involved in investigating digital information to get an indictment or initiate a criminal complaint. In fact, digital evidence is seized, essentially without asking, when probable cause exists and a judge or magistrate issues a search warrant.

A Digital Forensics Consultant's Role in Civil Cases

The use of digital forensics consultants in the civil sector is growing because attorneys are becoming more knowledgeable about gathering and analyzing digital evidence. This section gives you a brief overview of their role in civil litigation and general corporate matters.

This book uses the term "forensic examiner" to denote an employee status (mainly law enforcement or IT staff) as opposed to the term "consultant," which indicates a non-employee relationship.

In hospitals, medical offices, and other healthcare organizations, Health Insurance Portability and Accountability Act (HIPAA) privacy laws apply to medical records, and a digital forensics consultant might be involved in policymaking or investigations. As you learned in Chapter 2, HIPAA laws require healthcare providers to keep track of hardware and electronic media and the people responsible for this equipment, to make sure patient health information (PHI) isn't shared with an unauthorized party, and to ensure that someone is responsible for tracking the receipt and removal of hardware and software containing PHI.

If civil litigation is pending, potential litigants have a duty to preserve evidence, and a preservation hold or litigation hold notice might be issued. Digital forensics consultants might be involved in prelitigation corporate policymaking or postlitigation expert witness services to identify what digital material should be subject to a hold notice and how to comply with this type of notice.

A sample preservation letter is included in `Kroll Sample ED Docs.pdf`, available on this book's DVD in the Chapter04 folder.

The Sarbanes-Oxley Act and compliance with it might also fall under the purview of an IT professional with digital forensics knowledge. Digital forensics examiners or consultants can also be involved in family law cases in a variety of ways. For example, in a divorce proceeding, examination of a computer might reveal whether one spouse had bank accounts or assets the other spouse was unaware of.

After litigation in civil cases has started, the active process of discovery begins. Often an interrogatory is the first formal discovery request in civil litigation. Interrogatories are written lists of questions served on another party and should ask, among other things, who potentially has evidence, where it's located, and in what format. A digital forensics consultant can advise legal professionals on the interrogatory's technical aspects for specific case issues, such as questions on server backup frequency and storage, where Web sites are hosted, frequency of required password changes, and so on.

A sample interrogatory is included in `Kroll Sample ED Docs.pdf`, available on this book's DVD in the Chapter04 folder.

As discovery is gathered and reviewed, new custodians (that is, holders of potentially relevant information) might come to light or discovery might be broadened in some way, so having multiple interrogatories isn't unusual. The response to interrogatories often establishes how much further discovery progresses, including what evidence will be requested, who will be deposed, and so forth.

A **request for admission** is generally served on the opposing party at the beginning of civil litigation, too. This written document asks the opposing party to accept or deny certain facts of the case and respond in writing and under oath. For example, a digital forensics consultant might determine that only one person logged on to a computer during a specific period. The opposing party could be asked to state in writing whether that person's logon was, in fact, being used at that time.

A **request for production** typically happens later in the process than requests for admission or interrogatories; it's a written request for information (discovery) to be produced. Like interrogatories, multiple requests for production can be made during litigation as case knowledge increases and fact-finding broadens. A digital forensics consultant can advise legal professionals on the technical aspects of this document, such as encryption, security protocols, or whether server logs or backup tapes are required.

A sample request for production is included in `Kroll Sample ED Docs.pdf`, available on this book's DVD in the Chapter04 folder.

A **deposition** is taking an oral statement from a witness under oath before the trial. Witnesses are deposed in both civil and criminal cases. In a civil case, the opposing side is usually present for the cross-examination, and a court reporter usually records and transcribes the statement. Digital forensics consultants (or IT staff handling digital forensics) can also be deposed. They might be questioned on frequency and retention of server backup media, frequency of password changes, and other related topics.

A sample deposition notice is included in `Kroll Sample ED Docs.pdf`, available on this book's DVD in the Chapter04 folder.

Used in both civil and criminal cases, a protective order limits access to information or evidence. Documents filed with the court are public record, unless they're sealed from public access or otherwise protected. For example, in civil cases, a protective order could be applied to trade secrets or highly confidential documents, such as algorithms developed for the Department of Defense. In criminal cases, protective orders are usually applied to witness or informant identities to protect them from harm or intimidation. In civil or criminal cases, a digital forensics examiner or consultant can identify digital information that could be subject to a protective order or function as a court-appointed neutral coordinator (discussed later in "Special Masters and Forensics Mediators") to oversee discovery or digital forensics activities between litigants. A neutral coordinator is especially helpful in limiting or resolving disputes over data accessibility, handling of privileged or confidential information, and other cost issues related to e-discovery and digital forensics.

A Digital Forensics Examiner's Role in Criminal Cases

In most criminal cases, commissioned law enforcement officers or agents perform digital forensics examinations under strict protocols; in some cases, they carry out these examinations after patrol officers seize digital devices. The initial law enforcement investigation uses consultants only in rare situations.

Because of a constitutional expectation of privacy in the United States, digital forensics examiners are generally limited in an examination's scope, based on the search warrant's criteria. However, in some criminal cases, a search warrant might not be required to seize a digital device; for example, when evidence of a crime is in plain view, immediate seizure is allowed. In addition, "exigent circumstances" might exist when law enforcement believes evidence could be destroyed, or there might be an "incident to arrest," in which an arrest has taken place and evidence needs to be preserved or a safety risk to the public or officer is believed possible. Other circumstances exist, but this book focuses on these three. Nonetheless, a search warrant is typically obtained to perform the actual forensics examination (searching for files, looking at Internet activity, and so forth).

In corporate investigations, there's a possibility the case can turn into a criminal matter. You should be aware of constitutional privacy expectations in the workplace and when to contact law enforcement if criminal activity is suspected.

After the complaint or indictment has been filed, defense attorneys typically ask for details and evidence of the alleged crime before arraignment so that they can advise defendants of their plea options. A **bill of particulars** is used in criminal cases to get this information, much the same way interrogatories are used in civil matters. In this situation, a defense attorney might use a digital forensics consultant to review the digital evidence, the appropriateness of law enforcement's examination (based on the search warrant), and the validity of the methods or tools used. A consultant is used because defense attorneys rarely have forensic examiners as employed staff.

In corporations, a digital forensics examiner or consultant might be asked to determine whether espionage occurred and trade secrets were stolen or participate in network security policymaking or incident response.

Remember that in criminal cases, digital forensics examinations are typically carried out by commissioned law enforcement, who are referred to as "examiners" rather than consultants. However, criminal defense attorneys do use digital forensics consultants in both testifying and nontestifying roles.

Testimony by Digital Forensics Consultants and Examiners

Digital forensics consultants and examiners are often required to give testimony in civil or criminal cases at trial or in depositions or pretrial declarations. In pretrial declarations, a digital forensics consultant or examiner might be asked to provide a written statement under oath about a specific aspect of the forensics examination. These declarations are supportive statements that accompany a summary judgment or other motion filed with the court. A **summary judgment** is a formal request to the judge to determine facts of a case before trial in an attempt to erode a case bit by bit, until no core issues are left for trial. Attorneys often file multiple summary judgment motions, but getting a judgment can be difficult unless they can make a strong argument to the presiding judge. In this capacity, digital forensics consultants and examiners function as expert witnesses, and their testimony is usually in written form.

Remember that if you don't have access to Westlaw legal research, free legal research Web sites are available, such as *www.justia.com*, *www.plol.org*, and *www.findlaw.com*. You can search these resources for sample summary judgments and other court filings.

Under *Giglio v. United States*, 405 U.S. 150 (1972), anything affecting a testifying law enforcement officer or other government witness's credibility is discoverable, including personnel records and any negative off-duty incidents. Under Giglio, prosecution has a duty to discover this information and disclose it to the defense. This is known as **witness impeachment**.

To get an indictment in some criminal cases, a digital forensics examiner can be deposed or testify before a grand jury. Grand jury hearings are normally held in secret, so the opposing side isn't usually present or even aware of the hearing until the indictment is issued. As a result, the opposing side usually gets the digital forensics examiner's testimony transcript as part of the bill of particulars or under the Jencks Act.

Defendants in federal criminal cases can use the Jencks Act to discover witness statements the prosecution team has. For example, under the Jencks Act, an informant's testimony to a grand jury is discoverable by defense, as is any payment, reduction of prison sentence, or other benefits the informant receives.

As expert witnesses, digital forensics examiners are asked for their qualifications, and the judge determines whether these qualifications are enough for the examiner to testify as an expert. This process is referred to as a "Daubert hearing" (*Daubert v. Merrell Dow Pharmaceuticals, Inc.*, 1993) in federal civil or criminal cases. However, some states still use the Frye test (*Frye v. United States*, 1923). In short, from 1923 until Daubert, federal and state courts admitted evidence that was generally accepted in the scientific community, as indicated in Frye. In Daubert, the judge determined that the Federal Rules of Evidence superceded Frye and allowed alternative criteria to be applied.

Federal Rules of Evidence 702 also addresses testimony by experts. The following is an excerpt from this rule:

> *If scientific, technical, or other specialized knowledge will assist the trier of fact to understand the evidence or to determine a fact in issue, a witness qualified as an expert by knowledge, skill, experience, training, or education, may testify … in the form of an opinion or otherwise, if (1) the testimony is based upon sufficient facts or data, (2) the testimony is the product of reliable principles and methods, and (3) the witness has applied the principles and methods reliably to the facts of the case* (The Committee on the Judiciary, House of Representatives, 2010).

As you can see, there's a fair amount of latitude in expert testimony, particularly for the expert's background. In essence, expert testimony is permitted when it comes from a reasonably reliable source and is done in a way that can assist the jury (or judge) in understanding facts of a case. For example, the average juror might have difficulty understanding how computer files are stored in a hard drive or how they're deleted and later recovered. An expert can testify, usually with the aid of graphics, how this process is performed. As a result, experts are in demand partially for their ability to do the work, such as deleted file recovery, but also for their ability to communicate complex ideas to a judge or jury. The ability to convert "geek speak" to common language for a jury (or anyone working on the case, including legal staff) is as important for digital forensics experts as it is for a lawyer to convert legalese to understandable language for jurors.

Training and Experience for Digital Forensics Consultants

Both digital forensics and e-discovery professionals rely on tool-centered and academic training as well as actual case experience to gain a thorough knowledge of their specialties. Tool-centered training in digital forensics covers a wide variety of technology topics, ranging from hexadecimal (bit-level) analysis to user activity analysis. In addition to training from agencies such as the Secret Service and FBI, law enforcement officers often get training in digital forensics from the International Association of Computer Investigative Specialists (IACIS), which results in the Certified Forensic Computer Examiner (CFCE) certification. Starting in 2010, IACIS opened its training to non-law-enforcement applicants, too. Major forensics tool vendors also offer training and certification to law enforcement. For example, AccessData Forensic Toolkit, Guidance Software EnCase, and X-Ways Forensics are three forensics tools with corresponding certifications.

You can view IACIS Certification Competencies at *www.iacis.com/certification/certification_competencies* and X-Ways training options at *www.x-ways.net*.

IT professionals take a different path to digital forensics training because they already have a strong computer foundation, such as an A+ certification, followed by training and certification from a forensics software vendor. The SANS Institute (*www.sans.org*) is another source of forensics education.

The Association of Certified Fraud Examiners (*www.acfe.org*) has both beginning and advanced training in digital forensics as a continuing education option for the Certified Fraud Examiner (CFE) designation. CFEs are usually well trained in a variety of investigative techniques for fraud prevention and detection, and some specialize in digital forensics investigations. However, the CFE designation alone shouldn't be viewed as a substitute for digital forensics certification.

Licensed private investigators might be former law enforcement officers who have IACIS training, certification from the International Society of Forensic Computer Examiners (Certified Computer Examiner [CCE]; *www.isfce.com*), training with a forensics software vendor, or no digital forensics training at all. Further, each state has different private investigator licensing requirements, so there's no consistency in background or training requirements.

Although some states have enacted legislation requiring digital forensics examiners to have a valid private investigator license, in August 2008, the American Bar Association issued a recommendation that doesn't support this requirement (American Bar Association, 2008). The ABA recommendation identifies Texas, Georgia, North Carolina, Rhode Island, Michigan, and New York as particularly aggressive in their licensing requirements and goes on to state: "The public and courts will be negatively impacted if e-discovery, forensic investigations, network testing, and other computer services can be performed only by licensed private investigators because not all licensed private investigators are qualified to perform computer forensic services and many qualified computer forensics professionals would be excluded because they are not licensed."

E-discovery Consultants

E-discovery has been around for decades but took on new importance with the 2001 Enron bankruptcy and the millions of documents processed during the ensuing litigation. The industry began to grow rapidly, increasing from $40 million in 1999 to approximately $2.8 billion in 2009 (Greenwood, 2011). At first, the transition to the litigation databases used with e-discovery was gradual because law firms, by their own admission, are often slow to adopt new technology. However, when it became apparent that discovery volume was growing rapidly with the increase in computer-generated documents, law firms began to work more closely with software developers to improve litigation database tools. As mentioned, discovery documents were converted to TIF images and scanned with OCR software, and everything was processed into this uniform format to be included in a litigation database, regardless of whether the original discovery was paper or electronic. The TIF conversion also made it possible to redact material; at that time, technology for redacting native electronic documents without altering metadata didn't exist.

Anything in a digital format might become e-discovery, even paper documents and analog recordings that have been converted to a digital format.

As the use of litigation databases became more prevalent, vendors that previously handled large-scale paper copying started adding more database support services. At the same time, a handful of attorneys established themselves as e-discovery consultants. Today, **e-discovery consultants** range from highly skilled attorneys with digital forensics or programming backgrounds who often work as discovery neutrals (described in the next section) to poorly trained copy machine operators who might have only 30 minutes' training on database software. In addition, some law firms have established litigation support departments specializing in e-discovery, with staff having varying degrees of certifications and training or even including temporary workers with no training at all. Numerous groups now offer e-discovery certification, although caution should be exercised because the value of some groups is unclear. Ultimately, the American Bar Association or another credible national or international association will likely identify bona fide certifications in this area.

Although not the same as certification organizations, more organizations are contributing to the standardization of e-discovery, including The Sedona Conference, EDRM, Text REtrieval Conference (TREC) Legal Track (*http://trec-legal.umiacs.umd.edu/*), and Organization for the Advancement of Structured Information Standards (OASIS) (*https://www.oasis-open.org*).

The following sections describe the main categories of e-discovery consultants and their typical levels of training or experience.

Consultant Categories

E-discovery consultants come from a wide variety of backgrounds and disciplines and might include digital forensics consultants and examiners. In fact, few attorneys have formal training in digital forensics or experience in programming or other IT fields. Although rare, attorneys with this background can be a valuable asset in litigation involving substantial discovery and often function as court-appointed neutrals.

Next are attorneys who don't have specialized computer training but have chosen to focus on e-discovery case law and practice. As mentioned, some law firms have entire departments dedicated to e-discovery practice. In most cases, the attorney monitors constantly changing e-discovery case law and uses IT professionals to manage the technical aspects of a case.

IT professionals who began their careers as in-house support at law firms often move on to litigation support service providers or become independent consultants. With careful screening, the right IT professional can be a valuable asset to large-scale litigation in a law firm or used to monitor outside counsel's technical processes and costs for corporate clients.

Litigation support houses and Web-based service providers run the gamut of experience and background. Some companies are extremely knowledgeable and experienced and devote substantial resources to improving their products and services. They seek out experienced IT professionals with law firm experience to expand their operations and usually have e-discovery attorneys in management. However, this group of service providers might undergo frequent mergers or acquisitions by domestic or foreign companies, which can result in poor quality control and high staff turnover if not carefully managed.

Digital forensics consultants are now expanding their services to include broader litigation support, primarily litigation database management. This expansion is a natural and logical progression because these professionals are comfortable working with highly technical material as well as extremely large volumes of discovery. They often understand many legal concepts, including chain of custody and how to testify in court.

Some e-discovery consultants have a natural aptitude for computers and might begin their careers in copy houses as document reviewers and coders or learn database administration on their own. This group of consultants usually has some type of certification in digital forensics or as database administrators for litigation tools.

Last, but certainly not least, a number of large computer-related companies, such as Kroll Ontrack, IBM, Cisco, and Pitney Bowes, offer e-discovery and computer forensics services, as do accounting firms, such as KPMG and Ernst & Young. These companies usually have ready access to tech-savvy staff and sometimes proprietary litigation tools.

Tool-Centered Training On the technical side of investigating civil cases, law firms manage e-discovery and present the evidence *subjectively* to a judge or jury instead of testifying about the analysis of evidence, which is what a forensics examiner does. As a result, law firms often rely on untrained or less experienced staff to handle basic litigation database functions in civil cases, such as searching and coding, and use IT professionals or technically proficient legal staff to perform more advanced case management functions, such as creating and administering databases. Segmenting e-discovery processing in this manner enables law firms to increase their profit on cases.

Litigation software vendors usually offer two types of training to address how law firms are typically organized: end-user training and more advanced administrator training. You can see an example of iCONECT's two levels of training at *www.iconect.com/training-support/*. End-user training prepares people to use the software's basic features and is often structured for people with limited technical skills. The administrator training covers more complex end-user features as well as how to create the database and populate it with documents and data, perform database backups, manage network or security problems, and so forth. Certification usually accompanies satisfactory completion of either training.

Training is also available for document conversion tools, such as IPRO or ImageMaker products, which convert paper or digital documents into images (usually TIF with OCR), capture metadata, and create load files for importing into litigation databases or trial presentation software. Typically, converting documents and creating load files fall into the administrator category of training, designed for more technically proficient people. The IPRO training programs (*http://iprotech.com/training/*) are more complex than iCONECT's because they usually involve working with multiple platforms. For example, scanned paper documents or native files converted in IPRO are usually imported into iCONECT, other review platforms, or trial presentation tools. If the converted documents aren't processed correctly, they won't work with other e-discovery tools. Further, IPRO's system administrator training involves using a suite of tools, whereas iCONECT and other review platform training involves using a single tool.

Many litigation software products offer free training videos or webinars for beginners. For example, Concordance is a widely used litigation database with free training videos available at *www.lexisnexis.com/en-us/litigation/products/tutorials.page?tabs=Concordance*. If software vendor training isn't available, these videos can get you started, and reading the software's developer manual is a good way to learn its advanced features.

Academic Training Along with the growth in e-discovery and digital forensics, more academic institutions are establishing courses to train law students, paralegals, and IT professionals. Courses in law school, naturally, tend to focus more on e-discovery case law but might also include limited orientation to litigation database or trial presentation tools. Some law school courses have crossover discussions of digital forensics concepts but usually little or no hands-on training. Conversely, courses offered by college computer engineering or information systems departments tend to focus on the technical aspects of e-discovery and digital forensics and touch on case law only briefly. However, some two-year and four-year colleges are working to form certification programs that offer a good balance of case law review and hands-on technical training to move students through all stages of the e-discovery process with a basic knowledge of legal issues, using current software and hardware tools.

Some junior colleges that don't have a formal e-discovery program have creatively improvised by having a paralegal class and an IT class partner for a mock case, including a mock trial. This partnership mirrors the interaction between legal and IT staff that typically takes place in the real world.

Testimony by E-discovery Consultants

E-discovery consultants are sometimes asked to testify in court, although not as commonly as digital forensics consultants or examiners are. Usually, their testimony is limited to the methods they used to collect or process discovery. For example, what methods were involved in deduping? Did keyword searching include "fuzzy searches," a process of using wildcards or other methods to allow for variances in spelling, typing mistakes, poor spelling, and so forth? Most e-discovery consultants don't have the training to testify about evidence analysis used in digital forensics, such as who did what on a digital device. If evidence analysis and testimony are required, a qualified digital forensics consultant or examiner should be used.

Outsourcing E-discovery Consultants

Litigation involving e-discovery and computer forensics is complex. Even for small cases, finding staff with strong technical skills and using specialized software and hardware are important for e-discovery processing, but preparing to handle this task in-house can be a costly endeavor. As a result, many law firms outsource all or part of this process to vendors until they gain experience or have access to in-house resources. After getting this experience, many law firms establish departments dedicated to this process to increase profitability, and the full cycle of e-discovery is done in-house. Some corporations also establish in-house e-discovery departments, but the reason is to manage litigation costs better, not increase profits.

Regardless of whether e-discovery is managed by a law firm or in a corporate legal department, outsourcing all or part of the e-discovery cycle still requires knowledge of the process and tools and stringent quality assurance measures. For example, using a Web-based e-discovery repository shifts the bulk of the technical processing and, therefore, staffing and infrastructure to the hosting service and leaves legal professionals free to focus on a case's legal elements. However, without quality assurance checks and some reasonable technical skills, deliberate overcharging or preventable errors can result in excessive costs. For example, one national PDF repository charged monthly based on storage use, but many PDF files were scanned at higher than necessary resolution (which increased file size), and multiple copies of documents were loaded into the database. These practices increased storage charges substantially and created difficulties in downloading documents for trial. As a result, the law firm had to rebuild the database in-house one week before trial.

In addition, many vendors outsource part of e-discovery processing, such as document scanning and coding services, sometimes to foreign processing centers. Paper documents scanned at too low a resolution can result in poor-quality OCR, which means documents might be missed during database searching. Further, poor vendor communication can result in incorrect document coding, which also means documents can be missed during a database search. (Database text and field searching and OCR quality control are discussed in Chapters 5 and 6.) In short, when there's little or no quality assurance with outsourcing, the result is poor-quality products and possibly higher case costs to correct problems, not to mention possible adverse case outcomes.

On August 5, 2008, the American Bar Association issued "Formal Opinion 08-451: Lawyer's Obligations When Outsourcing Legal and Nonlegal Support Services," placing the responsibility for outsourcing results squarely in the attorney's lap. In part, it states: "A lawyer may outsource legal or nonlegal support services provided the lawyer remains ultimately responsible for rendering competent legal services to the client." It also states the lawyer has a duty to disclose outsourcing to the client.

Outsourcing is also used in criminal cases, although less often than in civil cases because of security, chain of custody, and other concerns. For example, in the case of *U.S. vs. Zacarias Moussaoui* (September 11th terrorist), discovery was hosted on a Web-based repository so that the defendant could review the case materials securely from jail while awaiting trial. This hosting option is being used more often in criminal cases because of increasing volumes of discovery and defendants' constitutional right to participate in their own defense, even if they're awaiting trial while in custody.

Special Masters and Forensics Mediators

In civil or criminal litigation, a **special master** is a person the court appoints to assist in performing specific functions in a pending action. These experts are essentially judicial adjuncts who are called different names, such as discovery master, neutral, neutral expert, coordinating attorney, referee, and other titles, all denoting a neutral role between parties in a case. A special master is often a lawyer or former judge; however, special masters who aren't attorneys but have expertise in e-discovery and computer forensics can also function in this capacity. E-discovery and computer forensics special masters, whether or not they're attorneys, can conduct on-site inspections of computer equipment and files, review sensitive data collections for relevance and privilege, and perform other tasks.

Although not as prevalent in criminal cases as in civil, the use of court-appointed neutrals is becoming more popular as judicial caseloads increase and digital case issues become more complex. In addition, time and budget constraints on law enforcement, prosecutors, and public defenders can make this role an attractive option in criminal cases.

If both sides agree, the court might appoint a special master under Federal Rules of Civil Procedure (FRCP 53) or a neutral expert witness or judicial assistant under the court's powers to manage discovery and mediate disputes under the Federal Rules of Evidence. For example, in the *World Trade Center Disaster Site Litigation* (2008 WL 793578, S.D.N.Y. March 24, 2008), a multidistrict insurance case, the plaintiffs objected to the court-appointed special master's recommendation that a third party build, maintain, and operate a discovery database. In approving the database's creation, the court held that with 10,000 cases before it, the possible benefits of managing large quantities of information in a central location outweighed the cost.

In another example, the judge in the case *Wachtel v. Health Net, Inc.* (239 F.R.D. 81, D. N.J. December 6, 2006) noted "a lengthy pattern of repeated and gross noncompliance with discovery." This pattern resulted in a "staggering" waste of judicial resources through years of policing discovery responses. In this case, the defendants ignored preservation obligations, delayed e-mail searches until after e-mail had been routinely destroyed, failed to inform its own outside counsel of the existence of relevant data, and ignored judicial orders to produce discovery. Sanctions were applied, and the court struck several of the defendant's pleadings, imposed costs, and appointed a special master at the defendant's expense. As this example shows, problems with discovery production generally result in disputes that consume a lot of judicial time and energy. This is financially wasteful to litigants and ultimately taxpayers, who pay for judicial salaries and court support.

In any court proceeding, judges often respond favorably to parties who show respect and consideration for the court's (including the judge, court staff, and especially the jury) time and financial constraints. Everyone on the litigation team, including digital forensics consultants and e-discovery consultants, should be conscious of this issue.

An article in the April 2010 issue of *Federal Courts Law Review* (Riedy et al, 2010) proposed the term **forensics mediator** for a new type of consultant. This person, instead of the plaintiff or defendant, would perform the actual discovery investigation. A forensics mediator would also facilitate agreements on production between both parties. Mediated investigative e-discovery might be the solution to achieving full and fair discovery efficiently, with minimal involvement by the presiding judge.

For an insider's perspective on the skills and knowledge needed as an e-discovery special master, *E-Discovery: A Special Master's Perspective* by Craig Ball (*www.craigball.com/EDD_SM_PERSP.pdf*, 2010), is an informative resource.

"Appointing Special Masters and Other Judicial Adjuncts: A Handbook for Judges and Lawyers" has a sample order for appointing a special master (available at *www.fjc.gov/public/pdf.nsf/lookup/ACAM2009.pdf/$file/ACAM2009.pdf*).

Best Practices in Selecting an E-discovery Team

Until e-discovery certifications have been approved and recognized by the American Bar Association or other credible entity, it's up to clients to screen law firms and consultants for suitable training and experience. Smart litigation consumers establish best-practice guidelines that combine technical certifications and ongoing legal training requirements for all law firm staff, as well as digital forensics and e-discovery consultants.

In criminal litigation, particularly for prosecutors, best practices extend to all discovery tasks, particularly exculpatory, impeachment, and protective order materials. Similarly, law enforcement agents, who also deal with huge amounts of discovery during investigations and trials, must stay abreast of new technologies and training. If law enforcement agents are testifying as experts, they should be mindful of their personal off-duty activities or other potential impeachment issues and how these activities could be used in court to impeach their current case testimony. Any potential concerns should be brought to the prosecutor's attention early in the case.

In addition to checking certifications and training, litigation consumers, particularly corporations, should develop methods to track case outcomes and costs. Many large corporations already require their outside counsel to use task-based billing, which is commonly known as **Uniform Task-Based Management System (UTBMS)**. In task-based billing, each legal task is assigned a code, and the time each staff member spends on this task is logged into a billing system with that code. Conversely, standard legal bills use narrative descriptions with a corresponding time unit to track activity. The downside of narrative billing is that corporate clients can't easily determine how much time was spent on an activity because several activities often take place in one time period and are blended into a descriptive paragraph. For example, a junior attorney does legal research and then begins drafting a motion to be filed in court; combined, these tasks take about an hour. A narrative entry describes both the research and motion drafting in one paragraph; with task-based billing, the research must be tracked separately from the motion drafting and gives clients a way to measure law firm productivity. Law firms prefer narrative billing for many reasons but mainly because writing a short summary at the end of the day is easier than tracking each activity in detail. Nonetheless, most insurance companies and many large corporations require task-based billing.

Using the UTBMS allows a litigation client (or law firm) to determine how much time is spent in each major category of the litigation process, including e-discovery, and formulate benchmarking systems. Through benchmarking, corporations can begin identifying which law firms manage litigation most effectively and can determine whether team changes need to occur or a consultant or IT professional should be brought in to manage processes better.

The electronic billing systems most law firms use are designed to accommodate task-based billing. In fact, many of these billing systems have adopted the e-discovery task codes ratified by the Legal Electronic Data Exchange Standard (LEDES) in July 2011. Two widely used billing systems are DataCert and TyMetrix. An added benefit of using these e-discovery codes is that they follow the EDRM process flow.

Visit *www.utbms.com* or *www.ledes.org* to review litigation task codes and e-discovery subcodes.

Chapter Summary

- The organizational concepts of discovery are the same today as in the past, before widespread use of computers. Index cards have been replaced with litigation databases, and discovery notebooks have been replaced with database folders and tags.

- As technology continues to develop, e-discovery becomes more complex—a task that shouldn't be underestimated in civil or criminal cases. This field is for people who enjoy continued learning because using e-discovery and computer forensics software and managing digital discovery require more training than traditional office software does.

- The industry has many consultants and experts. Some deserve these titles and enhance case management substantially; others don the title "expert" without having adequate hands-on foundation or experience. Corporations involved in litigation should establish best practices for selecting and monitoring e-discovery outside counsel, and law firms should establish best practices for selecting consultants and experts.

- Tool-centered training is available in both e-discovery and digital forensics. E-discovery training is divided into end-user and administrator levels; digital forensics training is more complex and unified.

- Digital forensics training for law enforcement officers can be obtained from a variety of sources, including IACIS and independent agencies. Non-law-enforcement training is available from IACIS, the International Society of Forensic Computer Examiners, The SANS Institute, and the Association of Certified Fraud Examiners.

- Digital forensics examiners and consultants often testify in court or in pretrial proceedings. Their ability to communicate complex technical issues to a judge or jury in simple language is important to success in most litigation.

- Law firms sometimes outsource legal and nonlegal support services but remain responsible for providing competent legal services to clients. In addition, lawyers have a duty to disclose the use of outsourcing to clients.

- The use of special masters, neutrals, and forensics mediators is becoming important in complex civil and criminal cases to minimize disputes and conserve judicial time and energy.

- UTBMS task-based billing can be used instead of narrative billing to establish case cost and efficiency benchmarks. Corporations can reduce the legal costs of e-discovery (and litigation in general) by using active rather than passive case monitoring.

Key Terms

bill of particulars   A request to prosecution for details and evidence of an alleged crime. *For civil cases, see* interrogatories.

consultant   A person or company offering services or professional advice; consultants can testify as experts if they meet the same qualifying standards.

deposition   Giving testimony under oath outside court; a key form of discovery.

digital forensics consultants   A person or company offering digital forensics services or advice; can subcontract some or all of the work.

digital forensics examiners   People who perform the actual forensics examination of digital hardware or software. They can give testimony on their findings or other related matters.

discovery   The process of identifying, locating, securing, and producing information and materials for use in litigation.

e-discovery consultants   People or companies providing a broad range of e-discovery services or advice, from digital forensics and data collection to file conversions, database administration, and hosting; these services sometimes include trial consulting.

evidence   The testimony of witnesses and the introduction of records, documents, exhibits, objects, or any other probative matter offered for the purpose of convincing a judge, jury, or other litigation party of a fact or belief.

expert   Under FRE 702, a person with special knowledge, experience, training, education, or skills; can also function as a consultant.

forensics mediator   A forensics expert who is neutral to the case and functions as a mediator between parties.

interrogatories   Under FRCP 33, written lists of questions served by one party to another. *For criminal cases, see* bill of particulars.

request for admission   Under FRCP 36, a form of discovery that asks the opposing party to accept or deny certain facts of the case in writing and under oath.

request for production   Under FRCP 34, a form of discovery, usually in writing, that requests documents, electronically stored information, or other tangible items; can also be used in criminal cases.

special master   Under FRCP 53, someone appointed by the court to perform a certain role or duties; can also be used in criminal cases.

summary judgment   A decision rendered by the court, usually before trial, that eliminates an issue in dispute.

Uniform Task-Based Management System (UTBMS)   A task-based billing system that assigns a code to each legal task.

witness impeachment   The process of attacking the accuracy of a witness's testimony or showing that a witness isn't credible.

Review Questions

1. Litigation databases replaced the use of what in organizing discovery? (Choose all that apply.)
   a. Interrogatories
   b. Index cards
   c. Word-processing documents
   d. Tape recordings

2. Digital forensics examiners can get technical training and certification from which of the following? (Choose all that apply.)
   a. The International Association of Computer Investigative Specialists
   b. Forensics software vendors
   c. The International Society of Forensic Computer Examiners
   d. Microsoft

3. In addition to the usual tasks of collecting and analyzing digital evidence, digital forensics consultants might be involved in which of the following activities? (Choose all that apply.)

   a. Corporate policymaking

   b. Offering technical advice on interrogatories

   c. Determining the appropriateness of law enforcement's examination

   d. Identifying digital information that's subject to a protective order

4. In which of the following circumstances is a search warrant *not* required to seize a digital device? (Choose all that apply.)

   a. Evidence of a crime is in plain view.

   b. Law enforcement believes evidence could be destroyed.

   c. There's a constitutional expectation of privacy.

   d. A safety risk is believed possible.

5. Digital forensics consultants are law enforcement officers. True or False?

6. Industry standards require e-discovery consultants to have certified training in litigation database, document conversion, and trial presentation software. True or False?

7. Which of the following is a proposed new type of consultant who would perform the actual discovery investigation instead of the plaintiff's or defendant's counsel?

   a. Forensics mediator

   b. Special master

   c. Coordinating attorney

   d. Neutral

8. Litigation database software training is usually divided into which two levels? (Choose all that apply.)

   a. End user

   b. Certified examiner

   c. Administrator

   d. Special master

9. E-discovery consultants do *not* testify about which of the following?

   a. Computer user activity

   b. Deduping methods

   c. Keyword search methods

   d. Accuracy of search results

10. Which of the following consists of written questions submitted for the purpose of gathering discovery along with written answers to these questions? (Choose all that apply.)

    a. Requests for admission

    b. Interrogatories

    c. Requests for production

    d. Depositions

11. Deputy Attorney General David W. Ogden's memo identifies the role of a(n) _____ for each U.S. Attorney's office.

12. According to the American Bar Association, when outsourcing legal services, the service provider is responsible for the results. True or False?

13. A court-appointed e-discovery neutral must be a former judge or lawyer. True or False?

14. E-discovery best practices for civil case management should include which of the following? (Choose all that apply.)

    a. Litigation software training

    b. Powerful workstations

    c. Tracking costs with the UTBMS

    d. Being able to sue the data collection company

Hands-On Projects

You can find data files for this chapter on the DVD in the Chapter 04\Projects folder. If necessary, be sure to copy them to your working directory on your machine before starting the projects.

Hands-On Project 4-1

In this project, you search the Internet for two e-discovery special masters, and write a one- to two-page summary of their curriculum vitae (CV): technical qualifications (if any), legal qualifications or degrees (if any), recent cases, and any other information, such as published books and articles. State briefly why you would or wouldn't use each one. You might want to review FRCP 53 (available at *www.law.cornell.edu*) for information on the use of special masters.

Hands-On Project 4-2

In this project, review the Sedona Conference "Best Practices for the Selection of Electronic Discovery Vendors, 2005," the EDRM "Project Management Guide" (*www.edrm.net*), and this chapter's material, and select two recommendations for choosing experts or vendors. Write a one- to two-page report summarizing why you chose these two recommendations.

Because the Sedona Conference material is lengthy, you can focus on "Section VI: What's for Sale: Electronic Discovery Services" and Appendix A-4, "Vendor Background" (*www.thesedonaconference. org/dltForm?did=RFP_Paper.pdf*). Browse through the rest of the document so that you know what information is covered for use in real-life situations or hands-on projects in later chapters.

Hands-On Project 4-3

In this project, you compare the information in a computer forensics report with the information you gathered in Chapter 3's hands-on projects to learn more about metadata. You use a sample report generated from Forensic Toolkit.

Internet Explorer 8 and Word 2010 are used in this project. If you're using IE 9 or Word 2013, steps might differ slightly.

1. Copy the **EnronFTKReport.zip** file in the Chapter 04\Projects folder on the DVD to your working directory. In Windows Explorer, right-click the file and click **Extract All**. Then click the **Extract** button to extract the report's contents. Navigate to and double-click the **Index.html** file to open it (see Figure 4-4). This file shows you what an FTK computer forensics report looks like; it uses the Enron PST as an example.

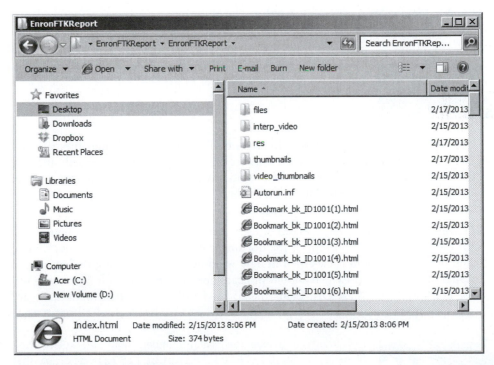

Figure 4-4 The FTK case report

Source: AccessData Group, Inc.

2. Navigate through the links in the navigation pane on the left and review the information briefly. Next, in the Bookmarks section, click the **Money_ASCII_Search** link to see this part of the report, which describes each document found during the search for "money" you did in Chapter 3. The first document you should see is files\[Fwd_Social Security].html (see Figure 4-5).

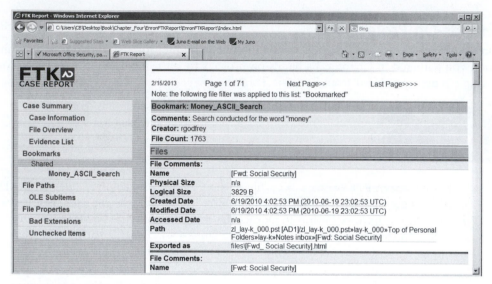

Figure 4-5 Viewing the Money_ASCII_Search section of the report
Source: AccessData Group, Inc.

All duplicates are included in criminal cases to comply with disclosure requirements related to exculpatory material.

As you can see, the information for each bookmarked file includes the path where it was located; its size; dates the file was created, modified, and accessed; and other OS information. Because the Enron PST is no longer on the host computer, OS dates aren't available in this example. However, in the Path line, you can see that the document came from the Notes inbox folder of Ken Lay's PST file.

3. Scroll down to the 03-06-01 minutes.doc file, and read the information in this part of the report. At the bottom of the document description, right-click the **files\03-06-01 minutes.doc** link and click **Open in new window**. In the Opening dialog box, click the **Open** option button (which should indicate opening the file with Microsoft Word by default), and then click **OK**. Using the F5 (or Find) key or other methods, search this document for the word "money." Note how long it takes to find all occurrences.

FTK inserts a unique identifying number inside brackets in the filename, as in 03-06-01 minutes[1572].doc, so that duplicate files aren't overwritten.

4. Close the Internet Explorer window. Right-click **files\03-06-01 minutes.doc** and click **Save target as**. Save the file in your working directory, and minimize the FTK Report window. In Windows Explorer, open the file. In Word, click **File, Info,** and then click the **Properties** list arrow in the right pane. In the drop-down list, click **Advanced Properties**. Review the information in the General and Statistics tabs. Figure 4-6 shows both tabs and their relationship to the application (Word), OS, and hard drive metadata. Figure 4-7 shows the hidden streams and objects that are linked and embedded (called "object linking and embedding [OLE]") in this file, focusing on the SummaryInformation stream. Streams and objects contain code used as an interface between the application (in this case, Word) and the OS. This OLE information remains in the document, even when it's been removed from the original computer.

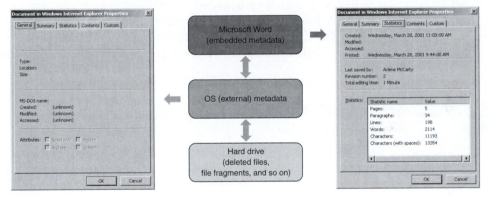

Figure 4-6 OS and application metadata

Source: Microsoft, Inc.

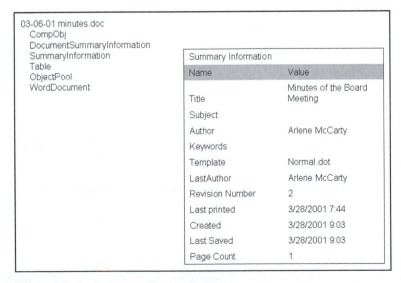

Figure 4-7 A compound file structure

Source: AccessData Group, Inc.

Files containing streams and objects, such as Word files, are called "compound (COM) files" or "structured storage."

5. Close the Properties dialog box and the 03-06-01 minutes.doc file. If prompted to save the changes, click **No**. Maximize the FTK Report window.

6. Continue to explore the FTK report to see what information is available. Because forensics examiners use the FTK tool, you'll find many types of information. Remember that numerous items were found in the "money" search, so clicking every link to review each item separately usually isn't practical. Importing these items from the report into a litigation database is often better for further review.

7. An FTK report is like a typical Web page, so several supporting files are generated in the EnronFTKReport folder. Close the FTK report. Now browse to and click the **files** folder to open it (see Figure 4-8). Sort the documents by clicking the **Type** column heading. If the **Type** heading isn't showing, right-click the column and click **Type**.

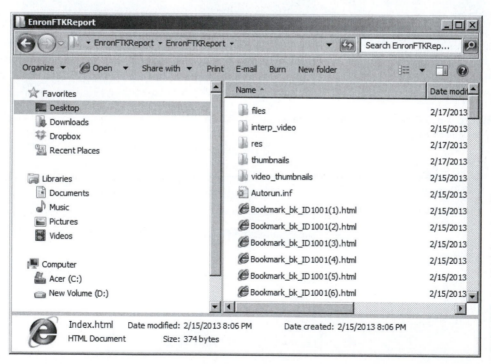

Figure 4-8 Sorting documents in a folder
Source: Microsoft, Inc.

These documents contain the word "money." The Office documents should have embedded metadata, as you see shortly. If you're working with a review platform such as iCONECT, Concordance, Summation, or another litigation database, you can load these documents into the software to make searching and organization easier, as long as there's searchable text. (Remember that you might not be able to search some PDFs and other files.) Although not ideal, by importing files into a review platform, you can at least search them globally for any case-related information. However, unlike in Discovery Attender, the e-mail attachments aren't matched with the original e-mails; they're separated.

8. Next, you practice copying one of the Word files in the files folder to a new location on your computer. Open the document you've selected, click **File, Info,** and then click the **Properties** list arrow in the right pane. In the drop-down list, click **Advanced Properties**. See whether any information in the Statistics or General tabs has changed, and then close the Properties dialog box.

9. Next, remove the read-only lock on the document by clicking **File, Info,** if necessary. Click the **Properties** list arrow in the right pane. In the drop-down list, click **Advanced Properties**. In the General tab of the Properties dialog box, click to clear the **Read only** check box. Now try different ways of moving files on your computer (such as dragging and right-clicking) and to a flash drive to see whether any metadata changes. Finally, try changing one letter in the Word document, save it, reopen it, and check the **General** and **Statistics** tabs in the Properties dialog box again.

These actions make you aware of how easily metadata changes in documents. Pay particular attention to the creation date. At some point, it should be newer than the other dates shown, which indicates the file could have been created on another computer and moved later. This information can be important in a criminal case and perhaps in a civil case. When embedded file metadata is available, comparing it with OS metadata in key case documents can reveal useful activity indicators.

The Sedona Conference Glossary includes definitions of metadata and different dates (creation date, for example) in an attempt to standardize the use of these terms. Interpreting dates in FTK and other discovery tools can be helpful, but compare the date and metadata definitions of your tool's manual with the Sedona Conference Glossary to be sure the terminology is used consistently in your reports, for case management purposes, and so forth. If there are differences, spell them out early in the report or other case management notes.

The structure of Office documents changed to Extensible Markup Language (XML) with Office 2007. Embedded document metadata still exists, but now it's carried in XML levels.

10. If time permits, start a Web browser, and go to **www.symantec.com/connect/articles/ microsoft-office-security-part-two**. Read the Symantec article on Microsoft Office security to learn more about hidden metadata in documents. Using the 03-06-01 minutes.doc file, practice the method described in Section 2.3 of the article, "Recover unseen metadata." Compare what you find with what was shown previously in Figure 4-7.

Case Projects

Numerous complaints and indictments were filed in the Enron case, but for simplicity's sake, the most recent (Lay_Indictment.pdf and lay_civil_complaint.pdf) are available on this book's DVD in the Chapter 04\Projects folder. You can find the original filings on the Internet, if needed.

Case Project 4-1

Using the ESI Letter 2011.pdf data file on the DVD as a sample, draft a preservation letter to Enron's agent of record for legal notice. If needed, you can use the information at *https://www.sos.nh.gov/corporate/soskb/Corp.asp?359194*.

Case Project 4-2

Using the SW.doc file on the DVD as a sample, draft a search warrant affidavit to seize and examine Ken Lay's computer in the Enron criminal case. Use your own information to fill in the blanks or the information at *https://www.sos.nh.gov/corporate/soskb/Corp.asp?359194* as well as the Lay_Indictment.pdf data file.

Case Project 4-3

Conduct a search at *www.microsoft.com* for the term "Document Inspector," and read about removing hidden data from Office documents. Similarly, search the Internet for "redacting pdf metadata" (all three words without quotes), and read a few articles that look interesting, preferably from *www.adobe.com*. Write a half-page summary of what you found for both Office and PDF documents.

Case Project 4-4

Search the Internet or other sources for three digital forensics experts, evaluate their qualifications, and select one you would likely use on a case in the future. If you find a company with multiple experts on staff, select one expert in the organization you want to use. Contact the three companies and explain that you're a student who's researching experts. Ask questions about their background and services, specifically whether they do criminal defense work. Remember that commissioned law enforcement personnel usually handle forensics work for the prosecution, but some civilians (typically with law enforcement backgrounds) might contract with prosecutors for case overloads or in rural areas, so client representation conflicts might exist if you need defense representation. Write a one- to two-page analysis of their qualifications and case experience, and explain why you would use the expert you selected over the others you researched. Include their responses about criminal defense work.

References

American Bar Association. "Formal Opinion 08-451: Lawyer's Obligations When Outsourcing Legal and Nonlegal Support Services," August 5, 2008, *www2.americanbar.org/calendar/ ll0508-2011-midyear-meeting/Documents/formal_opinion.pdf*.

American Bar Association. "Recommendation," August 11–12, 2008, *http://docs.google.com/ viewer?a=v&q=cache:ZV---FHmTWwJ:www.americanbar.org/content/dam/aba/migrated/ scitech/301.authcheckdam.doc+american+bar+august+2008+forensics&hl=en&gl=us&pid= bl&srcid=ADGEESh-VH19g9t2vVw7LeG1KBoiCpqbHf3p8mOXvRqZdZuHvr_o9zWtGiA W8tqmke_AxJC-uiPMdqJmbTlxPiY7V1pUPMxoCwtRryFJNzC6HabEqAvVJY-ld5aoKGVw AmhU8eMAIQv9&sig=AHIEtbTY9DLesMs6JBbwzNSul7oLtEQimw.*

Gifis, S. *Barron's Law Dictionary*, Hauppauge, NY: Barron's Educational Series, Inc., 1991.

Greenwood, A. "A New View, Part 2: E-Discovery Changes Have Some Seeing a Career in Document Review," *ABA Journal*, October 1, 2011, *www.abajournal.com/magazine/article/ a_new_view_part_2_e-discovery_changes_have_some_seeing_a_career_in_document/.*

Krause, J. "Businesses Head Off E-Discovery Costs," *Law Technology News*, February 25, 2011, *www.law.com/jsp/lawtechnologynews/PubArticleLTN.jsp?id=1202483163110& Businesses_Head_Off_EDiscovery_Costs&slreturn=1.*

Lee III, Emery G. and Thomas E. Willging. "Litigation Costs in Civil Cases: Multivariate Analysis - Report to the Judicial Conference Advisory Committee on Civil Rules," March 2010, *www.uscourts.gov/uscourts/RulesAndPolicies/rules/Duke%20Materials/Library/ FJC,%20Litigation%20Costs%20in%20Civil%20Cases%20-%20Multivariate%20 Analysis.pdf.*

Ogden, D. "Memorandum for Department Prosecutors: Guidance for Prosecutors Regarding Criminal Discovery," January 2010, *www.justice.gov/dag/discovery-guidance.html.*

Riedy, M., S. Beros, and K. Sperduto. "Mediated Investigative E-Discovery," *Federal Courts Law Review* 4: 1, April 2010, *www.fclr.org/fclr/articles/html/2010/Mediated%20 Investigative%20E-Discovery.pdf.*

The Committee on the Judiciary, House of Representatives. *Federal Rules of Evidence*, December 2010, *www.uscourts.gov/uscourts/RulesAndPolicies/rules/2010%20Rules/ Evidence.pdf.*

The Sedona Conference Working Group Series. "Best Practices for the Selection of Electronic Discovery Vendors: Navigating the Vendor Proposal Process," July 2005, *www. thesedonaconference.org/publications_html.*

The Sedona Conference Working Group Series. "The Sedona Conference Glossary: E-Discovery & Digital Information Management," September 2010, *www. thesedonaconference.org.*

chapter 5

Digital Evidence Case Flow

After reading this chapter and completing the exercises, you will be able to:

- Describe the procedures for preserving digital evidence
- Explain how to use Web-based repositories to process relevant data
- Use software tools to identify and review relevant data

This chapter describes the litigation process from the perspective of the party responding to a discovery request, and Chapter 6 describes the litigation process from the perspective of the party who initiated the litigation. In most cases, both parties seek and exchange discovery; they can be in the e-discovery cycle at any time, producing or receiving discovery, regardless of whether they're plaintiffs or defendants. As you can see in the EDRM, litigation isn't a linear process; there's a lot of back and forth.

In this chapter, you learn about preserving and processing digital evidence as well as identifying and reviewing relevant data. To see how to perform these tasks in a Web-based environment, you use tools such as iCONECT.

Preserving Digital Evidence

Because there's a risk that ESI can be altered inadvertently during collection if the correct tools and processes aren't used, the EDRM preservation stage is critical. The Electronic Discovery Reference Model defines preservation as "ensuring that ESI is protected against inappropriate alteration or destruction." The goal is to isolate and protect potentially relevant data to make sure it's legally defensible and in proportion to the discovery request; this process should also reduce the risk of altering data (*www.edrm.net/resources/edrm-stages-explained*). "Legally defensible" means the evidence is accepted by the courts.

For civil cases, Rule 26(f) recommends that both parties "address any issues related to disclosure or discovery of electronically stored information." The Sedona Principles (Second Edition, 2007) suggest including preservation and production methods in these discussions, and the parties should agree on their responsibilities and the scope of relevant data. Preserving electronic data in its original format is recommended; however, doing so can be a challenge. Electronic data is susceptible to changes and modifications caused by system activity and users accessing data. Therefore, expecting responding parties to take every conceivable step to preserve all potentially relevant data is unreasonable, but they aren't excused from taking reasonable steps to secure and preserve relevant data. In the litigation process, preserving data is commonly referred to as the duty to preserve, as you learned in Chapter 1.

Duty to Preserve

According to the Sedona Principles, organizations have a duty to preserve ESI if the data is expected to be relevant to litigation. A duty to preserve is also commonly called a "litigation hold," as defined by the court in the *Zubulake v. UBS Warburg LLC* case. The court ruled that "once a party reasonably anticipates litigation, it must suspend its routine document retention/destruction policy and put in place a litigation hold to ensure the preservation of relevant documents" (*Zubulake IV*, 220 F.R.D 216, S.D.N.Y 2003). Usually, relevant data that's produced is also accessible. However, the FRCP allows producing relevant but not accessible data (such as deleted data), for which advanced forensic or data recovery methods might be required to recover it (FRCP, 2006).

The responding party is responsible for evaluating which procedures and methods are best suited to meeting the preservation order and is obliged to preserve and produce relevant electronically stored data in good faith. To identify all relevant data, the responding party must use a variety of methods, and using electronic tools for search criteria and data sampling is preferred. Sanctions can be imposed if the court determines that the responding party had a clear duty to preserve relevant data but failed to do so, and this failure prejudiced the requesting party's case (Sedona Principles, Second Edition, 2007).

In criminal cases, prosecution and law enforcement have a duty to preserve all material, including anything that could be exculpatory or affect the trial's outcome.

Identification and Collection

In the EDRM, the identification stage is used to determine potential sources of relevant information. Because the scope of data being preserved and disclosed might not be known or might be subject to interpretation in the early stages of litigation, FRCP Rule 26(f) mandates what's called a "meet and confer." This meeting allows both parties to agree on what constitutes relevant data and what format should be used for data. Failing to meet and confer can result in court rulings that affect the case. For example, in *National Day Laborer Organizing Network et al v. U.S. Immigration and Customs Enforcement Agency et al* (10 Civ. 3488, SAS), the parties didn't meet and confer to settle details of the discovery format, resulting in the defendants producing files that didn't include metadata. In addition, because of the defendants' late response and their failure to object to the plaintiff's format requests, the court had to rule on these issues (S.D.N.Y., February 7, 2011). Judge Shira A. Scheindlin, well known for her decisions on e-discovery in the *Zubulake* case, wrote that "by failing to produce the records in a reasonably useful form and … in a form that makes it difficult or burdensome for the requesting party to use the information efficiently," the defendants violated FRCP 26(f).

In addition, referring to metadata being stripped from the files, Judge Scheindlin stated "that metadata is generally considered to be an integral part of an electronic record." She recommended including nine fields of metadata in any ESI production: identifier, filename, custodian, source device, source path, production path, modified date, modified time, and time zone offset value (the computer's time zone difference from Coordinated Universal Time [UTC]). She also recommended including these fields in all e-mail production:

- Sender and recipient
- CC and BCC recipients
- Date and time sent
- Subject
- Date and time received
- Attachments

Finally, Judge Scheindlin stated that the following metadata fields must accompany images of paper records: `bates_begin`, `bates_end`, `attach_begin`, and `attach_end`.

Many litigation databases, such as Concordance and Summation, require using an underscore instead of a blank space between words in some OCR fields. The underscore acts as a spacer to keep two words together in the same field during importing. Review the software manual to make sure you use the correct format.

This case shows a trend toward producing e-discovery data in native format. The courts prefer that requesting parties receive e-discovery data in the same form and with the same content as what the producing parties used. The objective is to prevent discovery being produced in a "litigation response" format, in which useful file metadata might be not be visible to the receiving party because the file format has been altered. For example, if the responding party stores documents in a Microsoft Word format but produces these documents in Adobe PDF format, the original file metadata is lost. If a requesting party receives electronic information with missing metadata, the courts might require the producing party to include relevant metadata. This case also emphasizes the importance of parties meeting and agreeing on discovery formats. If they can't agree, the issue can be referred to the court for resolution.

In criminal cases, identification and collection of discovery is subject to search warrants, court-ordered subpoenas based on probable cause, the plain view doctrine, and so forth.

The collection stage consists of acquiring ESI data that was specified as potentially relevant in the identification stage. Data is collected by using software tools, such as Discovery Attender and AccessData Forensic Toolkit, designed to retain metadata and protect files from inadvertent modification or changes. The EDRM recommends that litigation teams develop a collection strategy, prepare a collection plan, select the collection method, and then carry out the collection plan (*www.edrm.net/resources/guides/edrm-framework-guides/collection*). An important factor not mentioned in the EDRM is ensuring that technically qualified people are used to manage ESI data collection because they have expertise in knowing where different data types might be stored.

Processing Digital Evidence

After relevant information is collected, the processing stage takes place to reduce the volume of electronic data. In some cases, data must be converted into a format that's more suitable for review and analysis (EDRM, 2005–2012).

Requests for Data

Requests for relevant data can be received via a subpoena or an e-discovery request. The Sedona Principles and FRCP Rule 26(f) recommend that both parties discuss issues of preserving and producing electronic data to reduce misunderstandings as well as unnecessary motions and disputes. Discussions early in the litigation process improve the chance of discovery requests being clear and having a targeted scope.

Using a targeted scope for data collection requires configuring search criteria in the software tools used for collecting data. Search expressions can include proximity searches, keywords, or a combination of both. Other common search types are date ranges, e-mail addresses, and file types (such as PowerPoint or Word files).

In criminal cases, the discovery scope is much broader and should include exculpatory material or any material that could affect the trial's outcome.

Eliminating Duplicate Files

In many civil cases, processing data collections involves removing duplicate files. This task adds to the processing and review time because you must sift through redundant data. However, it's essential because duplicate files increase the data set's size and the cost of the production process.

Many e-discovery collection and review tools have built-in features for removing duplicate files. For example, you can select file attributes, such as filenames and create dates, to compare files. When the tool conducts a search based on these criteria, files with identical names and create dates are identified and can then be removed so that only one copy of a file is available for review.

Using Native or Converted Files

So far, you have gone through the litigation cycle to the EDRM processing stage. At this point, data sets are typically processed in one of two ways, depending on the file format both parties have agreed on. One method is to continue to the review stage with the files in native format, and the other is to convert the files into TIF with OCR or into searchable PDF files. (Both methods have variations, too.)

Both native and converted files have advantages and disadvantages. Deciding which method to use is often based on the attorneys' technical knowledge, skills, and experience. The review platform and the scope of the case are typically factors, too. Attorneys usually opt for converted files for a variety of reasons. The following sections examine these two main formats (as well as modified compromises between them), describe how they work in review tools, and discuss reasons for choosing one format over the other.

Native File Review   Most tech-savvy industry experts push for native file review because you don't have to spend time and money converting files that are already searchable and have intact metadata. However, these experts are comfortable with technology, which often isn't true for others in the legal community. Take a look at the `Kenneth_Lay_Rev1.pst` file produced in Chapter 3. Although it has been deduped, it still contains 1348 e-mail messages and 199 attachments of a variety of file types, including some less common ones (see Figure 5-1).

Although these files can be searched, you need a review tool that allows searching without altering metadata. Typically, the review process requires using the file's native application to open it for indexing and searching. However, opening a file might trigger hidden macros that change not only metadata, but also the file's contents. For example, Word documents can contain the Auto Date feature, which changes a document's date when it's opened. Similarly, when some Excel spreadsheets are opened, formulas are triggered. Even PowerPoint files can be set to open in Show mode, often with preset animation timings that alter the opened file. Automation and macro features in Office products can also affect discovery.

Discovery Attender and FTK are good tools for searching without altering metadata, but they don't have the organization features attorneys need for their work. (Because Discovery Attender and FTK don't have features for these organizational tasks, the following sections describe other desktop and Web-based tools you can use.) For example, processing software that automates functions such as Bates stamping is more efficient than manual organization

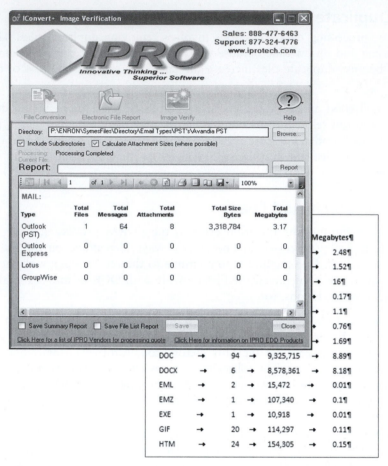

Figure 5-1 An IConvert report
Source: IPRO Tech, Inc.

methods using index cards and notebooks (discussed in Chapter 4). Bates stamping is a logical numbering system that uniquely identifies each page in documents produced for discovery and filed with the court. The Bates prefix denotes the document's source. For example, Acct-00001 means the first page of the first document from the Accounting Department. This useful system has been around since the late 1800s. Figure 5-2 shows an exhibit attached to a summary judgment with a Bates number identifying the document and page.

Bates numbering of documents is also known as "endorsing."

TEXAS COMMERCE BANK
NATIONAL ASSOCIATION

June 29, 1993

MARTHA D. VOSS
Private Banking
Vice President

Mr. Kenneth L. Lay
Chairman and Chief Executive Officer
Enron Corp.
1400 Smith Street
Houston, Texas 77002 - 7369

Dear Mr. Lay:

First, I would like to "introduce" myself as your new Private Banking officer at Texas Commerce Bank and I look forward to working with you in the future. I have been with Texas Commerce Bank for 12 years, most recently working in Gary Wright's Houston Corporate Banking Department.

I have met with Sally Keepers to discuss the pending issue of the renewal and consolidation of your two personal lines at TCB (including the $1.5 Million line formerly at First City and the $250,000 line at TCB). Sally requested that I write you a brief letter for our mutual discussion in order to outline the proposed terms and conditions as well as to point out the major differences between the existing and proposed line.

Attached you will find a brief summary of the proposed terms and conditions of a new combined $1.75 Million line. I believe there are several major advantages (both economic and administrative) of this proposed structure including:

(1) the two separate facilities are combined into one new facility;

(2) all fundings will be under one master note for a one-year period versus separate notes required every 90 days on the First City line;

(3) interest rate of Prime on a 365 day basis versus the current rate of Prime + 1% on a 360 day basis on the First City line (TCB's current rate on the $250,000 line is also Prime);

(4) collateral coverage of 150% on total outstandings versus the current "split" requirement of First City based on the type of stock pledged, i.e. "restricted" stock requires 175% coverage and "non-restricted" stock requires 150% coverage (TCB's $250,000 line is unsecured).

With regards to the latter point, the issue of "excess collateral" under your existing lines versus the current structure is worthy of a brief discussion. As of June 29th (see the attached Collateral Valuation), the collateral coverage of the total outstandings under both lines ($1,541,939 outstanding) would be 191% ($2,920,636 collateral value). Under either the existing or proposed structure, you would currently have the ability to borrow up to the full $1.75 Million line. However, it is fair to point out that the "excess" collateral is slightly different. Under the existing collateral and outstandings on the First City line, their is approximately $850M of excess collateral whereas under the new structure their would be slightly less excess collateral of approximately $625M.

GOVERNMENT
EXHIBIT
1045
Crim No. H-04-25 (S-2)

LAY-G34 0554

LAY-G34 0554

Figure 5-2 Example of a Bates stamp

Source: *www.justice.gov*

Searching without changing metadata and content is just the start. Many documents related to the discovery request might contain privileged or protected material. For example, in an internal management memo including a proprietary algorithm, the algorithm might be protected as a trade secret, but the rest of the memo is not. Legally, the unprotected portion must be produced, but **redaction** can be used to omit the protected data. Redacting part of a document—in this example, the algorithm—requires a tool that can handle this task without altering metadata. Redaction capabilities are often built into collection software.

After redacting protected data, attorneys consolidate all remaining data in one location for review and production. This data includes paper discovery, which is typically scanned and imported into the litigation database along with digital files, deposition transcripts, audio and video files, and so forth. Relevant documents should then be produced showing "alteration marks," which include Bates numbers and redaction marks. Documents containing these marks are called "burned-in," meaning Bates numbers and redaction marks can't be removed.

Web-Based Repositories For all but the smallest cases, Web-based repositories are a good option for review, and most can handle native file formats as well as paper. In addition, a hosting service manages converting data to the repository's platform. By using a Web-based repository, law firms and corporations can focus on a case's legal issues, leaving the problems of technology, infrastructure, and database administration to a third-party vendor. Typically, a Web-based repository service has clients transfer their collected data (including paper), maintain the chain of custody, and coordinate database configuration, such as field names and access rights. The result is secure Web access to a litigation database loaded with discovery files and ready for review. With quality control procedures, Web-based repositories can be an effective way for both novice and experienced law firms and corporations to manage e-discovery.

In addition to handling many technical support issues, Web-based repositories make it possible for multiple attorneys to access the data quickly if the case increases in scope. These attorneys can be located anywhere and can access the Web-based repository as long as they have Internet access. Repositories also make monitoring case progression easier.

Remember to consider software licensing requirements when choosing between in-house or Web-based review platforms; licensing can affect staff and co-counsel in remote locations. For example, the review platform's end user licensing agreement (EULA) might require remote co-counsel or staff to purchase their own licenses before they can be granted access to the review platform.

As discussed in Chapter 3, many e-discovery tools are available, and the market is quite competitive. In addition to getting recommendations from others, a good way to find reliable products is to sit in on free webinars offered by vendors. However, for the purposes of this chapter, you focus on iCONECT as a Web-based repository example. iCONECT, a software as a service (SaaS) product, came on the scene a decade ago. It can be hosted by a third party or on in-house servers. SaaS products offer technical support and bear the ongoing expense of improving their products to address rapid changes in digital technology and legal review requirements.

So why not use one of these cloud services if the process is easy? The American Bar Association opined that outsourcing services is acceptable, but the attorney of record is ultimately responsible for any problems resulting from outsourcing. Outsourcing raises security concerns because data is transported and stored offsite under the control of another organization. Therefore, security controls must be specified and included in agreements between the service agency and the data owner.

Web-based repositories of legal data can usually be accessed only by clients. However, the Federal Energy Regulatory Commission (FERC) Web site has a link to an iCONECT sample database containing data on FERC's Western Energy Markets investigation, which centered on Enron. This database contains Enron e-mails and .pst files, more than 150,000 scanned pages of documents, more than 85,000 records, and 40 transcripts related to the case. It includes a user guide and enables you to interact with a Web-based repository so that you can familiarize yourself with how these tools work. In the following activity, you connect to this sample database and explore using iCONECT to conduct searches.

Activity 5-1: Exploring iCONECT as a Web-Based Repository

Time Required: 45 to 60 minutes, depending on the Internet connection speed

Objective: Learn about iCONECT's features and view Enron data in a Web-based repository interface.

Description: In this activity, you connect to the iCONECT sample database and explore a Web-based repository tool. An Internet connection is required.

Internet Explorer is recommended as the Web browser for this activity. You must disable the popup blocker for these steps to work. If you have any trouble connecting to the database, consult the troubleshooting guide; you might need to contact the site administrator for help with licensing issues.

1. Start a Web browser and go to **www.ferc.gov/industries/electric/indus-act/wec/enron/info-release.asp.**

2. Click the **Search iCONECT nXT** link to open the iCONECT database with a guest login.

3. Figure 5-3 shows a list of available databases containing .pst files, documents, and transcripts, among others. Click the **ScannedDocuments** check box, and then click the **Open** button. If necessary, click **Run** in the Security Information message box. Close the Quick Tasks window that opens.

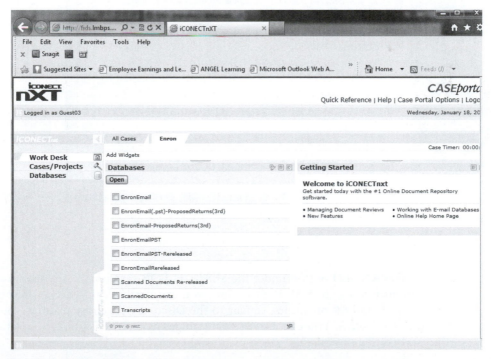

Figure 5-3 The database list

Source: www.ferc.gov

4. The ScannedDocuments window displays document 1 of the total 84,620 documents. This document contains four pages, as you can see by the numbers in the FIRSTBATES and LASTBATES fields (see Figure 5-4). Running vertically along the left side of the window are tabs you can use for a variety of tasks:

- *TOOLBAR*—Use this tab for searching and synchronizing the viewing window with selected documents.

- *REPORT*—Use this tab for creating reports that track review progress, the number of relevant and nonrelevant documents, and so forth.

- *EXPORT*—Use this tab to export data in a variety of formats, such as comma-separated values (CSV), and for applications such as Sanction II, TrialDirector Suite, and Concordance & Opticon.

- *PRODUCE*—Use this tab to print data, upload to network locations via FTP, or copy data to CD format.

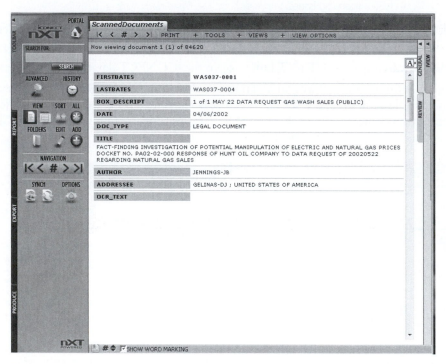

Figure 5-4 The ScannedDocuments window
Source: www.ferc.gov

5. Click the **ADVANCED** button under the SEARCH FOR text box to see advanced search options (see Figure 5-5). For example, you can do Boolean searches that enable you to use AND and OR operators, similar to the Discovery Attender features you explored in Chapter 3. You can also use date ranges, word exclusion, and several sorting and editing options.

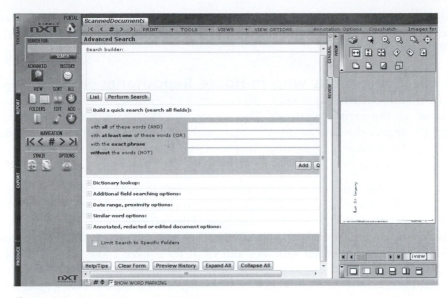

Figure 5-5 Advanced search options
Source: www.ferc.gov

6. You can also use the menu bar at the top for a wide variety of features. Click the **PRINT** and **TOOLS** menus to review what tasks are available; note that many are also available in the vertical tabs on the left. Next, click the **VIEWS** menu, and review the options for editing features used in different views.

7. iCONECT includes a help feature. Click **Help** to open the window shown in Figure 5-6. If necessary, click the **Contents** tab to see a detailed overview of categories and features in iCONECT.

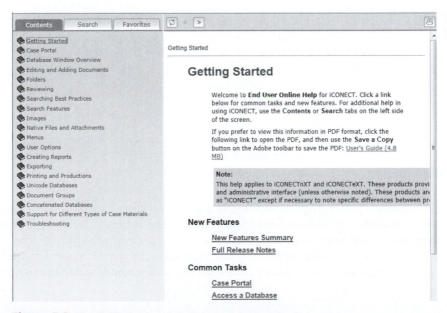

Figure 5-6 The iCONECT help window
Source: www.ferc.gov

8. Continue exploring iCONECT features, as time permits. For example, try conducting a search using the keyword "money" and review the results. When you're finished, exit the Web browser.

Native File Conversions with In-House Repositories
Say your corporation or law firm has decided to handle processing and review in house and purchased Concordance as the review platform. The native files that have been collected are just the start; you expect the case to grow substantially as both parties review the discovery. The attorneys have agreed to produce files in a stable format (TIF or PDF) for importing into Concordance.

Attorneys are usually most comfortable with searchable PDF files, largely because they're required to file documents with the court in PDF format. However, searchable PDFs might not be the best option for a litigation database. Files converted to TIF with OCR have some advantages over PDFs. For example, most litigation database and trial presentation tools were developed to be used with TIF and OCR files. Even those that can now handle PDFs and native files, such as Concordance and Summation, still work best with files in TIF format. There are some limitations in reviewing native files. E-mail (`.pst`) files, for instance, can be loaded in Concordance, but there's no reporting feature to check whether all files have been loaded. You must manually verify that all files were copied to the hosting platform when you're loading zipped and password-protected files or files created in applications that aren't installed on the host computer. Also, embedded files, such as an Excel spreadsheet embedded in a Word document, aren't extracted, so they can't be searched. With these limitations, the only practical use of these tools is for preliminary review of native files.

When discovery is converted to TIF with OCR, features such as Bates-stamping and redacting discovery are available, but metadata has to be captured separately. Despite this limitation, many law firms, corporations, and government agencies use Concordance and Summation for e-discovery management. If other tools are used that aren't capable of conversion to TIF with OCR, you can use special tools, such as ImageMAKER Discovery Assistant, LexisNexis LAW, AccessData Discovery Cracker, and IPRO eScan-IT, for this procedure. These tools work with a variety of native file formats and are capable of preserving metadata and Bates numbers, performing searches, cracking passwords, unzipping files, and handling decryption, among other tasks.

When you're evaluating processing tools, keep in mind that most cases have vast amounts of paper discovery as well as digital files. Some processing tools have no scanner interface for paper documents, so they can accommodate only digital files.

The final processing output from these tools is a group of files, usually TIF images, image logs, and load or data (`.dat`) files. These files populate the review platform with metadata, OCR content (extracted text), and coded information and operate as interlinking files, so clicking a field in the database opens the corresponding image in a viewer application. Typically, image logs contain a document's starting and ending identifiers (usually TIF references) as well as page count, parent-child relationships of any attachments, and so forth. A `.dat` file contains database fields, extracted document metadata, and/or OCR content (the actual document text). Depending on the program, OCR content is loaded in a field in the review database or stored in a separate file for searching. Review platforms vary in how load files are structured, but tools such as iConvert (free from IPRO) can be used to convert load files between platforms.

Figure 5-7 is an example of how these files are related. It shows the Enron iCONECT database on the left with the corresponding TIF image on the right. The `.dat` file (in the Notepad window under the database section) contains database field names as well as OCR. The image log file (displayed under the TIF image in the Notepad window on the right) shows code for finding the correct image in the database to display and lists a page count for each document. The actual TIF images are in a separate folder that's not shown; they're displayed in the viewer when activity occurs in the corresponding database field.

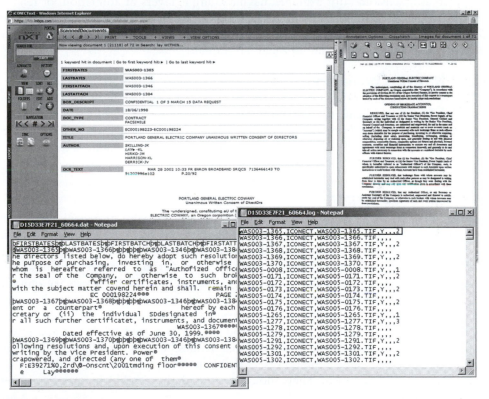

Figure 5-7 Load files

Source: www.ferc.gov

After the processed discovery is loaded in the review platform, additional database fields are coded with information similar to what was included on index cards (issues, privilege, and so on) in the past. **Coding** is the process of examining documents to identify names, dates, and relevant terms or phrases and entering the resulting information in database fields; this process can be done manually or with software. **Objective coding** is used with bibliographic data (for example, sender, recipient, date, and so on), and subjective coding is used to evaluate relevancy, legal issues, and so forth.

Coding provides information used in **fielded searching** and sorting, such as words or data that might not be in the document contents but are important descriptors. One example is issue coding, which determines whether the document's narrative content relates to case issues. You might have a database field called Issue, and this field's content could include items such as "breach of contract" or "harassment" for a lawsuit involving an employee's wrongful termination. Conversely, **full-text searching** involves all the document contents that have been converted to OCR.

Remember that you're taking native files from the applications in which they were created, forcing them into a "foreign" database, and converting them to flat TIF files. How are Excel spreadsheets and Access databases handled? Even relational structures might be evidence, such as those between fields, tables, and Web pages. PowerPoint files can also be considered dimensional (for example, having multiple layers or animation) or relational content (having calculations tied to another slide or an external document, for instance). All this potential evidence, whether it's dimensional or relational, is usually destroyed or corrupted in some way during processing to a flat TIF format.

Near-Native Conversion (the "Compromise Format") To solve the problem of Excel, Access, and other formats that don't lend themselves easily to TIF conversion, the "near-native" option can be used. With this option, you use TIF conversion for files that can be converted easily and preserve other files in their native format; these files are then linked to the database via hyperlinks. Hyperlinks reside in a database field for each document, and the native file is stored in a separate folder.

Then There's Paper

Almost all cases include discovery of paper documents, and attorneys want them to be searched in the review platform, too. Converting paper documents to TIF with OCR involves the same processing tools discussed previously as well as a scanner interface. Again, planning and communication are critical to getting consistent results. As you see in the hands-on projects at the end of the chapter, OCR quality can vary quite a bit; it's another quality assurance issue the review team should monitor. Search methods and field coding must be adjusted to accommodate problems with OCR quality, as shown in Figure 5-8. For example, subjective field coding is added to the database to improve search results for documents with particular names, words, or phrases, but this process can increase costs substantially. To offset the cost of manual coding, auto-coding tools have been developed. They should be tested thoroughly before using them in an actual case.

Coding manuals are often created to improve coders' consistency in data entry. However, when these manuals become too large, coding times slow down and costs increase. As a partial solution, review platform administrators often create authority lists, which are dropdown lists of defined coding responses tied to specific fields. Using an authority list eliminates incorrect field coding caused by typing mistakes.

Figure 5-8 An OCR file produced from scanning a paper document

Source: www.ferc.gov

Identifying and Reviewing Relevant Data

From a litigation support team's perspective, legal review begins after the forensics consultant, vendor, or IT staff have finished preserving, identifying, collecting, and preliminary processing, including deduplication. By this point, the choice of review platform has been made (Web based or desktop), and discovery has been processed and imported into the review platform. The legal team reviews the preliminary data sets to find relevant material and any material protected by attorney-client privilege or other privileges.

As the volume of discovery grows, difficulties in automated review of legal documents might crop up. Despite advances in review platforms, drawbacks still exist, such as failing to understand and use the technology correctly, poor communication between attorney and staff, quality problems resulting from staff turnover or outsourcing, and even linguistic issues in searching. Document review is a vast topic, and at the time of this writing, the EDRM manual's section on reviewing isn't complete. Therefore, this section just gives you an overview of the process and describes a few major difficulties in performing it.

The Sedona Conference and EDRM do have helpful materials on search functions. See "Best Practices Commentary on the Use of Search and Information Retrieval Methods in E-Discovery" (The Sedona Conference Working Group Series, August 2007) and the EDRM Search Guide (*www.edrm.net/resources/guides/edrm-search-guide*).

Ideally, each case should begin with a planning session, including a review manual containing all materials that members of the review team need. The first court filings are the core documents outlining the main legal issues in dispute. By reviewing the complaint as well as responses to early information requests, such as a request for admission or interrogatories, the legal team can put keywords, phrases, and players in context and question the relevance of similar words not initially included in searches as well as acronyms, initials, and so forth. If the complaint and other pleadings aren't included, there should be a case summary memo.

The entire legal team should have access to initial case documents. However, some law firms, in an effort to keep the review team focused, provide only limited access to this information. For example, temporary or contract employees might never have access to it. In either approach, the lead attorney is responsible for establishing and documenting a defensible review (one that will stand up to court scrutiny for errors).

After case issues, keywords, phrases, and parties have been identified, the lead attorney should explain the preliminary case strategies. Next is training in the review platform's search features. This training should cover the principles of fielded and full-text searching as well as keyword, Boolean, fuzzy, stemming, proximity, and wildcard searches (described in Chapter 7). Additional types of searches are available, such as concept searching and cluster searching.

All document reviewers should be given clear examples of potential search problems, such as poor-quality OCR, and workarounds for these problems. For example, some databases search only the first 60 characters of text in certain fields. Searching for dates can also be difficult because of different date formats, such as February 25, 2010; 2/25/2010; 2010.02.25; 2-25-10; and so forth. Additionally, a review platform might not recognize some symbols, such as a forward slash or an ampersand. Knowing how the review platform functions is critical for document search and retrieval.

Most review platforms can be configured to recognize special symbols.

Sorting Relevant and Nonrelevant Data

After training has been completed, the review for relevant materials can begin. This process is called a "first-pass review." Typically, the data set is divided into groups, and document reviewers are assigned portions of these groups to search and tag with suitable categories. In all but the smallest cases, document-by-document review can require excessive time and costs and isn't practical when the volume of discovery increases. Therefore, search protocols are typically used as a review filter. The lead attorney or project lead establishes search protocols that specify when to use wildcards, stemming, and other search methods usually based on OCR quality but also on the frequency of acronyms, misspellings, and other word deviations detected during periodic quality control sampling.

The first review should cover a small group of data so that quality control and metrics can be established. Manual review should reveal any errors requiring modification of search methods, further training, or improved communication about case issues. In addition, case management metrics are calculated, such as length of the initial review, number of staff required, error rates, and so forth. Many metrics are used, but a common rule of thumb is that one junior attorney or paralegal can review 40 to 50 documents per hour, with a "document" consisting of four to five pages. If a junior attorney is billed at $150 to $250 per hour, review can become expensive very quickly. As a result, review is often the most costly part of discovery, whether it's electronic or paper documents.

In Chapter 3, you used the keyword "money" to search Kenneth Lay's .pst file. E-mails in a data set typically contain a mixture of personal messages and spam as well as work-related messages. The goal was to identify all documents containing "money" that were relevant to the discovery request (the request for production, or RFP) from the opposing counsel, from the identified custodians (people), and over the period of time specified in the RFP. As you learned, discovery requests that are overly broad produce more documents of possibly little value, and all these documents need to be reviewed. Unless the attorneys agree to target their discovery requests, overly broad requests result in needless expense for both parties.

If the RFP has been written correctly and the collection tool allows targeted searching, you might not have many documents to review for relevance. For example, if the RFP restricts the collection to specifically relevant materials or types of data, the collection process might be adequate for the first-pass review. However, a random data review should be conducted to make sure the collection process identifies data relevant to the RFP.

In most review platforms, case documents are organized by using tags and folders. Tags are software features used to categorize a document or file based on specific criteria, such as privileged, responsive, e-mail thread, and so forth. At a minimum, each document should be tagged as privileged, responsive, nonresponsive, or further review (which the team leader can use to review questionable items). Tags can also be added to indicate "nonprivileged," "confidential," and so forth. It's all a matter of organization preference. Figure 5-9 shows folders and tags used in IPRO Eclipse. This document has been tagged as "Confidential" and is associated with a money fraud issue. The reviewer has used the "Attorney Work Product" tag to identify the document as work product, which in most cases isn't subject to discovery.

Remember that the requesting party can submit additional RFPs to expand the search if the first request doesn't yield the expected results.

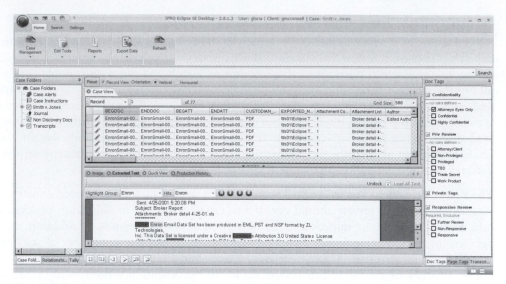

Figure 5-9 Eclipse folders and tags
Source: IPRO Tech, Inc.

Attorney-Client and Work-Product Privileges

Next is the second-pass review for material that's considered to fall under attorney-client or work-product privileges. Privileged communication can be written material as well as speech and actions. **Attorney-client privilege (ACP)** protects any communication between an attorney and a client; this communication is confidential and can't be disclosed without the client's consent. Communication between corporate counsel and employees, for example, might fall into this category. **Work-product privilege** protects any work an attorney has done in representing a client, including writings, statements, and testimony. It also includes an attorney's impressions, tactics, strategies, opinions, and thoughts. This privilege might also extend to work produced by consultants or experts.

Again, the review team should be given search terms for this procedure. Typical terms are names of attorneys, the words "privileged" or "confidential," e-mail addresses to or from legal counsel, and other words such as "lawsuit," "sued," "litigation," and so forth. In addition, the review team needs to know how to handle parent-child documents, as when an e-mail is privileged, but the attachment is not, or vice versa. Consistent review processes and procedures are essential to produce effective and defensible results. Before this review is considered complete, quality assurance checks should be done on a sample set of search results.

Remember that as the discovery volume increases, privilege review can inadvertently produce attorney-client and work-product privileged materials to the opposition. **Clawback agreements** negotiated during the meet and confer can be used later to identify and exclude these materials from being used by opposing counsel; however, these agreements shouldn't be the basis for poor review processes. There are differing legal interpretations of the **waiver of privilege** under FRE 502 and how it applies to clawback agreements (and other ways of managing privilege waivers) during e-discovery. Nonetheless, many problems can be avoided by documenting reasonable review processes and conducting sampling and quality assurance on results; in addition, a thorough understanding of the review tools and technology can help prevent common pitfalls. Using personnel with vendor certification in review tools to conduct the review process can improve the producing party's due diligence position if problems occur.

The case of *Holdings LTD v. Microsoft Corporation*, No. C-09-05535 EDL (N.D. Cal. March 11, 2011) is an example of due diligence and a defensible review. Because of a software glitch in a document review tool, some privileged documents were produced in a shortened format. The court ruled that this disclosure of privileged material was inadvertent. In addition, because the defendant's legal team had hired qualified attorneys to conduct the review for privileged material and a quality control team to review any documents still designated as privileged after the review, the court found that the defendant's legal team took reasonable steps to prevent disclosure of privileged material.

If discovery isn't deduped correctly, redacting or producing original documents instead of copies is a strong possibility because reviewers tend to treat documents differently. Inconsistent production of documents can affect rights under a clawback agreement or adversely affect the producing party's privilege position.

Protected Discovery

Review for protected material is often done during the privilege review stage. **Protected discovery** is any case material that needs to be shielded during the legal process. In a civil case, examples of protected discovery might be trade secrets, such as software code or algorithms. Even recipes might be considered protected, as for Pepsi, Coke, Kentucky Fried Chicken, and so forth. In criminal cases, protected material could be witness identities, phone numbers, addresses, and similar information. In both civil and criminal cases, Social Security numbers are usually protected. Because case documents filed with the court are normally a matter of public record, protection could be applied to anything that would cause harm to a person or business unless it's filed **under seal** with the court. Filing documents under seal keeps them from public access.

The Production Phase

After all review and quality assurance steps have been completed, documents are produced to the requesting party in the agreed-on format. A description of documents subject to redaction or withholding because of privilege or protection should be entered in a privilege log, and this log should be produced along with the remaining discovery.

FRCP 26(b)(5) "Claiming Privilege or Protecting Trial-Preparation Materials" states the following:

> *(A) Information Withheld. When a party withholds information otherwise discoverable by claiming that the information is privileged or subject to protection as trial-preparation material, the party must:*
>
> *(i) Expressly make the claim; and*

(ii) describe the nature of the documents, communications, or tangible things not produced or disclosed—and do so in a manner that, without revealing information itself privileged or protected, will enable other parties to assess the claim.

In other words, the objective of a privilege log is to disclose information to the opposition so that it's clear what has been specified as privileged and why. This log should include the following information for each document:

- Type (letter, memo, e-mail, schematic, YouTube video, Web page, and so forth)
- Author's name or other originator identification
- Names of recipients
- Date
- Title or description
- Subject matter
- The privilege claimed (attorney work-product, attorney-client communication, protected, and so forth)

Most review platforms can be configured to generate reports automatically that contain most of this information; however, some elements can be time consuming to track. For example, tracking e-mail threads when the topic changes mid-thread or parties in the communication change can be difficult.

After this phase, the producing party continues to organize materials related to case strategies, such as creating folders or notebooks for chronologies, witnesses, experts, and issues. The case is then prepared for trial, arbitration, or mediation, discussed in the next section.

Arbitration and Mediation

Many civil cases rarely go to trial; instead, they settle at some point, even the night before the trial. Civil cases can be settled before trial because of arbitration and mediation, which are methods of settling disputes outside a court setting—also known as **alternative dispute resolution**. An arbitrator is an impartial person chosen by both parties to solve their dispute, and his or her decision is held as binding or nonbinding, depending on the terms of the arbitration agreement. Arbitrators hear and evaluate evidence and make decisions. They follow court rules, although the setting might be less formal than court. A mediator differs slightly; this person brings parties together in some form of agreement but doesn't evaluate evidence or make decisions.

As mentioned in Chapter 4, special masters can be used in matters involving e-discovery, and they can function as mediators or arbitrators. As a mediator, a special master can be used to process and review discovery, such as computer hard drives containing privileged or protected materials, and turn the screened materials over to the appropriate parties. As an arbitrator, a special master can be appointed by a court to oversee e-discovery matters, such as disputes on forms of production, discovery accessibility, scope of discovery requests, and so forth. Typically, a court-appointed arbitrator's recommendations are binding.

According to some professionals in the field, strong presentation of discovery during arbitration or mediation is no different from presenting in front of a jury. However, mediation and arbitration are generally less formal, so the presentation format is left largely to the discretion of each party or the arbitrator. Arbitration and mediation usually take place in a conference room or similar facility, and using paper notebooks to present discovery isn't uncommon. If trial presentation software is used, refer to Chapter 6 for more information on using these tools in arbitration or mediation.

Chapter Summary

- During the meet and confer, parties should agree on preservation and production methods, their responsibilities, the scope of relevant data, and whether to produce native files or converted files.

- A duty to preserve obligates the responding party to evaluate which procedures and methods are best suited to meeting the preservation order and to preserve and produce relevant ESI in good faith.

- Targeted discovery scopes use search criteria that include search expressions, proximity searches, keywords, date ranges, file types, and e-mail addresses. Data collected with a targeted discovery scope can be deduplicated to remove identical files, which reduces data size and overall costs.

- Web-based repositories are a good option for novice and experienced litigators as well as corporate counsel. It can be used for large- or small-scale discovery review and gives remote staff access to case materials.

- Paper discovery is part of almost every case and often adds time and costs for manual or automated subjective and objective coding. OCR quality is particularly important with converted paper discovery, and search methods should be adjusted to allow for errors in OCR.

- Despite precautions and other due diligence measures, attorney-client and work-product privilege material might be produced inadvertently. Clawback agreements negotiated during the meet and confer can help in this situation but shouldn't be the basis for faulty review and production processes.

- Civil cases can be settled before trial by using arbitration and mediation, which are methods of settling disputes outside a court setting—also known as alternative dispute resolution. Arbitrators hear and evaluate evidence and make decisions. A mediator differs slightly; this person brings parties together in some form of agreement but doesn't evaluate evidence or make decisions.

Key Terms

alternative dispute resolution   A method of settling disputes outside a court setting by using mediation or arbitration.

attorney-client privilege (ACP)   This privilege protects any communication between an attorney and a client, which can include written material as well as speech and actions.

clawback agreements   Agreements negotiated during an initial meeting that allow the opposition to identify and exclude materials from use in the case.

coding   The process (automatic or manual) of examining documents to identify names, dates, and relevant terms or phrases so that information can be entered in database fields.

fielded searching   Searching for words or data that might not be in the document contents but are important descriptors; they're entered in database fields during the coding process.

full-text searching   Searching document contents that have been converted to OCR.

objective coding   Automated or manual coding done to search for bibliographic data (such as names and dates). *See also* coding.

protected discovery   Any case material that must be shielded during the review process, such as trade secrets or witness identities.

redaction   Obscuring or removing privileged or proprietary information from a file or document before it's produced.

under seal   This policy allows keeping protected discovery away from public access and review. *See also* protected discovery.

waiver of privilege   Usually an involuntary surrender of a right to attorney-client privilege under FRE 502; typically includes documents produced but not noted in a privilege log.

work-product privilege   This privilege protects any work an attorney has done in representing a client, including writings, statements, and testimony; also includes an attorney's impressions, tactics, strategies, opinions, and thoughts.

Review Questions

1. A duty to preserve is also called which of the following?

    a. Reasonable expectation

    b. Litigation hold

    c. Protected discovery

    d. Objective coding

2. Because the scope of data being disclosed might not be known in the early stages of litigation, FRCP Rule 26(f) mandates which of the following?

    a. Litigation hold

    b. Subjective coding

    c. Meet and confer

    d. Clawback agreements

3. The meet and confer enables both parties to agree on which of the following? (Choose all that apply.)

   a. Objective-coding guidelines

   b. What constitutes relevant data

   c. Details of the discovery format

   d. What constitutes privileged material

4. Typically, which process requires opening a file's native application for indexing and searching?

   a. Bates stamping

   b. Editing

   c. Reviewing

   d. Preserving ESI

5. Configuring search criteria in data-collection software improves the chance of targeting a discovery request's scope. True or False?

6. _____ agreements negotiated during the meet and confer make it possible to identify and exclude privileged or protected material from discovery.

   a. Counsel

   b. Documented

   c. Absent party

   d. Clawback

7. Protected discovery can include which of the following case materials? (Choose all that apply.)

   a. Trade secrets

   b. Witness identities

   c. Search keywords

   d. Review team members

8. Work-product privilege doesn't extend to reports and testimony from consultants or experts. True or False?

9. Case management metrics are calculated to determine which of the following? (Choose all that apply.)

   a. Length of time to conduct the first-pass review

   b. Number of staff members needed to conduct a review

   c. Keywords to use in searching

   d. Error rates in a review

10. Special masters can be appointed by the court only as arbitrators. True or False?

11. Subjective coding of database fields is used to evaluate bibliographic data. True or False?

12. In the production stage, a privilege log must be created that describes which of the following? (Choose all that apply.)

    a. Review team members

    b. Redacted material

    c. Protected discovery materials

    d. Case strategies

13. Which EDRM stage is often the most costly part of discovery, whether it involves electronic or paper documents?

    a. Collection

    b. Identification

    c. Review

    d. Production

14. Mediators hear and evaluate evidence and make decisions. True or False?

15. In criminal litigation, which members of the prosecution team have an obligation to preserve exculpatory evidence? (Choose all that apply.)

    a. Prosecuting attorney

    b. Any law enforcement agent or officer on the case

    c. Any government agency involved in the case

    d. Confidential informants

Hands-On Projects

These projects require Internet access.

Hands-On Project 5-1

This project gives you an opportunity to familiarize yourself with the software before using it in Chapter 6 projects. This tool isn't Web based, as iCONECT is; it's a desktop application that's loaded on your computer.

1. Start a Web browser, go to **www.indatacorp.com/trialdirectoreval**, and download and install the TrialDirector demonstration software.

2. Start TrialDirector by double-clicking the desktop shortcut.

3. Start a Web browser, and go to **www.indatacorp.com/TrialDirector-Support.html#Tutorials**, the Web site for TrialDirector tutorials.

4. Review the video tutorials for TrialDirector 5 and 6, particularly the module "A Tour of the TrialDirector 5 Interface," and try using some of the features in your

version of TrialDirector. You can also review the Quick Start User Guide by going to **www.indatacorp.com/TrialDirector-Support.html#UserGuide** and selecting the guide for the version you're trying. When you're finished, exit TrialDirector, but leave your Web browser running for the next project.

Hands-On Project 5-2

This project gives you more practice with iCONECT. It has features similar to what you find in desktop applications, such as Concordance, but it requires less technical skill to use.

1. Start a Web browser, if necessary, and go to **www.ferc.gov/industries/electric/indus-act/ wec/enron/info-release.asp**.

2. Click the **Search iCONECT nXT** link to open the iCONECT database with a guest login.

3. Click the **ScannedDocuments** check box, and then click the **Open** button. If necessary, click **Run** in the Security Information message box. Close the Quick Tasks window that opens.

4. Click the **TOOLBAR** tab, if necessary, and then click the **ADVANCED** button under the SEARCH FOR text box. In the "with all of these words (AND)" text box, type **trade, sell, markets, options**, and then click **Add**.

5. In the Search builder window, you should see "(trade, AND sell, AND markets, AND options)." Click the **Date range, proximity options** link.

6. In the "Narrow to a date range" drop-down list, click **AND**. In the Date Field list box, click **DATE, GE (>=), August 1, 2001**. In the AND list box, click **DATE, LT (<), September 8, 2001**. Click the **Add** button under the "Date range, proximity options" option. In the Search builder window, you should see the following displayed as the search criteria: (`trade, AND sell, AND markets, AND options )  AND` (`'DATE'  >= 01/08/2001 AND 'DATE' < 08/09/2001 )`.

7. Click the **Perform Search** button. The search should return four documents.

8. In the Export tab, click **Export To Another Program**. Export the search results to a folder on your computer, and make sure you select the **TrialDirector Suite** format. You use this exported data in Chapter 6 for extra practice, if time permits. Leave your Web browser running for the next project.

Hands-On Project 5-3

In this project, you download and install Concordance and compare its features with iCONECT.

1. Start a Web browser, if necessary, and go to **www.lexisnexis.com/concordance-downloads/**. Download and install the Concordance software.

2. To familiarize yourself with Concordance features, go to **http://law.lexisnexis.com/ concordance** for an overview of the software, **http://help.lexisnexis.com/litigation/ac/ cn_classic/index.html?pdf_documents.htm** to view user guides, and **www.lexisnexis. com/en-us/litigation/products/tutorials.page?tabs=Concordance** to see video tutorials.

3. Open the Concordance program you installed in Step 1. Use the Concordance user guides mentioned in Step 2 to review this tool's searching, production, export, and redaction capabilities.

4. Next, go to **www.ferc.gov/industries/electric/indus-act/wec/enron/info-release.asp**. Click the **Search iCONECT nXT** link to open the iCONECT database with a guest login.

5. Click the **ScannedDocuments** check box, and then click the **Open** button. If necessary, click **Run** in the Security Information message box. Close the Quick Tasks window that opens.

6. With both Concordance and iCONECT open, create a spreadsheet or table that compares the following features in both iCONECT and Concordance. Note whether each feature exists, and if it does, add descriptive details about it.

   - Searching and searching speed
   - Ease of use
   - Production capabilities
   - Exporting and importing data
   - Redaction capabilities
   - Security administration features for restricting modification of fields or data

Case Projects

Case Project 5-1

Conduct Internet research to find litigation cases in which the producing party screened data for privileged information, but an inadvertent disclosure of privileged data occurred despite its precautions. Choose a case, and write a one- to two-page report summarizing the case and details of the inadvertent disclosure. State whether the court concluded that the producing party took "reasonable steps" to avoid disclosure and what software features were used for these preventive measures.

Case Project 5-2

You're an IT staff member for a small pet supply company consisting of four stores and a warehouse. This company has 3 servers and 60 desktop computers. Your manager explains that a competitor has begun price-fixing litigation against your company, and relevant data must be preserved. Write a one- to two-page report describing ways to identify and preserve potentially relevant data.

Case Project 5-3

You're a paralegal assigned to the litigation team defending the pet supply company from Case Project 5-2. The IT Department has collected approximately 12 GB of potentially relevant ESI from the company computers, including e-mails, Office documents, databases, employee data from Human Resources, and financial data from the Finance Department.

The lead attorney has asked you to create a review plan or strategy to identify attorney-client and work-product privileged material. Write a one- to two-page memo to the attorney describing your recommendations and specifying suggested keywords. Also, recommend a litigation software tool that you believe will be effective in reducing the risk of inadvertent disclosures, and explain features of this tool to support your opinion.

References

EDRM, LLC. 2005–2012, *www.edrm.net/resources/edrm-stages-explained*.

Federal Rules of Civil Procedure. 2010, *www.uscourts.gov/uscourts/rules/civil-procedure.pdf*.

National Day Laborer Organizing Network et al v. U.S. Immigration and Customs Enforcement Agency et al, 10 Civ. 3488, SAS. Southern District of New York, February 7, 2011, *www.bc.edu/content/dam/files/schools/law_sites/library/pdf/Scheindlin_National_Day.pdf*.

The Sedona Principles, Second Edition. "Best Practices: Recommendations and Principles for Addressing Electronic Document Production," 2007, *www.thesedonaconference.org*.

chapter 6

Case Study: From Beginning to Trial

After reading this chapter and completing the exercises, you will be able to:

- Describe prelitigation e-discovery investigation practices
- Describe common e-discovery documents used when starting a formal lawsuit
- Explain e-discovery project management tasks, including sampling and metrics
- Explain fact-finding and pretrial motions
- Describe common technical and nontechnical considerations in trial presentations

In Chapter 5, you followed a theoretical case flow from a defendant's perspective, as a party producing e-discovery in response to a request for production after litigation has started, including data collection, internal review, and presentation during mediation or arbitration in a civil case. In this chapter, you follow a theoretical case from a plaintiff's perspective and go through the process of early case assessment and investigation—from filing a complaint and issuing a legal hold to receiving e-discovery from the opposing counsel or third parties and reviewing the discovery received, and then moving on to the trial. Notes are given when procedures in criminal cases differ. This chapter describes some rather detailed technical concepts, but they're critical to processing e-discovery.

Early Case Evaluation

Lawsuits generally aren't taken lightly, so formal litigation typically starts after reasonable due diligence investigation. Establishing the basis of a lawsuit involves early fact finding to lay a case foundation for the initial claims. However, it's not unusual for a case's basis to expand as investigation and discovery yield more information, as you have seen in the Enron case. The following sections outline important considerations in early case evaluation and investigation as well as the tools and sources of information that might be used. These sections fit into the first half of the EDRM cycle, which includes information management, investigation, preservation, and collection.

Prelitigation Investigations

Before filing a complaint (or indictment) in any litigation, a preliminary investigation should reveal some of the factual foundation for the litigation. In civil cases, the client is interviewed, and any preliminary evidence is evaluated. In criminal cases, investigations are often both open and covert; the covert portion includes wiretaps and body wires, for example. Many investigations are entirely covert, such as those involving organized crime. The information gathered in a preliminary investigation for a case, whether it's civil or criminal, becomes the foundation for the litigation.

For example, in the Enron case, the Federal Energy Regulatory Commission (FERC) began a fact-finding investigation into volatile price fluctuations in the bulk electric power markets in the summer of 2000. The Securities and Exchange Commission began investigating Enron in the summer of 2001, and the investigation later became a joint civil/criminal investigation when the Department of Justice joined in. Enron filed bankruptcy in December 2001 after financial statement reductions in excess of $1 billion revealed numerous accounting problems.

The civil complaint and criminal indictments for Jeffrey Skilling and Kenneth Lay are available as data files in the Chapter04 folder (`Lay_Indictment.pdf` and `lay_civil_complaint.pdf`).

During the investigation stage, capturing as much discovery as possible before litigation is critical, even before issuing a legal hold or notifying the opposition of potential litigation. This discovery might include capturing Web sites, YouTube video, social networking profiles, public information from government or media resources (TV, newspaper, radio, for example), geospatial or mapping data, webcam video, cell phone or voicemail recordings, and so forth. Pay particular attention to capturing volatile digital discovery—that is, information that can be destroyed deliberately or accidentally after notification of the investigation or litigation as well as records that can be destroyed in the normal course of business. Of course, all collections must be done with the correct legal authority and methods.

Common discovery sources include webcams (on highways, at public events, and so on), Google maps, Google Earth, and the commercial service DigitalGlobe. In most metropolitan areas, the state department of transportation installs webcams or other traffic-monitoring systems, and information from these sources can usually be requested as public records or via the Freedom of Information Act (FOIA). Similarly, Google maps and its street view option as well as satellite photos from Google Earth or DigitalGlobe can be helpful. Google Earth even has a feature that enables you to view places as they looked in the past. These resources can be useful in environmental, real estate, and insurance litigation, among others. For example, before-and-after satellite photos were used in litigation resulting from Hurricane Katrina, and many metropolitan areas have public crime maps that can yield interesting information. (See an example at *www.seattle.gov/police/crime/onlinecrimemaps.htm*.)

Tools and resources for a prelitigation investigation are abundant, and many are free or inexpensive. For example, you can do preliminary Web site capture with HTTrack (*www.httrack. org*), Web2Disk by InSpyder (*www.inspyder.com*), or the open-source Linux command wget, among others. With most Web capture tools, you can't copy server-side secure items, such as databases, code, and scripts; however, some type of Web capture is usually better than none at all. In addition, Web site history information is often available at the Wayback Machine (*www.archive.org*), but this site's terms of use don't allow copying information. Instead, consider issuing a subpoena to get Web archives legally. YouTube video can be captured with a number of devices, including RealPlayer SP. However, these preliminary captures should be supplemented with a formal request for production or even a subpoena, if necessary.

Screen captures can be a useful way to preserve potential evidence if other tools aren't available. Most computers have a function key for this operation, such as PrtSc or PrintScrn, that copies the screen image to the computer's clipboard. Then you can use Ctrl+V to paste the image into a document. For more information, search the Internet for "Windows screen captures," or visit *http://support.microsoft.com/kb/173884*.

More advanced investigative tools include visual analytic features; although they're marketed for law enforcement use, they're also used in civil litigation. Two examples of these tools are Analyst's Notebook and Social Network Analyzer from i2 Group, now owned by IBM (*www.i2group.com*). These tools create visual representations of large data sets, such as phone or bank records, IP addresses and traffic, social networking diagrams, link analysis, geospatial analysis, and tree maps. Visual analysis can help focus investigations on particular activities and connect pieces of information to form a cohesive story.

Always consider researching previous litigation the opposition has been involved in. Searching federal, state, and local jurisdictions can reveal evidence that could be useful to the current case, such as e-mails and other e-discovery.

Starting Litigation

After the preliminary case evaluation is done, formal litigation can start if enough information has been collected to pursue the case further. Starting litigation at this point involves a wide variety of documents to put the case on record with the court, notify potential parties of the litigation and their duty to preserve evidence, and undertake additional discovery in different forms. The following sections walk you through these steps and the use of common documents and helpful tools. You also learn about using experts and consultants to draft certain documents.

Legal Hold

After the preliminary case evaluation is finished, a legal hold can be issued, and a complaint can be filed in civil cases (or an indictment in criminal cases). A **legal hold** is an order to preserve data in anticipation of litigation, an audit, a government investigation, or another matter; it prohibits people from destroying or processing records. Similar terms include "litigation hold," "preservation letter," "suspension order," and others. For the most part, the terminology depends on the role of the party issuing the communication. For example, **preservation letter** might be used more often between opposing counsel to memorialize (that is, capture for legal purposes) the duty to preserve; "litigation hold" might be used more often in corporations between in-house counsel and IT staff, management, and so forth, to indicate that pending or actual litigation is likely. In this chapter, you focus on a legal hold from the perspective of the party requesting discovery and issuing a notice to opposing counsel to preserve records—the preservation letter. "The Sedona Conference Commentary on Legal Holds, the Trigger & the Process" (2007) is an excellent resource, although it focuses on triggers and an organization's internal processes when a legal hold is initiated.

It's also important to remember that legal holds are typically used in civil cases. Criminal prosecution more commonly involves using search warrants and seizing evidence during the investigation stage to prevent it from being destroyed by the accused. In addition, destruction of evidence by the prosecution (spoliation) is prohibited under the Brady doctrine, Jencks Act, and Giglio (discussed in Chapter 4), even without notice from the defense. However, the prosecuting attorney, much like in-house counsel communication with IT and management in civil matters, has an obligation to notify all members of the prosecuting and investigation teams to preserve discovery. In civil cases, deliberate destruction of evidence can result in criminal prosecution under the Sarbanes-Oxley Act (18 U.S.C.§1519) as well as legal sanctions in other matters.

In civil cases, the main reason for a requesting party to issue a preservation letter is to lay the foundation for sanctions in case of spoliation. However, a preservation letter generally isn't required because the duty to preserve begins when the opposing party has reasonable knowledge that the evidence could be relevant to future litigation.

A legal hold, in the form of a preservation letter, should be written in clear language and include the following items:

- Locations of possible data
- Possible types of relevant data
- List of key custodians

- List of things not to do (such as defragmenting, upgrading, and opening, moving, deleting, or overwriting files)
- Contact person for questions

You saw a sample preservation letter, `Kroll Sample ED Docs.pdf`, in Chapter 4. It's on the DVD in the Chapter04 folder.

Request for Admission

After the preservation letter is issued, a request for admission (RFA) usually follows. As specified in FRCP 36, this written statement asks a party to admit or deny certain case facts to ascertain what items aren't in controversy and, therefore, limit further investigation and discovery. Responses to an RFA can include production of documents. Some courts might deem a failure to respond as an admission of the facts addressed in the RFA.

An RFA involving Enron (`FERC_Enron RFA.pdf`) is on the DVD in the Chapter06 folder.

Depending on the nature of the case, having an IT or computer forensics person help address technical issues in drafting an RFA to opposition can be useful. For example, you might want to have the opposition confirm the scripting directives (commands) for links or the methods of data collection used on certain Web sites. In the Enron case, multiple trading databases were used, and an RFA might be the best time to confirm activity of this type and any case-related implications. Note that all legal team members should have access to RFA responses because they can clarify the context of keywords, names, and phrases during discovery searching and organization.

In criminal cases, the prosecution is required to prove its case, so any form of "admission" is done during arraignment when the defendant pleads innocent or guilty.

Interrogatories

After an RFA is issued, more detailed interrogatories usually follow. FRCP 33 governs the use of interrogatories, often informally called "rogs." As you learned in Chapter 4, interrogatories are a written form of information gathering that the recipient responds to in writing and under oath. They're often combined with a request for production (RFP) of discovery and possibly supplemental RFAs. In criminal cases, FRCrP 16 governs discovery, and the criminal counterpart to an interrogatory is called a bill of particulars. A motion for a bill of particulars requests details of the crime's when, where, and how.

Meet and Confer

At this point, both parties have done a fair amount of preliminary investigation and fact-finding through written requests for information. Armed with this preliminary information, the courts usually require a **meet and confer** (introduced in Chapter 5) between the parties. FRCP 26(f), "Conference of the Parties; Planning for Discovery," requires the parties to meet as soon as practical or before certain court deadlines. The scope of the meeting is intended to encourage the parties to agree on litigation issues early in the case, including the possibility for prompt settlement or other case resolution, or to develop a discovery plan.

With e-discovery, the meet and confer should address such topics as the types and forms of ESI to be produced as well as paper discovery. For example, if both parties are using the same review platform, **cost sharing** can be used by hiring one vendor to process native files to TIF for all parties (plaintiff and defendant), if TIF is the agreed-on format. Additionally, discussion on the types of native file formats to produce might reveal a need for specialized software. For example, some large corporations have developed in-house software for special processes, and the opposition needs access to this software if conversion to a nonproprietary format could destroy metadata or other critical file information. In addition, if the case involves intellectual property claims related to software code and development, access to code in the compiled or executable files might also require specialized software.

Similarly, if computer hard drives are to be examined for user activity or recovery of deleted files, the meet and confer is the time to agree on access to the computers or servers in question and on procedures to follow. Identifying, preserving, and retrieving files on legacy media might also require in-depth planning.

Last, but certainly not least, search procedures should be established, including keywords, custodians, date ranges, locations, and other matters to identify discovery as specifically as possible without being overly burdensome or broad. Keyword search parameters are particularly important and should address Boolean, fuzzy, stemming, and other search methods. In addition, locating nonsearchable files should be addressed (that is, PDF, TIF, JPG, and other image files that contain text but can't be searched), and attention should be paid to additional time and expense involved in processing large volumes of this type of discovery.

The meet and confer is intended to reveal potential disputes on schedules and discovery, such as adequacy of production. The courts expect both parties to participate in this process in good faith, and failure to do so can result in court sanctions. If the process is successful, it should limit the courts from intervening in disputes as the case goes to trial.

Although criminal cases aren't directly affected by FRCP 26(f), the courts always encourage early case resolution and/or discovery planning in civil or criminal cases. In criminal cases in particular, issues of access to electronic discovery by defendants must be addressed, including defendants in custody in detention centers, jail, or prison. E-discovery presents unique problems for the Department of Corrections and similar institutions because their core functions don't address supplying equipment for inmates to review digital evidence, largely because of budget constraints and security risks. Nonetheless, most courts uphold a defendant's constitutional right to review all case materials and require some type of accommodation for this procedure. In addition, although most criminal cases have defense counsel assigned, some defendants choose to represent themselves, called "pro se" representation. Pro se representation adds complications to the case, particularly if the defendant is in custody. Further, some criminal defendants have literacy or foreign language issues or have no computer skills. All these factors affect how e-discovery is processed and should be addressed early in the case.

In public defense matters, the courts often require the party with the most resources (usually the government) to process evidence into a common format. In-custody review of case materials might affect discovery formats and conversion as well as production timing, which should also be addressed early. Cost sharing of discovery processing can be beneficial in criminal cases as well and is often encouraged when public defense resources are involved.

In civil or criminal cases, timing strategies can affect when case materials are produced to the opposition. For example, it's not unusual for the prosecution in criminal cases to withhold some materials at first in an attempt to push for a plea agreement. In civil cases, all discovery must be exchanged before trial per a formal case schedule.

In civil or criminal cases, encrypted or password protected files might require specific legal authority before access or processing, as there might be an expectation of privacy, Fifth Amendment privilege against self-incrimination, or other legal concerns beyond those of the core discovery.

Request for Production

The meet and confer should lay the foundation for additional discovery; a case settlement or plea agreement usually hasn't been achieved at this point. As a result, the case typically continues with a request for production (RFP), which is the main form of requesting discovery in civil cases. An RFP can be combined with interrogatories or an RFA. In criminal cases, a motion for discovery is the counterpart to an RFP.

Discovery requests identify the information being sought and can include data, documents, formulas, recipes, voicemails, videos, bank records, access to land and buildings, expert witness work product—in short, anything in a party's possession or control that's related to the litigation, except attorney-client and attorney-work-product privileged material. Information in the discovery material that's produced can be useful for dispositive motions, depositions, settlement proposals, and trial. A "dispositive motion" is any motion seeking to resolve all or part of a case. For example, a motion for summary judgment is a dispositive motion that usually incorporates some form of evidence supporting a request for the judge to take some action and is typically used in civil cases. A motion to dismiss, the counterpart in criminal cases, is often used to request that all or part of the criminal indictment be dismissed.

In civil cases, volumes of nonrelevant material might be produced as part of the strategy to inundate the opposing side with material and hide relevant documents. Today, these "document dumps" are likely to be challenged in court. This challenge might be upheld if document production is found to be excessive, and sanctions could result. In fact, despite the broad ability to request discovery, **proportionality** considerations usually apply. FRCP 26(b)(2)(C)(iii) states that discovery can be limited when "[T]he burden or expense of the proposed discovery outweighs its likely benefit, considering the needs of the case, the amount in controversy, the parties' resources, the importance of the issues at stake in the action, and the importance of the discovery in resolving the issues." Rule 26 applies other considerations to discovery with the purpose of requiring each attorney to consider the request's legitimacy, the response, or an objection.

Conversely, in criminal cases, the prosecution often produces all material, even if it isn't relevant, to avoid violating the Brady doctrine, which requires disclosing all discovery that might show innocence (exculpatory) or otherwise affect a trial's outcome. As a result, proportionality considerations don't apply to criminal cases because the burden of proof lies with prosecution. However, public defense criminal cases are likely to be subject to budgetary restrictions, and proportionality (as it relates to discovery and case budget) might be applied more strictly to lower-level offenses but more loosely in cases involving sentences of long-term incarceration. In other words, the courts usually direct more funding and resources to a defendant who might be sentenced to death or life in prison than to a defendant who might be incarcerated short term for drug trafficking.

In both civil and criminal cases, subpoenas can be used in addition to RFPs or discovery motions. FRCP 45 governs using subpoenas in civil cases, and FRCrP 17 governs their use in criminal cases. There are two main forms of subpoenas: a subpoena and a subpoena duces tecum. A subpoena is a command for a person to appear to give testimony. A **subpoena duces tecum** is a command for a person to appear with certain evidence, such as books, records, or other tangible items, or to permit inspection of property, for example. It's a command rather than a request because subpoenas are issued by the court and can be signed by an attorney as an officer of the court. Record custodians in large government agencies and corporations usually respond to these subpoenas in writing instead of appearing in person.

When seeking discovery stored or transmitted over the Internet, such as e-mails, voicemails (which use VoIP), or information stored in the cloud, the Stored Communications Act (SCA) can apply. The SCA lists five ways these records can be obtained:

- Subpoena
- Subpoena with previous notice to the subscriber or customer
- Court order
- Court order with previous notice to the subscriber or customer
- Search warrant

The main difference between a subpoena and a search warrant is that a subpoena commands the person to produce something (testimony, records, access to property, and so on), whereas a search warrant permits law enforcement to search for and seize evidence if there's probable cause that a crime has been committed. Both instruments can be challenged in court: the subpoena before the response and the search warrant after the search, if it's believed to be improper. For example, Enron filed a **motion to quash** four subpoena duces tecum for digital discovery that the plaintiff requested shortly before trial. This motion cited the discovery request as being overly burdensome and asked for attorney-client and work-product privileged material, among others. It also sought a protection order to limit discovery. A copy of the motion is included on the DVD in the Chapter06 folder (`Enron_Motion_Quash.pdf`).

Plaintiffs' E-discovery Management

Before receiving discovery under an RFP, a preliminary project management plan should be created as a result of the groundwork laid during an investigation, early discovery in the form of an RFA or interrogatories, and a meet and confer. In addition, when producing discovery as outlined in Chapter 5, a project management plan is important. Project management, in this context, is the same as project management in manufacturing or IT and software development. In its basic form, a project management plan should identify the project team, technology and tools, quality control points and methods, potential vendor support, project budget and timeline, and case goals and objectives. For litigation, goals and objectives are fairly simple: Collect, organize, and present evidence to refute the opponent's claims, prove your client's claims, or both.

A preliminary project management plan is updated as the case progresses, depending on factors such as volume and types of discovery, changes in case strategy, and so forth. Keep in mind that mistakes and problems are likely despite planning, especially when there's a large volume of e-discovery, so having a well-documented discovery review process is helpful in defending against possible negative allegations, including court sanctions or malpractice. Good documentation of the discovery review process should be supplemented with e-discovery best practices that include using up-to-date workstations with fast processors, large amounts of RAM, and dual monitors as well as networks with the capacity to handle simultaneous users running complex queries and other processes for a large volume of e-discovery. Also, litigation staff should stay abreast of advancements in industry hardware and software and take certified training as often as possible.

When discovery is received from opposing counsel (or another source via subpoena), a discovery or chain-of-custody log should be created that includes details of the items received, such as date, type of media, media label data, and other descriptive information.

Be careful to preserve the metadata of any files on the medium and even metadata *about* the medium. For example, a DVD's creation date might be evidence, in addition to dates and other file metadata on the disc.

Some preliminary information about the discovery is usually gathered at this point from a standalone computer isolated from any network or Internet connection. You should inventory and copy the entire medium, and then place the original in a secure location. Working from a copy makes it possible to keep the original intact even when errors inevitably occur. Methods for copying and inventorying media include special tools, such as FTK and Discovery Attender, and command-line scripts, such as xcopy and dir with switches (see Figure 6-1). For example, issuing a dir command without switches lists all files and subfolders in the current folder. To list only the names of subfolders and files without any metadata (such as file size), use dir /b. Using dir /s lists files in the current folder and all subfolders. Last, using dir /s/b>inventory.txt sends a bare inventory (without file details, such as dates) of the current directory and subfolders to a text file in that directory. In e-discovery, you use this feature often to inventory discs and other media. At the command prompt, type help followed by xcopy or dir to see the syntax and other information on working with these commands.

Whatever method is used, it must be tested before working on a live case.

Figure 6-1 Running a script at the command line
Source: Microsoft, Inc.

In addition to free or low-cost tools, such as FileMonkey (*www.monkeyjob.com*), Total Commander (*www.ghisler.com*), UltraEdit, and TextPad, command-line scripts and batch files are used for e-discovery file management. Learning basic command-line and batch file scripting is strongly recommended for anyone dealing with e-discovery, even attorneys. Several online resources are available, such as *www.computerhope.com*, or search for "command-line reference" or "batch files" at *www.microsoft.com*. Use quotes around these phrases to narrow the search.

Using a command-line inventory, IPRO iConvert, or other preview software, assess the volume and types of files on the medium. Be sure to note any unusual file types (extensions) or file types that you don't have the software to open. Print and maintain any reports, and attach them to the discovery log or chain-of-custody log.

Sampling and Metrics

Sampling and metrics are important components of project management plans, and some of the first adjustments to plans take place at this stage in both civil and criminal cases. As you've learned, sampling is done to test a variety of files for application compatibility, viewing, and processing. It's also used to review files for additional keywords or review information to broaden the discovery scope. Metrics are activity measurements to gauge how much time (and, therefore, cost) is needed to process and review certain quantities of e-discovery.

As mentioned in Chapter 5, you must consider several factors when dealing with native files before you can start the review process and, therefore, sampling and metrics. For example, based on the preview or inventory, do you have applications to open and search each file type? Can you determine whether any files are password protected or encrypted? If so, do you have resources to open them? In criminal cases, do you have legal authority under a search warrant or other court order to open password-protected or encrypted files that might be subject to additional privacy rights? Are there any compressed or zipped files, and do they need manual processing? Are there Excel spreadsheets or databases, such as Access or SQL, that can't be loaded in a review platform? Do you have PDF, JPG, TIF, or other files that can't be searched and need to be converted with OCR? Are there voicemails or wiretaps that need a lot of manual processing (such as transcription) or special hosting?

For example, in the Enron case, Snohomish County Public Utility District spent more than $200,000 to transcribe some of the 2800 audio recordings of Enron traders. Body wires, wiretaps, and video surveillance recordings are no longer used exclusively in criminal cases; many civil cases now involve voicemail (including VoIP), video from security cameras or webcams, YouTube video, and so forth. Although voice recognition technology is improving, generally it's not practical for most litigation recordings because of poor sound quality and multiple speakers. Therefore, manual review and transcription are often necessary, including activity transcripts in video surveillance when sound isn't captured. Activity transcripts log timestamps of important surveillance activities instead of the spoken word.

Quick View Plus (*www.avantstar.com*) is a file viewer, widely used in e-discovery, that you can use to view more than 300 file types, often without having to purchase a file's native application.

Before copying native discovery files to a company network, you need to determine whether any files have viruses. However, virus scanning can alter file metadata, so you must use tools to capture metadata on a standalone computer before scanning the files. On a standalone computer isolated from the network, you can run tools to extract file metadata and preserve it, and then identify encrypted, virus, or other problem files known as "exceptions." LAW, Discovery Cracker, IPRO eScan-IT, and ImageMaker's Discovery Assistant are a few tools you can use for this task. For example, eScan-IT has an eQC module for processing exceptions and unknown files (see Figure 6-2).

If virus scanning isn't a concern, you can load native files into Concordance, Summation, or another review platform on a standalone computer to do some preliminary searching or sampling. Be aware, however, that these tools might not load all native files, so make sure you enable error logs so that you can identify files that don't load correctly. Quality assurance procedures should be used to compare the number of files loaded in the review platform with those listed on the discovery inventory. Any missing files should be noted as well as the actual or suspected reason for the failure to load.

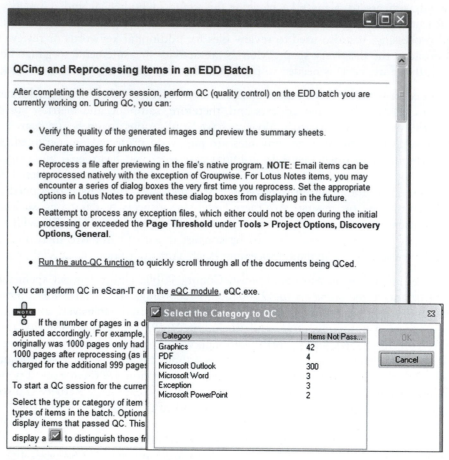

Figure 6-2 Using the eScan-IT eQC module
Source: IPRO Tech, Inc.

Although native file review platforms have improved substantially, there are still surprises with many products on the market. Before buying any review platform, be sure to test it with as many sample file types as possible and evaluate error logs after loading files. Also, review technical notes that might alert you to potential limitations or bugs.

Some files might contain commands that corrupt your computer or possibly your network server. For example, files ending in .bat can cause problems. Be sure to do research before opening or viewing any unfamiliar file types, or open unfamiliar file types on a standalone computer.

If the case is expected to grow substantially, involves a foreign language, or has many unusual or problem-prone file types (exceptions), outsourcing the discovery process to a vendor might be wise. A good litigation support vendor usually has the tools and technical staff to process files (including metadata in load files) into a format that can be imported into the review platform you choose.

Review platforms and trial presentation tools require load file formats that use delimiters. Delimiters are characters used to separate information, such as commas used in comma-separated values (CSV) files or tabs used in tab-separated values (TSV) files.

Sampling is done to establish metrics, identify unknown file types that might need special software or viewers, verify the accuracy of search methods, identify keywords to expand search parameters, and other reasons. For example, say the requesting party receives the `Kenneth_Lay_Rev1.pst` file you produced in Hands-On Project 3-3. A search for the keyword "money" should be done, and the team leader should review the results in a variety of ways. Search methods that use fuzzy, wildcard, or stemming procedures produce different results. In addition, you might find that certain e-mails or other documents containing the keyword are sent regularly to certain custodians, who could become the subject of additional discovery requests or perhaps depositions. In the Enron case, the keyword "money" appears frequently along with other keywords, such as Ricochet and Raptor, that weren't considered relevant before, so other keywords might become the subject of additional discovery requests.

Technical or legal staff who encounter privileged material should consult with the lead attorney immediately. Case law as well as national and local bar association ethics directives from the national and local bar associations might dictate how to treat this material. For example, the receiving party might be required to notify the producing party of the disclosure or turn the matter over to the court for disposition.

Metrics are gathered to estimate the time and costs to manage, process, and review discovery and to verify the accuracy of searching and review procedures. Most case metrics divide these procedures into stages that mirror the EDRM. In fact, the EDRM has a draft metrics code set (*www.edrm.net/resources/standards/edrm-metrics/edrm-metrics-code-set*). Similarly, "The Sedona Conference Commentary on Achieving Quality in the E-Discovery Process" (May 2009) covers the main purposes and factors in e-discovery project management, quality measures, and metrics. It also offers a primer on using sampling procedures (see Appendix A).

Project Management Resources

After doing metrics and sampling, you should select tools, vendors, and staff members. These resources have been covered in previous chapters, so the following sections simply summarize what you've learned so far.

Selecting Discovery Tools
In civil or criminal cases, multiple tools are usually needed to copy, inventory, manage, and review the full spectrum of e-discovery. Forensics tools, such as Forensics Toolkit or Imager, are usually needed to preserve and copy digital discovery, including metadata of the OS, files, and possibly storage media. For example, the creation date of a seized CD/DVD might be crucial in establishing the timeline in a criminal case, but this data might be altered if the medium isn't copied correctly. In the production phase of discovery, software such as Discovery Attender can quickly search and identify files containing keywords and generate a report for early discovery assessment without altering metadata. IPRO iConvert is a free preview tool for determining file types in the discovery material.

PDF, TIF, JPG, and other image files should be sampled to determine whether they contain text that can't be searched and need further processing. For example, many banks now photocopy the front and back of checks, and these copies might contain text that would be useful to search. Unless your review platform tool can convert these files via OCR or unzip, decrypt, or crack passwords, you must do further processing with tools such as LAW, IPRO, ImageMaker, Discovery Cracker, and so forth.

Audio, video, and files created with proprietary software require special tools to play or view these files. Typically, the producing party Bates stamps the discovery of audio and video files by adding the Bates number to the filename as a prefix or suffix. These details should be discussed during the meet and confer.

In addition to free viewers from Microsoft and other vendors, Quick View Plus (*www.avantstar.com*) is often a useful tool. A Web-based reviewing platform can also be helpful for viewing or processing unusual file types. However, the original application might be required to view some files; in these cases, you must pay the vendor for the tool or get it via an agreement with the opposing counsel or under a court order.

New tools come on the market frequently, and existing tools are improved regularly. For example, Clearwell, now owned by Symantec, has become a popular e-discovery tool for managing the EDRM life cycle. It has features for reviewing and converting native files and for importing and exporting load files in addition to foreign language support and visual analytic tools. However, it can't be connected to a scanner for processing paper discovery.

As mentioned, Web-based review platforms are good for novice e-discovery teams and when the case size is expected to exceed what in-house staff can handle. Make sure you check periodically for changes in fees and to compare vendors for costs of these tools. Some vendors charge per document, per user, by bandwidth used, or by amount of storage space. Additional fees might be charged for converting native files.

When considering a Web-based review platform, make sure you ask about storage capacities for audio and video files. Some companies, such as Kroll Ontrack, ZyLAB, Autonomy, and Fios, offer this support, but most e-discovery vendors don't because of the increased bandwidth needed to play these files over an Internet connection.

Another factor in selecting tools is determining how key discovery material (known as "hot docs") is going to be used during trial, arbitration, or mediation. In particular, note what file formats (TIF, PDF, or native files) will be imported into trial presentation tools, such as TrialDirector, Sanction, and Visionary.

Selecting Team Members Selecting e-discovery team members depends on what tools are used for review and organization, the nature of the discovery (such as file formats, exception processing, and so on), the complexity of case issues, the expected size of the case, and case deadlines. In some situations, such as civil cases involving protected case material, security can also affect staffing decisions.

As mentioned, documenting due diligence in e-discovery processes can be beneficial in case of unforeseen problems, and this procedure includes documenting staffing decisions.

A review team of experienced paralegals, junior attorneys, and IT staff with adequate technical training or certifications usually manages cases better, particularly if the lead attorney is skilled at project management planning and communication.

In addition to the review team, experts or consultants might need access to some case materials. In this case, having these personnel use litigation software for review off-site can be helpful. IPRO has developed a portable litigation database (iPublish, *www.iprotech.com/ipro-products/*) as part of its e-discovery tool suite, and it's ideal for experts' use or for investigators and agents in criminal cases because additional licensing isn't required.

Vendors often play an important role in e-discovery, and they can include digital forensics consultants, Web-based review platform providers, litigation support processing houses, document review services, and even trial consultants. Applied Discovery, the e-discovery arm of LexisNexis, has expanded its outsourcing services to include document review. Similarly, Discover Ready (*www.discoverready.com*) and Kroll Ontrack (*www.krollontrack.com/e-discovery/review-and-production/document-review-services*) offer review staff and systems and have both domestic and overseas operations.

E-discovery Organization

During the EDRM stage between collection and presentation (trial, arbitration, or mediation), discovery is organized in notebooks or folders to keep track of chronology, issues, witnesses, experts, and trial outlines. Review platforms help with this organization by offering features such as tags, folders, and sorting categories (see Figure 6-3).

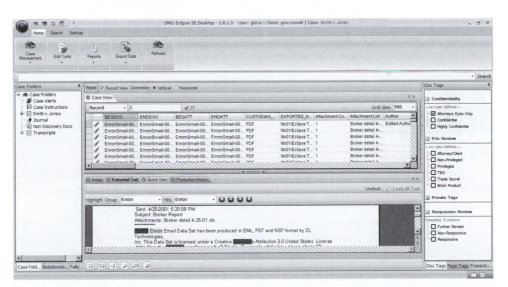

Figure 6-3 Eclipse folders and tags
Source: IPRO Tech, Inc.

In addition to using built-in organization features in review platforms and trial presentation tools, you can find software for more detailed or specific case organization, such as LexisNexis CaseMap and TimeMap. CaseMap can be used as a standalone tool or integrated with Concordance, iCONECT, and other review platforms. It organizes facts, documents, issues, characters (key people), and case law for easy analysis. TimeMap is a timeline graphing tool used for case organization and presentation. You can download both tools at *www.casemap.com*.

The following sections cover many aspects of e-discovery organization, including identifying case issues and strategies (which is the basis of all further organization). Another task is database configuration, which includes field naming for issues. After e-discovery is imported into a database, document coding for each item is done to identify which items relate to what issues, among other things. Quality assurance checks the consistency and progress of coding, search methods, and other key information, and metrics review evaluates case progress in time, deadlines, and budget.

Case Issues and Strategies

Preliminary case issues and strategies are generally formed during the initial investigation but can be revised during the meet and confer, again when discovery is received and reviewed, and after depositions and other fact-finding probes. For example, in the Enron case, the civil complaint against Kenneth Lay identified securities fraud as a key issue, with the claims that financial results had been manipulated and misleading public statements were made. As a publicly traded company, the litigation investigation could include financial reports from the Security and Exchange Commission (SEC) and its online Edgar database (*www.sec.gov/edgar.shtml*) as well as recordings, transcripts, and press releases of quarterly stockholder or financial analyst meetings. Newspaper articles or other media reports could be useful if the source of the information can be verified. Similarly, tracking stocks sold by Enron officers could reveal patterns that correlate with inflated earnings reports or unexpected write-downs. Publicly traded companies are required to file information about executives' company stock holdings with the SEC, and as the Enron investigation and discovery progressed, it became apparent that the accounting firm of Arthur Andersen could be implicated. As a result, the discovery scope was broadened, and case strategies and issues were adjusted.

Many publicly traded companies have an investor relations section on their Web sites containing financial statements as well as recordings or transcripts of quarterly earnings conference calls. Some news services, such as SeekingAlpha, Reuters, and Morningstar, also maintain a database of these transcripts.

The Enron matter was complex and had many case issues. Fortunately, complex cases aren't the norm. However, civil law firms tend to inflate the number of case issues to sometimes unmanageable levels, possibly to impress clients with the complexity of the review or perhaps as a result of the lead attorney's lack of clarity or communication. In reality, when case issues move past 30 to 40, the resulting confusion often means review staff can't organize large volumes of discovery correctly or consistently. In addition, most trial consultants advise against presenting too many issues to a jury because this practice leads to confusion, and important issues get lost. The lead attorney's lack of trial experience could be the basis of this problem. Interestingly, case issues are often managed far more efficiently in criminal cases than in civil cases because criminal attorneys simply don't have the time, money, or resources for unfocused fishing expeditions. Ideally, case issues should be well focused and grouped from the start so that the review staff can work with consistency. The team leader should conduct quality control frequently to detect where problems might happen.

Database Configuration

Project management includes database configuration. This process of identifying and naming database fields takes into consideration factors such as the nature of the case; file types; number and location of review team members, co-counsel, and other parties who need access to the database; security; and potential legal issues. Databases have **key fields**, which are unique numbers or identifiers used for image and data files. Typically, Bates numbers are used for identifiers because these alphanumeric series are unique for each item of discovery.

A field type tells the database how to allocate space and formatting for all cells in that field, much like Microsoft Excel cell formatting. Identifying field types includes designating numeric fields for dates and phone numbers, text fields for short entries (such as names of people or businesses), and paragraph fields that allow lengthier entries, such as OCR material.

You also need to set up security and access rights for reviewers, remote staff or consultants, and other database users. A database administrator, for example, has full access rights to import and export data, perform regular backups, solve network problems, and other administrative tasks, such as creating the database and **authority lists**. As described in Chapter 5, authority lists are drop-down lists with entries used to improve database-coding accuracy and consistency, particularly when you have multiple reviewers (see Figure 6-4).

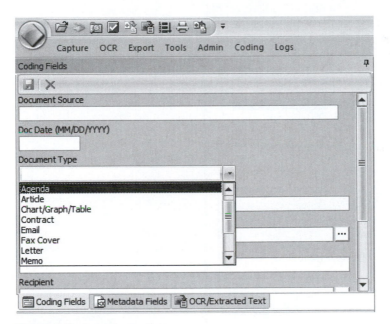

Figure 6-4 An authority list
Source: IPRO Tech, Inc.

The team leader or project manager should have broad access rights to monitor the review team's activity, keep track of metrics, and use the database's reporting features. The lead attorney and review staff usually have more limited security and access rights because they're mainly searching and tagging documents. They don't need rights to add fields, create authority lists, load and delete documents, and perform administrative duties, such as database backup. The lead attorney, however, might need rights to run reports and evaluate metrics, too.

Document Coding

Although native files contain metadata that can be extracted and used for case organization, some metadata requires normalization to be entered in a database easily. In addition, hand-written or paper documents scanned into TIF or PDF format or documents with marginalia (written comments in the margins) don't contain metadata, so coding must be done to enter these materials in a database.

Document coding involves entering data in a database field manually or automatically; manual coding is quite expensive if it's done on a large amount of discovery. Metadata often needs additional processing, too. For example, if e-mail files have been collected from one custodian who uses multiple computers, the username on each computer might be different, so this piece of metadata might have to be entered manually. Similarly, date formats can vary when people work in multiple countries. In the United States, the date format month/day/year is typical; in Europe, the date format is usually day/month/year. This difference carries over into e-mail and document metadata. **Normalization** involves coding or reformatting this information (manually or automatically) to a consistent syntax that allows accurate field searching or sorting (see Figure 6-5).

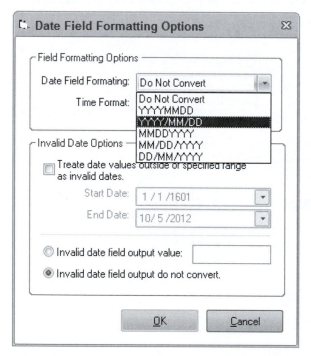

Figure 6-5 Normalizing date formats in eScan-IT
Source: IPRO Tech, Inc.

Coding can be objective or subjective, as you learned in Chapter 5. For example, when paper discovery is scanned and converted to TIF or PDF files, objective coding is used to capture bibliographic information, such as date, author, recipient, title, subject, and so forth. Subjective coding is typically used to identify documents pertaining to certain case issues or designate privileged, attorney-work-product, and protected materials.

Organizing discovery also involves the time-consuming process of **unitization**, which is assembling separate items, such as pages or attachments, into complete documents. Unitization can be physical or logical. For example, the combination of a paper memo stapled to a spreadsheet is considered a "document" in physical unitization. However, if you notice that the spreadsheet was stapled to the memo accidentally, you might decide to separate these two items and treat them as different documents, which is known as logical unitization. Unitization is used with electronic discovery, too. Indicators such as page numbers, titles, and headers and footers in digital files are ways to identify logical documents. For example, faxed documents often have transmission dates and times printed on them that could be indicators of logical unitization. Figure 6-6 shows eScan-IT options for changing a document's unitization by defining its "boundary." Typical options are Box, Folder, Document (Parent), Child (Attachment), and Page/Remove Boundary. These options are fairly common of other e-discovery processing tools, review platforms, and trial presentation tools.

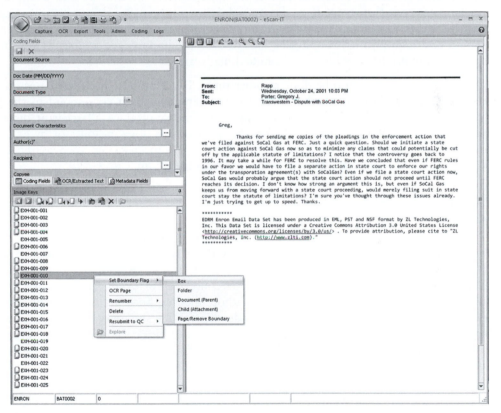

Figure 6-6 Unitizing documents
Source: IPRO Tech, Inc.

E-mail can be produced without attachments, with attachments in place, or with attachments separated. Similarly, Word documents can be produced with embedded or linked Excel charts and spreadsheets or without them. During the meet and confer, both parties should specify how to assemble these types of documents and their attachments to save time and effort. Unitization on a large scale is time-consuming and, therefore, expensive but can usually be done in most review platforms or processing tools, such as LAW, IPRO, and Discovery Assistant.

The goal of coding, normalization, and unitization efforts might depend on whether a document's content is important or whether the way documents were handled is crucial to the case's storyline or issues. For example, a physician's orders attached to the wrong patient's record might prove malpractice or other patient care issues. Similarly, if a law enforcement professional seizes a stack of documents from a table and mixes up their order inadvertently, the evidence might be altered if the document order is relevant to the defendant's activities or the overall case storyline. Creating a coding manual or project manual and using authority lists can help prevent problems and ensure that team members' work on coding is consistent.

Quality Assurance

For in-house e-discovery processing at corporations, law firms, and government agencies, best practices include quality assurance checks at every phase, and litigation managers should be prepared to handle problems that come up. Discovery inventories and chain-of-custody tracking are critical, too. OCR quality (which relies on the paper document's physical condition), scanning resolution, and other factors should be checked often; this type of verification should be a high priority. Monitoring logs of database imports and exports is also important to make sure no discovery has been omitted inadvertently.

Quality checks should also be done at other times. For example, check the Bates numbers of received discovery to see whether there are any gaps that don't correspond to the privilege log. Missing numbers could mean the opposition didn't produce all relevant discovery, or processing errors have occurred, whether the processing is done in-house or by external vendors. Most review platforms have features for doing gap checking, such as the Gapcheck CPL in Concordance (*http://law.lexisnexis.com/literature/Gap_Check.pdf*).

Metrics Review

Metrics are typically gathered in several stages of case processing, often at the same time quality checks are done. The EDRM and Sedona Conference have metrics recommendations, but each case is unique. The LEDES Uniform Task-Based Management System code set for e-discovery, discussed in Chapter 4, can also be helpful for tracking metrics by stages. Metrics are used to evaluate time and budget concerns. For example, most cases have fairly rigid case schedules filed with the court. Without metrics, knowing whether certain stages of e-discovery could be completed before the deadline to file summary judgments or whether a case will be ready to go to trial on time would be difficult. In addition, without metrics, most cases would go over budget. Clients who are charged $1 million in legal fees for a lawsuit filed for only $500,000 are likely to be quite unhappy, to say the least.

Fact-Finding

Fact-finding is the process of reviewing discovery to gather evidence that's relevant to case issues. It usually begins during the prelitigation investigation to determine the case's underlying merits and supporting case law, but it continues throughout the case life cycle and through trial or even appeals. As applied to e-discovery, fact-finding can involve computer forensics examination and is used to review and organize e-mail, documents, audio, video, and other case materials, including responses to requests for admission, interrogatories, and depositions. At this point, key evidence is identified and tagged or put in folders (refer back to Figure 6-3) for pretrial motions and, if necessary, trial. For example, all e-mails about an older employee's age might be placed in a database folder or tagged accordingly, along with copies of case law notes related to age discrimination and wrongful termination. So fact-finding includes organizing evidence by issue, case strategy, and relevant case law and can encompass attorney analysis and conclusion notes. It should also include evidence supporting legal assertions and evidence that the opposition could use to dispute a variety of assertions; in other words, it should include material that can support both sides of an argument. This process relates to the FIRAC method (facts, issues, rules and references, analysis, and conclusions) discussed in Chapter 2.

Search Concepts and Methods Review of e-discovery can be done methodically—that is, starting with the first page of the first document in a database and reviewing one page at a time through the entire database. Many cases were managed in this fashion until the volume of discovery became extensive. However, this method of review is now impractical and cost prohibitive for most cases because of the overwhelming number of documents. As a result, different search concepts and methods are used instead, depending on factors such as the nature of the case and skills of the legal staff. These other methods include fuzzy, stemming, and wildcard searches. A second method should still be used to verify whether the search results are acceptable because some studies have shown that these types of searches can overlook some items.

Many attorneys new to e-discovery strongly resist any review methods other than page-by-page for fear of missing something and because this method can result in higher case fees. However, in both civil or criminal cases, budgetary restrictions dictate the feasibility of using page-by-page review versus a well-documented and defensible search and review process.

Early case organization and fact-finding are necessary to file pretrial motions and prepare effective trial presentations. Unfortunately, many attorneys delay these steps in the hope that the lawsuit will be settled before legal fees are incurred. This approach is usually too haphazard with large cases, and it often contributes to poor case management and costly mistakes later when legal staff must rush to accomplish these time-consuming, detailed tasks. Best practices dictate early and orderly case management.

Pretrial Motions

Both civil and criminal cases usually involve several pretrial motions, including motions for summary judgment (civil) and motions to quash evidence (criminal). Pretrial motions are used to eliminate legal contentions or limit evidence before trial. These motions often result from facts discovered from key documents or other evidence found during discovery review, expert consultation, and information revealed during depositions and other sources.

Filing pretrial motions or responding to motions filed by the opposition can happen abruptly, and there are usually court rules with specific deadlines for filing motions and responses. As most attorneys handle multiple cases simultaneously, it's not unusual for the lead attorney to be absent from the case for periods and have to ask for collection of all documents related to motions with little or no advance notice. The requested documents and other evidence are usually included as exhibits to the motion or exhibits attached to expert affidavits or declarations. Because the review team and legal support staff must be prepared to gather motion information quickly, maintaining regular quality checks as discovery is reviewed and organized helps them respond to these requests promptly and accurately.

When communication between opposing counsel is poor or contentious, discovery might be produced in an inadequate format or be incomplete or untimely, and a **motion to compel** discovery is issued, often because the format or other production concerns aren't addressed adequately during the meet and confer. One common tactic in the past was for the responding party to produce PDF files that couldn't be searched, making them difficult to review and destroying native file metadata. Other forms of inappropriate production included e-mail with missing fields or documents with extremely small or white font. Today, these forms of production might result in sanctions.

Similarly, discovery in criminal cases might be subject to the Federal Rules of Civil Procedure on the form of ESI production and other matters. For example, in *United States v. Briggs, et al* (2011 WL 4017886; W.D.N.Y. Sept. 8, 2011), the government prosecutor produced nonsearchable PDF and TIF files of wiretap transcripts. U.S. Magistrate Judge Hugh Scott applied the FRCP and required that native or searchable files be produced.

Trial Presentation

You're now at the end of the EDRM cycle, which is trial presentation. Trials are expensive, so most people try to avoid them. Nevertheless, cases must be prepared for this possibility. Some law firms, however, have a policy of not processing e-discovery until the last minute in the belief that the case will be settled. Unfortunately, last-minute processing of e-discovery for trial usually results in costly mistakes and a poor outcome, not to mention nondefensible case management processes that can result in spoliation, court sanctions, or malpractice. Whether e-discovery is processed early in the case or at the last minute, however, costs for processing and organization are high, but these tasks make quick retrieval of key information for pretrial motions or trial presentations possible.

Trial Tools

In addition to PowerPoint, the three most widely used trial presentation tools are TrialDirector (*www.indatacorp.com*), Sanction (*www.sanction.com*), and Visionary (*www. visionarylegaltechnologies.com*). They have been developed to work with files processed in Concordance, Summation, iCONECT, and other e-discovery review or processing platforms. TIF images and load and data files of hot docs from these platforms can be imported into trial presentation tools along with native and PDF files. In this chapter, you use TrialDirector; you can download a 140-day demo version at *www.indatacorp.com/ trialdirectoreval*. In addition, it helps to be prepared to use all manner of equipment during trial, including digital whiteboards, videoconferencing, real-time court reporting software, and virtual reality displays.

 "Effective Use of Courtroom Technology: A Judge's Guide to Pretrial and Trial" (2001) is an excellent resource commissioned by the Federal Judicial Center (*www.fjc.gov/public/pdf.nsf/lookup/cttech00.pdf/ $file/cttech00.pdf*).

In addition to trial presentation software, trial hardware might be needed, and it's not supplied by the court. This hardware can include monitors, screens, projectors, audio/sound systems, wiring, printers, and so forth. Computers and laptops must be equipped with RAM and CPU speeds capable of running all required software without disruption.

Exhibit Organization and Migration

Until now, most case materials have been reviewed and organized in review platforms such as Concordance, Summation, or iCONECT and consist of tags, folders, and fielded data usually entered manually, such as issue categories. Anything that would be entered in index cards in the paper review described in Chapter 4 is included in a field in the review platform as part of the overall case organization.

At this point, exhibits for trial are created, numbered, filed with the court, and exchanged with opposing counsel. In the past, exhibits were numbered during presentation at trial, but now pretrial numbering is usually assigned based on the numbering series agreed to during the meet and confer. Typically, plaintiff exhibits are numbered first—say, from 1 to 500—and defendant exhibits are numbered next (see Figure 6-7). When both plaintiff and defendant are using the same exhibit, both sides should use the same number so as not to confuse the jury.

Figure 6-7 Exhibits shown in TrialDirector
Source: InData Corporation

Trial exhibits can be organized and assigned exhibit numbers in the review platform and then transferred to the trial presentation tool, or exhibit numbers can be assigned in the trial presentation tool. Either way, both the trial presentation tool and review platform should have exhibit numbers synchronized so that you always know what documents have been or will be presented during trial. As you see in the hands-on projects, most trial presentation tools accept common review platform load and DAT (data) files or have features for converting common formats to make exchanging materials easier. As mentioned, good project management takes into account this stage of file migration and organization to avoid unnecessary reprocessing costs and confusion at the last minute before trial. In short, take the time to know the technical requirements of your trial presentation tools early in the case, such as maximum number of characters per field, filename syntax, symbol compatibility in filenames, preferred format of scanned documents, and so forth.

Quality control in exhibit organization involves comparisons to make sure the same trial exhibits are in the review platform and the trial presentation tool. Be careful that no exhibits are lost when you're migrating evidence between tools. Figure 6-8 shows a simplified case, in which item counts from eScan-IT reports are compared with TrialDirector item counts and double-checked against Bates number sequences. You should also verify that documents in both tools are compared with presentation outlines prepared by the lead attorney, as these outlines can change unexpectedly.

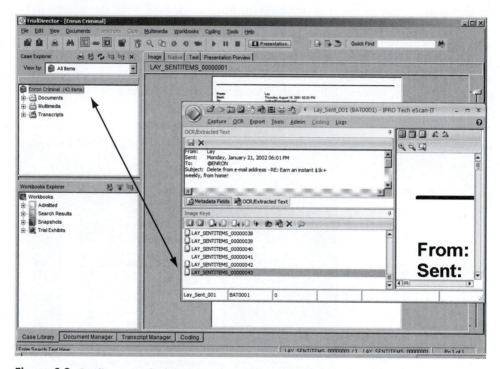

Figure 6-8 Quality control when migrating evidence from eScan-IT to TrialDirector
Source: IPRO Tech, Inc. and InData Corporation

After all exhibit numbers have been assigned, and this information has been entered in both the review platform and trial presentation tool, trial notebooks are usually created in paper format. However, using paper notebooks is optional because tech-savvy litigators can use trial presentation tools to set up a dual-screen presentation (one screen viewed by the jury and one seen only by the presenter). Notebooks usually contain exhibits in numerical order and have a separate tab (or separate notebook) with exhibits organized in chronological order. In addition, trial exhibits are exchanged with opposing counsel and filed with the court, and opposing counsel's exhibit numbers are entered in both the trial presentation tool and review platform. Take extra care to ensure accuracy during this process because most judges think poorly of errors that waste time for the court and jury.

Courtroom Facilities

Many courts have updated their facilities to accommodate modern courtroom technology; however, some have not. It's important to visit the court well before the trial to examine the facilities for technical and presentation concerns and speak with the judge's clerk or bailiff about acceptable types of presentation if this information isn't available elsewhere from the court. For example, some judges don't allow Internet access, which could affect your presentation or trial coordination. Similarly, some judges object to placing screens in certain parts of the courtroom or restrict the use of certain electrical outlets for safety or other reasons. Older courthouses might have limited circuit loads that affect the amount or type of equipment you can use.

Many courts in metropolitan areas have designated technology training days that allow pretrial review of the court's technical capacity and preferences. They might be offered frequently or just once a month, so plan to visit the courthouse at least 60 days before trial and again 1 to 2 weeks before trial to make sure you have addressed all potential concerns.

Security Considerations

In some criminal or even civil cases, security can be an issue. For example, cases involving organized crime usually have increased security that affects access to the courtroom, or cases involving child pornography might have special rules for presenting evidence. Remember that most court proceedings are open to the public and media, so anticipate how this factor might affect your operations and what's presented, including protected material for trade secrets. In addition, determine whether equipment or other materials need to be stored in the courtroom during recess and other times. Some courts have a workroom attached for attorneys' use or a jury room with storage accommodations. Again, advance planning is crucial.

Jury Considerations

As mentioned, trial presentation requires unique communication and technical skills. Knowing what information should be presented—and how and when it should be presented—to a jury or judge is an art. To help with achieving this goal, trial presentation software has many benefits over the flip charts, projectors, and other methods used in the past. For example, when cross-examining a witness, documents can be shown on a screen for the jury to see, and key text can be highlighted or expanded for emphasis. Similarly, two documents can be presented side by side to point out alterations, for instance.

With trial presentation software, video-recorded depositions can be replayed while synchronized to the transcript, and relevant exhibits can be displayed simultaneously. This multimedia presentation improves the jury's understanding of the case and recall of important facts during deliberations. Jurors who are more visually oriented can watch the deponent giving testimony, and jurors who want to see more text-based evidence can monitor the transcript and supporting exhibits.

When presenting evidence in a digital format, be prepared to give the jury the same evidence in a portable format if jurors ask to review evidence again during deliberations before delivering a verdict. The judge determines whether this request is reasonable, but generally, it's granted. Occasionally, if the opposing counsel has no objection, some materials can be converted to a format that's easier for jurors to use, as long as the content isn't altered. For example, it's unrealistic to expect jurors to know how to operate trial presentation software, especially when the deposition video and transcript play back in a synchronized fashion. The two components can be separated into formats that jurors can view in more familiar tools, such as Windows Media Player and Microsoft Word. Of course, they lose the synchronization feature, but this drawback can be explained to the judge and jury. Know ahead of time how to do any necessary conversions, and make sure you have the correct codecs and other tools handy.

Judicial Considerations

In most metropolitan areas, judges have become accustomed to trial presentation technology. In fact, courts generally approve of using technology because studies have shown that trials proceed faster when it's used. However, the use of special technology during trial generally requires the judge's approval in advance. Always be prepared to communicate simply and clearly what equipment you plan to use and anything unusual about how it works.

Regardless of whether the presiding judge is comfortable with technology, it's a good idea to have **demonstratives** available to help the judge understand the technology you're using in case he or she has questions. Demonstratives are any type of evidence used to explain something, such as flip charts, PowerPoint slides, physical models, videos, and so forth. If there's a problem you aren't prepared to address, you can try contacting the software or equipment vendor and explaining the situation. For example, the judge might ask how to verify that a copy of a wiretap recording is the same as the original recording. An affidavit from the vendor who made the copy or matching certified transcripts might be suitable. As a simple solution, playing the same random parts of the two recordings might be adequate. Most vendors have encountered similar problems and are willing to assist.

Finally, keep in mind that exhibiting professionalism and efficiency to the judge, court staff, and jury go a long way toward a successful case outcome. Even if the case is lost, judges will remember your behavior in future cases.

Chapter Summary

- Early case evaluation includes prelitigation investigation, interviews, and preliminary discovery, which often includes capturing Web-based and other digital evidence from public and private sources.

- Formal litigation begins with filing a complaint in civil cases or an indictment in criminal cases. In civil cases, a legal hold is issued to notify parties of their obligation to preserve data. Legal holds aren't required in criminal cases because of the prosecution's duty to preserve evidence under Brady, Jencks, and Giglio. Formal civil discovery starts with requests for admission, requests for production, interrogatories, depositions, and other fact-finding processes. Criminal cases use different discovery documents, such as a bill of particulars.

- A meet and confer is the time to agree on all technical and nontechnical discovery requirements, such as whether OS metadata or deleted files are needed. Additional discussions should cover keyword and other searching parameters, whether native files will be produced, the format of converted files, and whether cost sharing is suitable. Both parties should specify the correct handling of native files that require special software as well as encrypted and password-protected files.

- Project management involves sampling and metrics. The project manager selects the tools and resources for each case and monitors case processing with software reports and other sampling methods and metrics calculations. Project management includes devising methods to adhere to case budgets and notifying the lead attorney when issues that can affect the budget or schedule come up. Project managers should keep good documentation and stay abreast of changing e-discovery technologies.

- The basis of e-discovery organization lies in case issues and strategies, which can often change and broaden as discovery is reviewed. E-discovery is imported into review databases, which are configured for case needs and the legal staff who use them. Document coding involves both subjective and objective data capture. Authority lists and restrictions of database access are used to prevent user entry errors and accidentally deleting information. Quality assurance is done to monitor the consistency and accuracy of discovery organization, and a metrics review is used to assess case progress, budget, and schedules.

- Fact-finding is the process of identifying evidence to support or refute case allegations. It no longer involves page-by-page document review; instead, it relies on well-documented and defensible search concepts and methods done in review databases.

- Pretrial motions are used to eliminate legal contentions (dispositive) or limit evidence before a trial. Some common forms of dispositive pretrial motions include a motion for summary judgment or a motion to dismiss. A motion to quash can be used to prevent evidence from being used in a case. A motion to compel is used when discovery isn't produced or isn't produced in an acceptable format.

- Judges have complete control over their courts and often have restrictions on placement or use of certain equipment in court, or they might limit or deny Internet access. Security concerns can also affect trial setup and presentation, particularly in cases involving trade secrets, organized crime, national security (the PATRIOT Act), and child pornography. Three widely used trial presentation tools are TrialDirector, Sanction, and Visionary. Early case processing should take into account tool specifications for file types, file formats, naming conventions, and other requirements. Anticipating these requirements prevents reprocessing costs and errors before the trial. Be prepared to have digital evidence in a portable format for jurors, if they request it during deliberations.

Key Terms

authority lists   Lists created for use in databases to improve accuracy and consistency of document coding.

cost sharing   The process of plaintiffs and defendants sharing resources voluntarily to reduce case costs; can also apply to third parties. It's the opposite of cost shifting, which is usually involuntary.

demonstratives   Evidence other than testimony intended to clarify case facts, usually presented during a civil or criminal trial; can include animated videos, charts, timelines, and models.

fact-finding   The process of reviewing discovery to find evidence related to case issues.

key field   A database field used to hold a unique record identifier.

legal hold   An order to preserve data in anticipation of litigation, an audit, a government investigation, or another matter; it prohibits people from destroying or processing records. *See also* preservation letter.

meet and confer   A meeting required by FRCP 26(f) that takes place between opposing counsel and unrepresented parties to address potential problems of discovery, scheduling, and other case matters.

motion to compel   A form of legal pleading used to force the opposition to produce evidence previously requested but not delivered.

motion to quash   A legal procedure used to reject, invalidate, or suppress evidence.

normalization   The process of standardizing data formats.

preservation letter   Same as a legal hold but typically used between opposing counsel. *See also* legal hold.

proportionality   Under FRCP 26(b)(2), the process of limiting the burden of discovery by weighing it against its likely benefits. This concept can also be applied to criminal cases.

subpoena duces tecum   A written command issued by the court (or a lawyer as an agent of the court) to appear with certain evidence or to permit some action, such as inspecting property.

unitization   The process of organizing documents and attachments. Physical unitization uses physical features (date, title, staples, folders, and so on) of pages to identify a complete document. Logical unitization uses human interpretation of page content to identify a complete document.

Review Questions

1. Information from public sources of discovery can be requested via the Freedom of Information Act. True or False?

2. Which of the following is an order to preserve data and prohibit destroying or processing potentially relevant records?

   a. Meet and confer

   b. Legal hold

   c. Motion to quash

   d. RFP

3. Which of the following is a legal document used to *request* discovery from opposing counsel? (Choose all that apply.)

   a. RFA

   b. Motion to compel

   c. RFP

   d. Subpoena

4. A legal hold should include which of the following? (Choose all that apply.)

   a. List of key custodians

   b. Possible types of relevant data

   c. Crime maps

   d. Preservation letters

5. A request for admission must precede a preservation letter. True or False?

6. During a meet and confer, the discovery plan should include which of the following? (Choose all that apply.)

   a. Discussion of cost sharing

   b. Search parameters

   c. Choice of trial presentation tools

   d. Production formats

7. _____ considerations can be applied to limit discovery if the burden and expense are likely to outweigh the benefits.

8. According to the Stored Communications Act, discovery that's been stored on or transmitted over the Internet can be obtained in which of the following ways? (Choose all that apply.)

   a. Subpoena

   b. Interrogatory

   c. Search warrant

   d. Court order

9. Identifiers for key fields in a litigation database are usually based on which of the following?

   a. Dates of documents

   b. A numbering sequence determined by the judge

   c. Bates numbers

   d. None of the above

10. Unitization is the process of coding information in a consistent syntax to improve the accuracy of searching and sorting records. True or False?

11. Which of the following is used to improve the consistency and accuracy of coding database entries? (Choose all that apply.)

 a. Coding manual

 b. Authority lists

 c. Bates numbers

 d. Field types

12. What are some built-in features that software tools include for organizing discovery?

13. Documenting staffing decisions for review teams is an important part of due diligence in e-discovery processes. True or False?

14. Which of the following is used to force opposition to produce evidence that has been requested but not provided?

 a. Summary judgment

 b. Subpoena

 c. Motion to compel

 d. Motion to quash

15. Describe one quality control measure you should use when organizing exhibits.

16. Describe one feature of trial presentation software that improves jurors' understanding of a case's facts and evidence.

17. Which of the following should you prepare to help judges understand the technology being used to present a case?

 a. Exhibits

 b. Demonstratives

 c. Subpoena duces tecum

 d. Load files

Hands-On Projects

You can find data files for this chapter on the DVD in the Chapter06\Projects folder. If necessary, be sure to copy them to your working directory on your machine before starting the projects.

Allow extra time for the projects in this chapter.

Hands-On Project 6-1

In this project, you use eScan-IT for creating load files and OCR text files and for Bates stamping (endorsing) documents. Your results might vary depending on the applications installed on your computer. eScan-IT requires two authorization numbers for installation: a serial number (given in Step 2) and a validation number that you get by calling IPRO support while you're installing the program.

Make sure the `zl_lay-k_000.pst` file you used in Chapter 3 has been copied to your hard drive, preferably near the root. Don't copy it to an external drive or a thumb drive.

If you're using Office 2013, you might need to install Microsoft Office Document Imaging to do this project. Click Start, All Programs, Microsoft Office, Microsoft Office Tools, and then Microsoft Office Document Imaging. (For more information, search at *www.microsoft.com* for "Microsoft Office Document Imaging.")

1. Go to the **Software\IPRO** folder on the book's DVD, and copy the **eScanIT3_2_0.exe** file to your working directory. Go to the **Chapter06\Projects** folder on the book's DVD, and copy the **Ch6_eScanIT.wmv** file and the **Documentation** folder to your working directory. Review the **IPRO eScan-IT Install Guide.pdf** and the **eScanITCard.pdf** files in the Documentation folder so that you know where to look if you have questions.

2. Install eScan-IT by opening Windows Explorer, right-clicking **eScanIT3_2_0.exe**, and clicking **Run as administrator**. Follow the installation instructions. The serial number you need is SCND-01-00688-4042E2GDAH49. To validate the software, you must call IPRO support (877-324-4776, option 2) Monday through Friday between 7 a.m. and 5 p.m. MST while you're at your computer.

3. After the software has been installed, double-click the **eScan-IT** desktop icon to open the software. If prompted to establish a valid system directory, browse to the correct location or accept the default, and then click **OK**. Play the **Ch6_eScanIT.wmv** video, and follow along on your computer to process the **zl_lay-k_000.pst** file, pausing the video as needed. (*Note*: The location of files on your computer might differ from what's shown in the video.)

4. Use these metadata fields for this project when indicated in the video:

• BEGATT	BEGDOC	ENDATT
• ENDDOC	OCRTEXT	Author
• BCC	CC	Creation Date
• Creation Date[E]	Date Created	Entry ID
• From	Last Accessed	Last Modified
• Location	MD5 Hash	MD5 Hash[E]
• Message ID	Page count	
• Sent Date	Subject[E]	

5. When you're finished processing the PST file, navigate to the **Export** folder and review the files in the **IMG_0000001** subfolder, which contains both image (.tif) and OCR (.txt) files. Also, review the **IPRO.LFP** file in the BAT0001 subfolder. You can open LFP and OCR files with Notepad. You use these files in Hands-On Project 6-2.

6. Exit eScan-IT, and close any open windows.

Hands-On Project 6-2

In this project, you migrate the LFP and OCR export files you processed in Hands-On Project 6-1 to a new case created in TrialDirector. You also set a path (link) to where image (.tif) files are stored.

The TrialDirector demo license is valid for 140 days.

1. Start a Web browser, go to **www.indatacorp.com/trialdirectoreval**, and download TrialDirector, if you didn't download and install it in Chapter 5. You might also want to download the TrialDirector Sample Data files (available at the TrialDirector download link) so that you can explore the TrialDirector sample case organization later.

2. In Windows Explorer, go to the location where you stored the downloaded file. Right-click **TD6WebSetup.exe** and click **Run as administrator**. Follow the installation prompts.

3. Double-click the TrialDirector desktop icon to start the program. Play the **Ch6_TrialDirector.wmv** video and follow along to set up your case and migrate the files from Hands-On Project 6-1. Pause the video as needed.

4. Be sure to verify that all files processed in eScan-IT have been imported into TrialDirector correctly (refer back to Figure 6-8), including placeholder (exception) documents.

5. If time permits, import the file you created at the end of Hands-On Project 5-2 into TrialDirector; refer to the user manual or Help menu, if needed. This step gives you practice importing load files from different sources, especially review platforms such as Concordance and iCONECT.

6. Exit TrialDirector, and close all open windows.

Hands-On Project 6-3

In this project, you take a virtual tour of a real federal courtroom and review guides for equipment setup requirements.

1. Start a Web browser, and go to **www.wawd.uscourts.gov/attorneys/trial-support/ virtual-tour-seattle**. Take the virtual tour, making notes as you watch. Move the mouse over the courtroom photo to trigger hotspots containing more information, and make sure your speakers are turned on so that you can hear the audio dialogue.

2. Next, go to **www.wawd.uscourts.gov/attorneys/trial-support/courtroom-technology-overview**, and read the Courtroom Technology Overview.

3. Write a one-page paper on what you observed about the courtroom setup, and state whether you understand the types of computer and AV cables or connectors needed for trial presentations. Include descriptions of the prosecution and defense tables, witness stand, jury box, podium, and courtroom deputy station. You can use your personal or classroom computer as an example for the connection setups.

Case Projects

CASE PROJECTS

Case Project 6-1

You're an intern with a nonprofit consumer watchdog group and have been asked to join its Oil and Gas Price Fraud Working Group, which is the nonprofit counterpart to the group formed by the Department of Justice (*www.justice.gov/opa/pr/2011/April/11-ag-500.html*). Apply what you've learned about Enron's inflated earnings and energy price manipulation to conducting a mock investigation into petroleum price inflations that occurred between 2008 and 2012. The objective is to identify 5 to 10 sources of potential e-discovery to lay a foundation for further investigation or even litigation. Consider a number of sources, such as oil company financial statement filings with the SEC/Edgar, recordings of conference calls with oil company executives (often available on company Web sites under "Investor Relations"), newspaper or TV commentaries, Yahoo! financial charts for particular stocks, petroleum trade association publications or Web sites, government investigations, petroleum pricing regulations, and so forth. List sources of e-discovery that might reveal relevant information, both good and bad.

Write a two-page paper on the e-discovery you would capture online or download and the discovery you would get with a subpoena, a search warrant, or an RFP. Describe what tools you would use to collect and preserve this material.

References

Federal Judicial Center. "Effective Use of Courtroom Technology: A Judge's Guide to Pretrial and Trial," 2001, *www.fjc.gov/public/pdf.nsf/lookup/CTtech00.pdf/$file/CTtech00.pdf*.

Stored Communications Act. 18 U.S.C. §§ 2701-2712, 1986.

The Electronic Discovery Reference Model. EDRM Metrics Code Set, *www.edrm.net/resources/standards/edrm-metrics/edrm-metrics-code-set*.

The Sedona Conference Working Group. "Commentary on Achieving Quality in the E-Discovery Process," May 2009, *www.thesedonaconference.org/content/miscFiles/Achieving_Quality.pdf*.

The Sedona Conference Working Group. "Commentary on Legal Holds, the Trigger & the Process," 2007, *www.thesedonaconference.org*.

United States v. Briggs, et al. 2011 WL 4017886; W.D.N.Y., September 8, 2011.

chapter 7

Information Governance
and Litigation Preparedness

After reading this chapter and completing the exercises, you will be able to:

- Ascertain which laws, rules, and regulations apply to your organization
- Describe systems used to assist with litigation preparedness
- Plan for multiple litigations that draw from similar sets of data
- Evaluate an organization's readiness to respond to a litigation hold

In this chapter, you see how to ascertain which rules, laws, and regulations apply to your organization. As you've learned in previous chapters, the question isn't whether a company will be involved in litigation, but when. The way information is handled, stored, and retrieved affects how easy or difficult e-discovery will be, so information governance is a crucial part of a company's policies. In addition, when dealing with multiple litigations, a company might have data that's used in a variety of cases. The data custodian, who can be a network administrator, an attorney, or another employee, must organize data in a way that makes it easy to retrieve. Due diligence requires collecting e-discovery to make sure assets and liabilities are analyzed thoroughly.

Examining Information Governance

The term "information governance" has gained popularity. Defined in Chapter 2 as a way of ensuring that data is managed correctly from the top down, it essentially means an organization must assume that sooner or later it will be involved in litigation, whether it's civil or criminal. The Gartner Group defines information governance as follows:

> *The specification of decision rights and an accountability framework to ensure appropriate behavior in the valuation, creation, storage, use, archiving, and deletion of information. It includes the processes, roles and policies, standards, and metrics that ensure the effective and efficient use of information in enabling an organization to achieve its goals.*

Whether you're using a broad or targeted e-discovery scope (covered in Chapter 3), the e-discovery process can be simplified by creating an information architecture and ESI procedures. This chapter delves into how companies should use internal policies and procedures to fulfill legal and regulatory responsibilities for preserving and organizing information. Figure 7-1 shows the Information Governance Reference Model you saw in Chapter 2. In this chapter, you focus on the sections labeled IT, which deals with efficiency; Privacy and Security (added later, after this model was created), which address risk; and Legal, which also addresses risk. IT efficiency includes storing, purging, backing up, and restoring data as well as deleting and archiving files. Legal staff should determine what needs to be stored and how long. Privacy and security must be considered when deciding what part of data is stored, encrypted, or purged.

Information governance requires determining which laws and regulations apply to your organization. For example, hospitals certainly fall under HIPAA; attorney-client privilege applies to law firms; government agencies must deal with the Freedom of Information Act (FOIA); and schools must adhere to the Family Educational Rights and Privacy Act (FERPA). Banks, mortgage firms, and brokers must follow Security and Exchange Commission (SEC) regulations in one form or another. After the legal staff determines which rules apply, the IT staff must create policies and procedures to comply with discovery orders or litigation holds.

As you learned in Chapter 2, the Sarbanes-Oxley Act of 2002 (Pub.L. 107-204, 116 Stat. 745) was created in response to an era of financial scandals, including Enron and WorldCom. This act is sometimes referred to as the Public Company Accounting Reform and Investor Protection Act and the Corporate and Auditing Accountability and Responsibility Act. Sarbanes-Oxley

Information Governance Reference Model (IGRM)

Linking duty + value to information asset = efficient, effective management

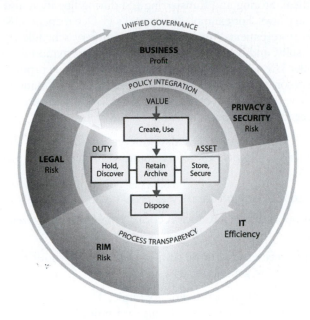

Duty: Legal obligation
for specific information

Value: Utility or
business purpose of
specific information

Asset: Specific container
of information

RIM = records information management

Figure 7-1 The Information Governance Reference Model

Source: *EDRM.net*

was intended to protect investors by improving the accuracy and reliability of publicly traded companies' disclosures for compliance with securities laws. It created new standards for corporate accountability and penalties for violations and changed how boards of directors and executives interact with each other and with corporate auditors. One critical standard of Sarbanes-Oxley is that an organization's governing management, such as the CEO, CFO, and board of trustees, must be accountable for financial oversight. A key point concerns conflict of interest; in other words, the accounting firm chosen to do audits can't have employed the CEO, CFO, or similar person of authority within a year of the audit.

Sections 302 and 303 of Sarbanes-Oxley cover audits and internal controls that apply to accurate reporting of a company's finances. In addition, Section 404 requires both management and external auditors to examine internal controls, so a Section 404 audit is conducted to monitor what's happening financially and examine the IT aspects of the business flow model. This audit also inspects controls to detect and prevent fraud. Sections 802, 906, and 1107 address criminal penalties for certain acts. Section 802 covers altering evidence or otherwise interfering with a government investigation. Section 906 imposes heavy penalties if the CEO, CFO, or a similar person of authority swears to and affirms false statements about the company's financial health. Section 1107 has equally severe penalties for those who go after whistleblowers.

Privacy Laws

Privacy laws must be considered when designing networks, databases, e-mail systems, and the processes that go along with them. Storing and transferring ESI during litigation also require paying attention to applicable privacy laws. For example, a hospital's IT Department must ensure privacy when setting up servers to store patients' medical histories, surgery schedules, patient appointments, prescriptions, test results, and other patient information. Information governance dictates storing records that fall under HIPAA protection separately from general corporate records. If the hospital is state run, some records would fall under the Freedom of Information Act (FOIA). Of course, no patients want their records to become public knowledge, so measures must be put in place to keep this data segregated from what's available via the FOIA.

Another critical question is who's storing ESI that's accessible online. Is it the health care facility or a third party? PrivacyRights.org offers some cautions on the pros and cons of third-party storage systems:

- A third party might not be subject to HIPAA regulations.

- If a third party is subpoenaed to produce records, it might have to release your organization's medical information.

- A third party's user agreement might be subject to change without notice to facilitate advertising or other revenue-generating measures.

Health care and finances go hand in hand. For example, HIPAA doesn't cover financial records, but someone examining your credit card bills and point of sale (POS) activity could easily discover items of your medical history. The **Gramm-Leach-Bliley Act** offers protection against this invasion of privacy. One provision of this act, which was created to address consumers' financial privacy, is that financial institutions must tell consumers who has access to their information and what third parties their information might be shared with. Although consumers can usually opt out of having their information shared, in some specific instances they can't. For example, they can't opt out when third parties are hired to process or store consumer data, when general or combined data (that doesn't list names) is used for marketing, and, most critical, when law enforcement or legal proceedings require the information. If, for example, a financial institution is required to share data during civil litigation, what steps must be taken to protect consumers?

 Keep in mind that the term "financial institution" doesn't apply only to banks, credit unions, and credit card companies. It includes check-cashing institutions, mortgage brokers, debt collection services, and real estate investment firms.

The most important step in protecting consumers is following the regulation that **nonpublic personal information (NPI)** can't be shared, except under the circumstances listed in the preceding paragraph. NPI includes information that can specify an individual. (For example, statistics categorizing Pacific Islander males or Hispanic females aren't considered NPI, but Social Security numbers are.) Therefore, a third-party organization a company hires to process data falls under these exceptions. Although a third-party organization can share NPI, the information must be transmitted in encrypted form and preferably over a secure line. When HIPAA was first enacted, pharmacies handed people a disclosure form stating who they would be sharing patient data with. Now when you go to a doctor's office for an initial consultation, typically you must sign a form stating that you understand your information might be shared with a billing agency, the insurer, your referring physician, and other third parties, such as laboratories. HIPAA addresses **personal health information (PHI)** and the electronic version, abbreviated as "ePHI." In other words, any personally identifiable information is protected under this act. When dealing with ePHI, the same precautions used with NPI must be taken. When storing or transmitting information, files should be encrypted, and vendors hired to process the information must abide by applicable privacy laws.

In addition, Web sites regularly collect information from users, and precautions need to be taken when dealing with personal information. The **Children's Online Privacy Protection Act (COPPA)** is a law that addresses NPI. It deals with Web sites that collect information from children younger than 13 and is different from the Child Online Protection Act (COPA), which sought to protect children from potentially harmful Web site content. The bill effectively died in 2009 when the U.S. Supreme Court refused to hear arguments on it. COPPA addresses the fact that when collecting information from children, sites also gather details about parents, family members, and friends, and all this information is protected. The importance of COPPA is related to Web sites and personally identifiable information.

For more information on COPPA, see *www.business.ftc.gov/documents/ Complying-with-COPPA-Frequently-Asked-Questions.*

Another law regulating privacy issues is the **Family Educational Rights and Privacy Act (FERPA)**; it falls under the U.S. Department of Education and was created to protect students' educational records. It requires that IT staff at K-12 schools and institutes of higher learning maintain student records on separate network segments. Information on employees' payroll records, retirement benefits, and so forth is covered under a different law. Legal staff at educational institutions should be aware of applicable laws and assist the IT staff in deciding how information is organized and determing policies and procedures.

Freedom of Information Act

The **Freedom of Information Act (FOIA)**, enacted in 1966, specifies that the U.S. government must disclose in full or in part documentation requested by the public. There are nine exceptions to the rule, including national security matters, patients' medical records, trade secrets, records of cases still in litigation, and records covered under another statute. Some states have their own FOIA that applies to records maintained at the state level. The 1996 Electronic Freedom of Information Act Amendments required government agencies to make records available in electronic format.

How does the FOIA affect ESI? When employees of government agencies are hired, for example, they're informed that the contents of their computer files and e-mails are in the public domain. Some states require retaining e-mail backups for seven years, and often the salaries of all state employees can be accessed online (as in the state of Washington, for example). This information isn't considered NPI because their Social Security numbers aren't published. Student e-mail, however, is a different story. Normally, FERPA applies to this information, but if a student's e-mail address is in the form *student@institution*.edu, the e-mail could be accessible under the FOIA. The FOIA doesn't apply to student e-mail hosted by a third party, but it would be protected under the Electronic Communications Privacy Act (ECPA).

For a good history of the FOIA, go to *www.justice.gov/oip/foia-leg-mat.html.*

As technology advances, most state and federal courts are leaning toward a broad interpretation when defining what constitutes a "public record." Like private businesses, government agencies' communications use a wide variety of electronic media and devices, so the definition has been stretched to include, among others, tweets, text messages, e-mails, Web pages, blog posts, photographs, recordings, databases, Webcasts, phone records, and server logs. All these items are accessible under the FOIA.

The procedure for requesting public records varies with each federal agency and from state to state. In general, however, an agency identifies a central contact, sometimes called a public information officer or an FOIA officer, to whom all requests are directed. Requests can be made in writing or sometimes online. Many agencies require you to confirm that the information you're requesting won't be used for commercial purposes, and reasonable copying fees might be charged. The process is usually simple, but identifying the records you want as specifically as possible is recommended. If you want metadata included, you must ask for it. Records such as death certificates, title transfers, and court documents are part of the public record, so generally there are no restrictions on getting this information. You might run into restrictions for records such as birth certificates if you aren't a relative of the person whose records you're requesting. For example, many agencies or states require that a person must have been deceased for 75 years before a birth certificate for him or her is released to another party.

In some states, a preliminary response is required in five business days or fewer; other states have no mandatory response time. At the federal level, the required response time is 20 days. At both the state and federal level, response times can be extended under circumstances such as the need to review a large quantity of records or retrieve information from multiple offices.

To find information on the FOIA officer for the White House Office of Management and Budget, learn how to obtain records, and see answers to other frequently asked questions, go to *www.whitehouse. gov/omb/foia_default.*

As with e-discovery, if part of a record is confidential or exempt, the agency must produce the nonconfidential portion and typically uses redaction techniques on the confidential portions. Keep in mind that paper records are usually redacted manually, which is time consuming, and redacting electronic records can alter metadata. Even electronic redaction takes time and might require extracting metadata to a separate file before redacting the remaining record. The average number of requests per year since 2008 have been more than 500,000, and in 2012, 651,254 requests were made (*FOIA.gov*, 2013). Although improvements in the process have been made, more than 70,000 requests were backlogged at the end of 2012.

As you have seen, the Federal Rules of Civil Procedure guide e-discovery in civil matters, but the FRCP doesn't address digital evidence in criminal cases or public records. The FRCP mainly deals with search and seizure law when examining ESI. However, when litigation involves criminal cases or public records, judges who handle e-discovery in civil matters sometimes apply the FRCP to these matters. Remember that the rights of the individual come into play with criminal cases. For example, in *National Day Laborer Organizing Network et al v. United States Immigration and Customs Enforcement Agency, et al* (2012 U.S. Dist. Lexis 97863; SDNY, July 13, 2012), Judge Scheindlin, of the landmark *Zubulake* case, initially applied FRCP 34 to producing metadata in a FOIA request from the plaintiff. However, Judge Scheindlin subsequently retracted the ruling, so the question of metadata being included in FOIA requests is still unresolved.

The FOIA and the FRCP have different legal standards for determining whether information must be produced. The FOIA relies on whether a request is "reasonable," and the FRCP uses the term "proportional." Document retrieval can be time consuming and costly, and defendants often claim that an e-discovery request is unreasonable because the cost to convert or retrieve data is prohibitive. The *Zubulake* case introduced proportionality, meaning the party with the most resources pays for data retrieval. In other words, the government doesn't have to produce public records when processing them is overly burdensome. However, if the FRCP guideline is followed, the cost is split proportionately.

At the state and lower levels, several public data request cases have involved metadata. Starting with *Lake v. City of Phoenix* (218 P.3d 1004; Ariz. 2009), the state supreme court determined that metadata is part of the original electronic record and must be produced along with the records. However, Maryland, for example, allows removing metadata before producing the requested records.

NOTE Other noteworthy cases with similar responses include *Hearst Corp. v. New York* (882 N.Y.S.2d 862; NY Sup. Ct., Albany Cnty. 2009); *O'Neill v. City of Shoreline* (240 P.3d 1149; Wash. 2010); and *Irwin v. Onondaga Cnty. Resource Agency* (895 N.Y.S.2d 262; NY App. Div. 2010).

Systems to Assist with Litigation Preparedness

In response to the need to preserve and organize ESI for compliance with regulations and as part of litigation preparedness, document management systems have been created that are capable of handling large volumes of information with assisted or automatic filing features. A **document management system (DMS)** can act as a decision support system that monitors a user's actions and then mimics them later. For example, a DMS records where a user, such as a paralegal or an attorney, files a document or e-mail. The next time the user files a similar document, the system automatically prompts him or her to specify whether the document should be stored in the same location. This feature helps sort the large amount of electronic data stored on the terabyte hard drives and even larger servers that are common today. Many DMS solutions also offer features for creating and assembling documents based on standards or preapproved expressions and other improvements in collaboration and cooperation in document handling. "Preapproved expressions" are terms in document titles or e-mail subject lines that prompt the DMS to store records in specific locations to improve sorting and retrieving. For example, a DMS might be used to automatically store all HIPAA-protected records on the same network drive.

 Decision support systems (DSSs) are software tools that examine data such as sales trends, purchasing trends, vendor use, and so forth to help companies make important decisions.

The purpose of DMSs is to keep information in a centralized location. Going from paper documents to ESI makes records easier to locate and minimize retrieval time. When choosing a DMS, companies should evaluate the following features:

- Document imaging features
- OCR capability
- Multiuser access
- Full-text searching
- Multiple security-level access and monitoring
- PDF conversions
- Central document repository
- Backup and restore (disaster recovery)
- E-mail support

Because mobility is a growing trend in document management, companies must address **bring your own device (BYOD)** issues. The plethora of mobile devices used creates security vulnerabilities in information infrastructures. As a result, DMS vendors are adding features for securing remote access and mobile devices. Many employees have to bypass company firewalls and store documents on cloud services so that they can access them from anywhere, particularly via smartphones and tablets, and cloud storage has increased the demand for DMSs. In the past, corporate information stored on file servers or desktop PCs wasn't accessible from mobile devices unless a VPN had been set up, but with a DMS's central storage location, employees can access files from almost anywhere. Allowing employees to set up their own access to information can be a major security risk, however, because companies have little control over who can access files outside the infrastructure. By establishing a **central document repository** and security levels, companies can monitor and control who's examining documents and what information is being accessed. Security levels include varying degrees of read/write privileges applied to files.

Another trend is a platform approach to document management, which is finding one system to solve several problems instead of trying to stitch together uncoordinated systems to achieve the same goal. Using five DMSs in separate departments to manage files, for example, results in little consistency. In addition, the terminology used in different DMSs varies, so these departments might have difficulty communicating. Trying to make different systems work together can also result in conflicting data.

The main reason law firms purchase a DMS is to avoid the situation of each attorney and paralegal having his or her own storage location. A DMS also helps in meeting document retention obligations and eliminates a lot of paper after documents are scanned and stored electronically in a central repository. However, corporate legal departments in particular are concerned about security, especially because of laws such as the **Health Information Technology for Economic and Clinical Health Act (HITECH)** and HIPAA. HITECH was created in 2009 to encourage placing health records online, but online storage increases the potential for unauthorized access. Therefore, legal departments are more vigilant about controlling which DMS users can view or download documents and encrypting documents when they're stored or passed to others. Medical data should also be stored in encrypted format.

Planning for Multiple Litigations

The volume of documents and e-mails stored in a central repository can measure in the terabyte range, and all these e-mails and documents might be needed for multiple litigations or investigations. The Gartner Research Group states that **business process management (BPM)** "provides governance of a business's process environment to improve agility and operational performance" (2013). BPM aims for more flexibility than the traditional management approaches of hierarchical companies. By putting customers' needs first, companies can serve them in a more responsive and efficient way. BPM attempts to use a "holistic" approach to business, which takes into account the way clients prefer to work and the best way to accommodate these preferences. Methods and processes must be broad in nature so that companies have the benefits of ease of use and flexibility while meeting clients' demands.

The EDRM, introduced in Chapter 2, was developed to codify the work done in e-discovery cases. Part of this process involves culling and redacting files and making decisions about what data is needed for a particular case. Having a DMS simplifies searching files, but a BPM is needed, too. This section describes some companies that have developed BPM products.

Daegis, an e-discovery software vendor, has trademarked the term **Cross-Matter Management**, which is a product that identifies, collects, and processes data for a case and then hosts all data for related cases in a single repository, so data and attorneys' work product can be reused easily for subsequent cases (*www.daegis.com/solutions/daegis-for-cross-matter-management/*, 2013). Cross-Matter Management is useful when a company is facing multiple litigations. In this situation, attorneys have to examine the same documents multiple times when using many of the DMSs currently available. By using Cross-Matter Management, they can reduce the time and costs of litigation because all related documents are stored in the same location, and redaction has to be done only once on these documents.

Another vendor, Exterro (*www.exterro.com*), offers Exterro Fusion, which can be administered locally or in the cloud. This enterprise-level application adheres closely to the EDRM, with the goal of sifting through large volumes of information efficiently. Exterro also offers Fusion Genome Data Mapping, which creates an inventory of a company's IT infrastructure so that you can determine where data is stored and what litigation holds might affect it. It also works with third-party software, such as tools used for human resources. When examining software packages, such as Exterro, for creating a BPM, IT support staff must determine whether other software used at the company works with the BPM package. For example, companies such as Barracuda Networks (*www.barracuda.com*) gear their products for e-mail archiving and compliance with laws such as HIPAA as well as handling deduplication and attachments. Insight by Catalyst (*www.catalystsecure.com/products/catalyst-insight*) is another product aimed at analyzing a large amount of data, and it includes a cloud option.

To understand the importance of data storage and retrieval and central document repositories, think of the General Petraus case, which is a good example of how an investigation can grow quickly and spin off into other areas (see Figure 7-2). Beginning with one accusation, more than 20,000 e-mails were examined, which resulted in another general being investigated and many other people scrutinized.

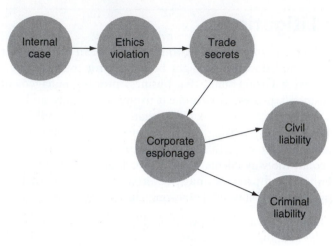

Figure 7-2 A potential internal investigation
© Cengage Learning 2014

Next, take a look at a typical internal investigation. An employee is being investigated for conducting an outside business while on the job. During the standard examination of his e-mails and Internet access, it becomes apparent that he has been involved in a serious ethics violation with another employee. The two have been accessing data on a drive they shouldn't have access to, thereby violating the Computer Fraud and Abuse Act (that is, exceeding their privileges). The IT investigating team realizes it has a new case on its hands. A partner company then brings accusations of its trade secrets being leaked and names one of the employees currently under investigation in the suit. Another e-discovery team is assembled to handle this trade secrets incident, which eventually develops into a full-blown corporate espionage case with federal investigators involved, and a third team is assigned to this case. In this example, a criminal case has spun off from the original civil litigation, and multiple teams of six or more people are analyzing data that probably overlaps.

If the company is using a DMS, applying a multiple-litigation tool, such as Cross-Matter Management, can eliminate some redundancy in redacting documents and determining what files are relevant. With a central document repository, most documents and e-mail are already in one location. The risk of a central repository, however, is inadequate security controls. Even encrypted data should be in restricted-access folders or directories.

To move from simply reacting to responding efficiently, companies should evaluate their litigation readiness (Zylab, 2010). The first step is to determine what type of ESI is stored. Because most legal holds involve e-mails, be sure to know where all e-mail is stored, including backups, scheduled purges, and so forth. Next, you should know about the company's storage area networks (SANs), sharepoints, mobile devices used by employees, and cloud storage.

In Chapter 3, you learned the basics of what to do after receiving a litigation hold. The process is summarized in the following list:

- Do retention policies exist and apply for the ESI your organization has produced?

- What are the account deletion and data retention policies for information stored by former employees?

- Does the backup policy specify where data is stored and how long it's retained?

- How long are deleted messages retained on e-mail servers? Does a policy exist for specifying the retention period and server settings?

- Do IT personnel have the training, skills, and tools for acquiring data in a manner that preserves its integrity?

- If a third-party vendor is used to collect data, what steps must be taken to grant access to the company's systems? Will the vendor have access to the data and system tools needed to carry out the data collection? Is the vendor likely to be an asset or an impediment?

Spoliation is a major concern when evaluating litigation readiness. When a litigation hold is issued, employees need to know what's required of them, so established, repeatable procedures must be in place to ensure that the company is ready for litigation. (Ensuring that a company follows standard processes that are done the same way every time cuts down on the possibility of errors.) One stumbling block for many companies is retaining backups correctly. The wide variety of economical choices for retaining backups means judges expect companies to have information readily available. If processes are in place and communicated to employees effectively, avoiding the inadvertent destruction of backups is easier.

Another stumbling block involves e-mail. Because e-mail is a common method of tracking negotiations in business settings, policies for retaining e-mail messages must be established and followed. For example, a company receives a litigation hold, but several employees have been deleting e-mails pertaining to the litigation. The company generally keeps e-mail backups for at least 90 days, however, so these deleted e-mails are still available for a short time. Increasing the retention period for e-mail backups might be wise, in this case. Many organizations now transfer their corporate e-mail accounts to cloud storage, which reduces hardware purchases, increases flexibility, and allows file access from almost anywhere in the world. What policies, agreements, and contractual obligations need to be in place for backing up these systems? When evaluating a service provider, a company needs to know whether backups are stored on site, how often backups take place, and how long file restorations take. Third-party hosting can make e-mail backup and storage more complex, however, and you can't assume it will be the same as having your IT staff manage e-mail. Among other questions you should investigate, determine whether the hosting company is obligated to adhere to litigation holds and what notifications you must send the hosting company about following litigation holds before signing an agreement and moving your storage to the cloud.

Mergers and Acquisitions

In addition to facing multiple litigations, many companies at some point become involved in a merger and acquisition. Mergers and acquisitions (M&As) require that the acquiring company show due diligence in the evaluation phase of the target company. Any litigation holds and relevant ESI of the target company must be examined and isolated from the acquiring firm's data

(Garrie, 2009). The IT infrastructure, storage practices, and ESI processes also need to be examined before, during, and after an M&A. To see how to conduct basic risk management, you examine four hypothetical M&As in this section (illustrated in Figure 7-3):

- The target company has no e-discovery experience and no litigation holds. This type of M&A is usually the easiest to handle, as long as the acquiring company is careful about what data is destroyed during the merger.

- The target company has good e-discovery protocols in place and few ongoing litigation holds (or is managing its litigation holds well). The acquiring company, as part of its due diligence, knows what ESI must remain isolated and not be destroyed or purged.

- The target company uses a DMS, has established some e-discovery protocols, and has some ongoing litigation holds. This type of M&A costs the acquiring company in terms of time and legal counsel, so it must be examined carefully for its effect on the return on investment (ROI).

- Although the target company has good qualities, it has been poorly managed, and its bookkeeping and document-tracking practices are slipshod. It might also be involved in ongoing litigation. The cost to acquire this company might be excessive, so the benefits and drawbacks should be weighed carefully.

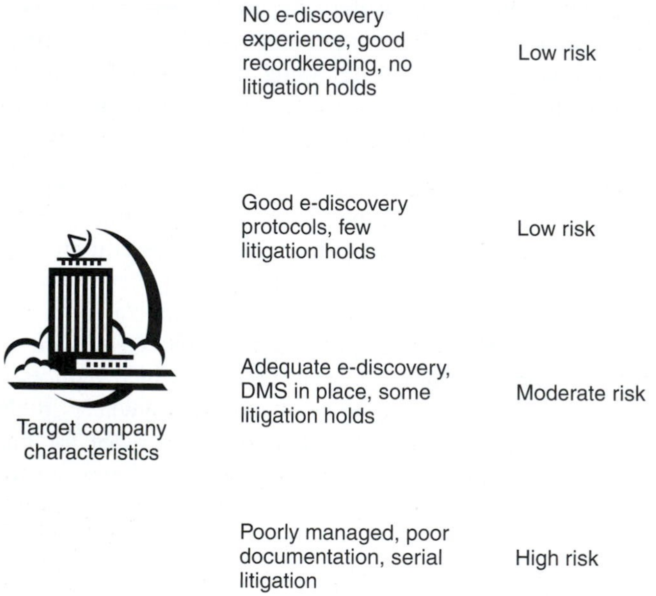

No e-discovery experience, good recordkeeping, no litigation holds	Low risk
Good e-discovery protocols, few litigation holds	Low risk
Adequate e-discovery, DMS in place, some litigation holds	Moderate risk
Poorly managed, poor documentation, serial litigation	High risk

Target company characteristics

Figure 7-3 Examining the risks of mergers and acquisitions
© Cengage Learning 2014

The acquiring company should strive to treat the purchase as a friendly litigation and must examine accounting details, legal issues, and employee records thoroughly. The Hewlett-Packard purchase of Autonomy PLC, a software company, is an excellent example of what can go wrong when acquiring companies neglect these thorough checks. Autonomy had doctored its books, and as a result, Hewlett-Packard paid $8.8 million more for the purchase than it was worth. The problem with conducting due diligence for M&As is that investigators rely on the documentation the company gives them, so the process includes looking at the contract, reviewing stock certificates and records of previous owners, and so forth. A friendly litigation approach serves the acquiring company better by not assuming the target company was telling the truth; in this case, the acquiring company might dig deeper. Autonomy had a good reputation in the industry, so it was considered to be above suspicion. However, after the sale, employees came forward with the information about the books, and Hewlett-Packard discovered its error (Svesson, 2012).

Speeding Up Searches

Because of technological advances, there's far too much data for attorneys, paralegals, and investigators to sift through. A typical case can involve terabytes of data, so learning efficient methods of finding the data you need is crucial. In this section, you examine traditional search methods, such as indexes, and two new methods.

As part of preparing for litigation, several tools are available to index information and identify it as confidential, proprietary, or privileged. Indexing information in this way makes it easier to negotiate what information should be excluded from discovery and simplifies preparing a **motion for protective order**. This motion is used to prevent confidential information, such as a company's trade secrets, from becoming public domain. You also need to be able to search files for relevant information when preparing for a case. As you've learned, a variety of software tools for searching and indexing are available, such as IPRO, VeBridge Summation Software, Sherpa Software Discovery Attender, AccessData eDiscovery, and others. Some newer ones include Daegis and Exterro, discussed earlier in this chapter. When you move beyond simple keyword searches, you have to use more sophisticated techniques. Many of the document and e-mail search tools in both e-discovery and digital forensics are based on the dtSearch engine (dtSearch Corporation, 2011). dtSearch is useful for indexing large volumes of documents and can index according to file type and words. For example, it can tell you the number of times a particular word occurred and where it occurred in the files.

After indexing, you can use several options to search documents. Most people are familiar with using search phrases in Internet search engines. If you want to search for a specific phrase, such as "e-discovery search techniques," you enclose the entire phrase with quotation marks. With dtSearch, you can also specify how far apart words should be. For example, "attorney not w/27 state" means that the word "attorney" isn't found within 27 words of the word "state."

Although dtSearch is the main engine of several search products, other search engines use the same principles discussed in this section.

Another dtSearch method is **fuzzy searching**, which enables you to find words even if they're misspelled. When converting paper documents to electronic form with OCR, the recognition of letters and numbers isn't always precise; therefore, the letter "b" might show up as an "8" or the letter "l" as the number "1." When searching these files, the fuzzy searching method is especially useful. In some software tools, you can specify the degree of fuzziness. For example, a degree of 1 allows the spelling to be off by one character, a degree of 3 allows it to vary by three characters, and so forth.

Another search method is **stemming**, which is used to find all variations on a word. For example, searching for the word "obtain" would also return "obtains," "obtaining," "obtained," and so on. In addition to variations on a word, stemming algorithms can search for grammatic differences. For example, searching for the noun "fish" also yields the verbs "fishes" and "fishing."

Phonic searching is another search method, which is especially useful when examining documents written by a non-native speaker. For example, a non-native speaker might write the word "hole" instead of "whole." Therefore, you would search for both "hole" and "whole." Phonic searching is also used for variations on spelling, such as the British "grey" and the American "gray."

Using **synonym searches** means loading a thesaurus to find words with similar meanings. For specialized fields, such as forensics and medicine, a user-defined thesaurus might be needed. For example, if you're searching for the term "confidential," a thesaurus might return the synonyms "secret," "private," and "classified."

Using **Boolean operators** such as AND, OR, and NOT is an effective way to fine-tune searches. Say you're searching for "Kansas City," and you want to include the cities in both Missouri and Kansas. In this case, your search expression would be "MO" OR "KS". If you're using exclusionary logic, such as searching for a document with the file extension .xlsx and containing the word "payment," your search expression would be "file type = *.xlsx" AND "name = *payment*".

Wildcard searches must be used with caution to avoid getting false positives. Using a question mark (?) in a search to represent a single character might return unrelated results or results that aren't useful. For example, using "b?t" can yield "bit," "but," "bat," "byt," and so forth. The asterisk as a wildcard means any combination of characters, so searching for "*.docx," for example, returns far too many results.

A **pattern search** is useful when you're looking for credit card numbers. Most people have seen the XXXX-XXXX-XXXX-XXXX format for VISA and MasterCard account numbers. Outside the fields of digital forensics or finance, however, people might not be aware of other common patterns, such as the following:

- VISA card numbers start with 4, MasterCard numbers start with 5, and Discover card numbers start with 6.
- JCPenney card numbers follow the pattern XXX-XXX-XXX-X-X.
- American Express card numbers follow the pattern XXXX-XXXXX-XXXXXX.

Pattern searches are also useful with IP addresses, phone numbers, and so forth.

Although this chapter doesn't cover the UNIX/Linux grep command-line tool, this free tool can perform sophisticated searches. Using it requires some training and practice, but often you can get more positive hits than by using only simple keyword searches. In addition, grep can save time and help you avoid costly sanctions as a result of inadequate searches.

The volume of ESI has led to the development of **predictive coding**, which combines computer speed with human reasoning in a form of artificial intelligence. Although dtSearch is a reliable method of searching large volumes of data, it can't make decisions. Predictive coding, on the other hand, allows a computer to learn and make decisions. A professional sorts and codes a set of control documents, and then the computer generates algorithms based on the patterns it finds in the control documents. Using these algorithms, it sorts the remaining documents. This method isn't foolproof and is heavily debated. However, two cases stand out to illustrate its emergence as a new technique. In *Global Aerospace Inc. et al., v. Landow Aviation, L.P. dba Dulles Jet Center, et al*, Judge James Chamblin allowed the defense to process ESI with predictive coding. In *Da Silva Moore v. Publicis Group* (No. 11-CV-1279, 2012), Judge Peck ordered the use of predictive coding, citing FRCP 26(b)(2)(C) and the fact that more than three million documents had to be processed. However, he cautioned that predictive coding might not be suitable for all cases.

Another method getting attention lately is **forensic linguistics**, which is based on the theory that a person's language—word choice, pattern, and flow—is as unique as a fingerprint. You probably use this method subconsciously, such as saying "That doesn't sound like her" or "He would never use that word; he would use this term instead." Roger Shuy is considered the pioneer of forensic linguistics. Although these methods haven't been accepted fully, people do use them. For example, in a murder case, a consultant noticed the way a suspect used punctuation and was able to use that information find the killer. Formally, this method is defined as combining linguistics, language, and the law.

Chapter Summary

- Information governance requires determining which laws and regulations apply to an organization's operations, such as HIPAA, FOIA, and Sarbanes-Oxley.

- The Sarbanes-Oxley Act, created in response to the Enron, WorldCom, and other scandals, specifies internal financial controls a company must have in place. Sections 302 and 303 cover audits and internal controls that apply to accurate reporting of a company's finances. Section 404 also covers audits, and Sections 802, 906, and 1107 address criminal penalties.

- Privacy laws to consider when setting up network storage include HIPAA, the Graham-Leach-Bliley Act, the Family Educational Rights and Privacy Act, and the Children's Online Privacy Protection Act.

- Public records of government employees, including e-mail, text messages, blog posts, and so forth, are accessible under the Freedom of Information Act.

- A document management system helps sort large amounts of data and has features for retrieving documents based on standards or preapproved expressions.

- The plethora of mobile devices used creates security vulnerabilities in information infrastructures, so companies must address bring your own device (BYOD) issues. To meet this need, DMS vendors are adding features for securing remote access and mobile devices. Companies can also establish a central document repository to monitor and control who's examining documents and what information is being accessed.

- Software tools that incorporate business process management can help streamline e-discovery, particularly when facing multiple litigations at the same time.

- E-discovery tools include sophisticated search methods, such as fuzzy searching, stemming, and phonic searching. New methods being developed include predictive coding and forensic linguistics.

Key Terms

Boolean operators The AND, OR, and NOT operators used when performing keyword searches on documents and other ESI. These values return true or false values that specify whether a keyword meets the search criteria.

bring your own device (BYOD) The use of personal mobile devices on a corporate network.

business process management (BPM) A practice that aims to improve the effectiveness and efficiency of processes by being more flexible than traditional hierarchical management approaches.

central document repository A network location for storing all documents related to a case or project so that searching and sorting files are more efficient.

Children's Online Privacy Protection Act (COPPA) A U.S. federal law intended to protect children's privacy; it sets guidelines for collecting information via a Web site from people under the age of 13.

Cross-Matter Management Created by Daegis eDiscovery, it's a procedure for handling multiple litigations that involves identifying and collecting custodian data, processing it, hosting it in a single repository, and then reusing the data and resulting work product for subsequent cases.

document management system (DMS) A system that uses a central repository to help sort documents according to their relevance and applicable regulations. *See also* central document repository.

Family Educational Rights and Privacy Act (FERPA) An act created to protect students' educational records. It allows parents or students to examine records and request corrections and prevents this information from being shared without their written permission.

forensic linguistics A new method that relies on a person's unique use of language to determine who wrote a particular document or e-mail.

Freedom of Information Act (FOIA) An act that allows requesting information stored by the U.S. federal government. Exceptions to this rule include items of national security, trade secrets, medical records, and cases in the process of being litigated.

fuzzy searching A sophisticated search method that finds even misspelled words.

Gramm-Leach-Bliley Act An act that restricts the disclosure of nonpublic personal information stored by financial institutions. *See also* nonpublic personal information (NPI).

Health Information Technology for Economic and Clinical Health Act (HITECH) An act created to allow placing patients' healthcare records online to improve the efficiency of physicians accessing their records.

motion for protective order This motion is filed to prevent records (such as those involving a company's trade secrets) from becoming part of the public domain.

nonpublic personal information (NPI) Data that can specify an individual, such as Social Security numbers.

pattern search A search method used to find items that follow a specific pattern of letters or numbers, such as phone numbers, credit cards, and IP addresses.

personal health information (PHI)   Confidential information collected by a medical practitioner for the purposes of treatment; includes medical tests, lab results, insurance data, and so forth. This information is protected under HIPAA.

predictive coding   A new search method that combines computer speed with human reasoning in a form of artificial intelligence, used to sort and index files. It's useful in dealing with large volumes of data efficiently.

stemming   A search method that finds all variations of a word.

synonym search   A search method used to find words with similar meanings. Typically requires uploading a thesaurus.

wildcard search   A search method that uses a question mark (?) to search for a single-character variation or an asterisk (*) to match a combination of characters.

Review Questions

1. A health insurance company might be required to adhere to which of the following regulations? (Choose all that apply.)

    a. HIPAA

    b. FOIA

    c. SEC

    d. Sarbanes-Oxley

2. Having a central document repository helps with which of the following? (Choose all that apply.)

    a. Efficient access to files

    b. Monitoring access to secure files

    c. Preventing inadvertent deletion of files

    d. Adhering to protocols

3. Cross-Matter Management is useful in handling several simultaneous lawsuits.

    True or False?

4. Which of the following search methods enables you to find words even if they're misspelled?

    a. Synonym searches

    b. Fuzzy searching

    c. Stemming

    d. Boolean operators

5. Sarbanes-Oxley applies to which of the following?

    a. Privately held corporations

    b. Publicly traded corporations

    c.   Limited liability corporations

    d.   Sole proprietorships

6. For publicly traded companies, which sections of Sarbanes-Oxley apply to audits? (Choose all that apply.)

    a.   Section 302

    b.   Section 404

    c.   Section 802

    d.   Section 1107

7. NPI includes which of the following data? (Choose all that apply.)

    a.   Demographic data

    b.   Social Security numbers

    c.   Salaries of non-government-agency employees

    d.   Property lienholders

8. When health information is available online, which act applies?

    a.   HIPAA

    b.   Sarbanes-Oxley

    c.   HITECH

    d.   Gramm-Leach-Bliley

9. Explain how BYOD can pose a problem when dealing with ESI.

10. A proximity search does which of the following?

    a.   Doesn't allow returning words within 15 feet of the search term

    b.   Eliminates certain words

    c.   Finds words if they aren't closer than a specified number of words from the another term

    d.   Looks for words that stand alone

11. Under the Freedom of Information Act, states must release the birth record of a person who's currently alive to anyone requesting it. True or False?

12. A third-party storage service is always subject to HIPAA regulations. True or False?

13. Which of the following protects the privacy of student e-mails hosted by a third party?

    a.   FOIA

    b.   ECPA

    c.   COPPA

    d.   Sarbanes-Oxley

Hands-On Projects

Hands-On Project 7-1

E-discovery software packages, such as AccessData FTK, EnCase, and Discovery Attender, and others, use search expressions to find terms matching specified conditions. Using the Linux grep command, the search expression for finding VISA or MasterCard numbers is \<((\d\d\d\d)[\-]){3}\d\d\d\d\)>. This expression specifies three groups of four digits (represented by d) separated by hyphens, followed by the last four digits. Create a grep search expression to find American Express card numbers and another to find JCPenney card numbers.

Hands-On Project 7-2

Using a search engine, find three or more document management systems. Compare their costs, features, and user interfaces. If you were part of a consulting firm, which one would you recommend to a client, and why?

Case Projects

Case Project 7-1

Because BYOD has become widespread in companies, the location of files when a litigation hold has been issued can be complicated. Based on the discussion in the chapter, find an article that discusses processes and policies that can be used to solve this problem. Write a two- to three-paragraph summary of the article's recommendations.

Case Project 7-2

Find the Web site for the International Association of Forensic Linguists. Read the association's goals and descriptions of uses for forensic linguistics. What recent cases are cited to support its use? Write a one- to two-page paper summarizing your findings and explaining your opinion of the usefulness of this search method.

References

Garrie, Daniel. "ESI and Technology Issues When Performing Mergers and Acquisitions," 2010, *www.lawandforensics.com/esi-technology-issues-when-performing-mergers-acquisitions/*.

Gartner Research Group. 2013, *www.gartner.com/technology/core/products/research/topics/businessProcessManagement.jsp*.

Svesson, Peter. "HP Says Autonomy Corporation PLC, Which It Purchased for $10 Billion in 2011, Lied About Finances," 2012, *www.huffingtonpost.com/2012/11/20/hp-autonomy-corporation-plc-finances_n_2164056.html*.

Zylab. "8-Point Inspection to Gauge Litigation Readiness," 2010, *http://media.insidecounsel.com/insidecounsel/historical/WebSeminars/Documents/ZyLAB%208%20Point%20Inspection%20of%20Litigation%20Readiness.pdf*.

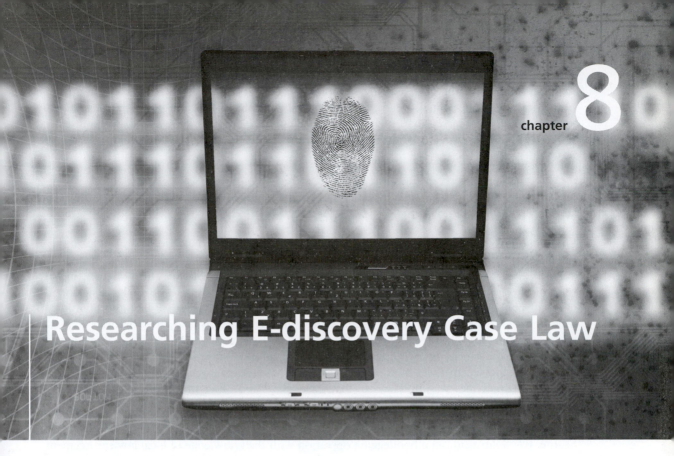

chapter 8

Researching E-discovery Case Law

After reading this chapter and completing the exercises, you will be able to:

- Describe the appeals process
- Describe commercial and free resources for researching case law
- Explain the implications of civil case law on e-discovery, including e-mail issues and litigation holds
- Explain how criminal case law applies to e-discovery
- Summarize the issues in multijurisdictional and international cases

In the e-discovery process, both people and corporations can appeal verdicts, so you need to understand how the appeals process works. In addition, case law changes constantly in both the civil and criminal arenas, and you must be able to research cases that can affect your case and anticipate what might be needed. You also need to be aware of multijurisdictional and international cases and how laws can vary from state to state and from country to country.

Understanding the Legal Appeals Process

Common law countries use case law as a guide when there are no existing statues that apply specifically to a case. Case law determines how laws are applied and is based on previous rulings. New technology, such as smartphones, text messaging, Skype, and Google+, introduce situations for which no existing case law applies, so these cases must be tested in a court of law. Although it's the lawyer's responsibility to assess new case law and give legal advice, other people, such as the head of the e-discovery team lead, the forensics expert, and paralegal staff, need to know case law, too. Because it changes so rapidly, being knowledgeable of the latest cases is important. If the situation a case involves hasn't been tried before, precedent can be set by the case's outcome. Unfortunately, rulings can be overturned later. Sometimes they're simply called "bad case law," and other times they cause confusion until definitions are changed.

For example, the famous case *Olmstead v. United States* happened during Prohibition in Seattle. Roy Olmstead ran a bootlegging operation with the knowledge of local law enforcement and business owners. In 1924, federal agents began wiretapping his phone without a warrant. Because the definition of eavesdropping meant more of a physical intrusion, the case sparked a debate about the rights of individuals to privacy of communications. Its ruling was later overturned by the case *Charles Katz v. United States* (1967), which set two conditions for determining these rights. First, is there an expectation of privacy? Second, is this expectation reasonable? A person closing the door to a phone booth expects privacy, and a reasonable person would agree with this expectation. Although these cases happened several decades apart, the *Katz* case is referred to as overturning *Olmstead* in the matter of wiretaps.

When reading case law, it helps to have a general understanding of how the U.S. court system is organized. The judicial branch of the U.S. federal government is represented in all 50 states. State courts deal with cases such as divorce, probate, real estate, and criminal cases. Each state has its own hierarchy of courts ending in a state supreme court for appeals. Each state also has federal courts that address issues dealing with the U.S. Constitution, bankruptcies, treaties, and so forth (United States Courts.gov, 2012). Ninety-four federal districts are grouped into 12 circuit courts, also known as **appellate courts**. Each state has at least one federal district court. Cases heard in district courts feed into the appellate courts if challenged. So if you hear references to cases being heard in the Ninth Circuit Court, you know that the original case was in one of the western states, as shown in Figure 8-1. The Ninth Circuit Court is the largest and a good example of the variety resulting from states' populations. For example, Hawaii, Idaho, and Montana have only one federal district, but California has four: the Central, Eastern, Northern, and Southern Districts. The Twelfth Circuit Court of Appeals is the smallest, encompassing only the District of Columbia. At the top level, of course, is the U.S. Supreme Court, which has final say in matters of the U.S. Constitution.

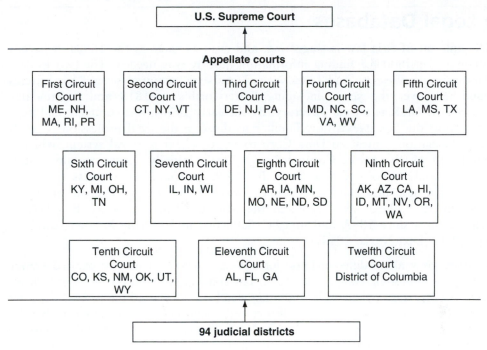

Figure 8-1 U.S. circuit courts and the appeals process
© Cengage Learning 2014

The process of appeals for a federal case is straightforward. If plaintiffs or defendants disagree with the judge or jury's verdict, they can take it to a court of appeals or a district court. The appellant has to prove that a legal aspect of the case is incorrect. When addressing e-discovery, the appeal might be based on an overly broad discovery order or use of cell phone data, for example. Appeals can be written briefs or oral arguments.

A good example of a series of appeals is a recent case on privacy. The BALCO scandal involved major league baseball players' use of steroids, and federal agents began an investigation in 2002. During the course of the investigation, agents seized the records of the Bay Area Lab Cooperative (BALCO), which had not only records of the players being investigated, but also those of more than 100 others. These names were leaked to the press, and many careers were ruined. The Major League Ball Players association filed charges in Nevada and other states, and the cases were appealed in several district courts, including the districts of Central and Northern California. The question was whether the warrant allowed agents to examine electronic evidence that wasn't part of the original warrant. In essence, they should have separated out the records of players who weren't included in the investigation. The argument became what constitutes "plain view"? If you have a suspect computer, are all files considered to be in plain view and, therefore, don't require an additional warrant? After appeals taking place from 2004 to 2009, the cases—which all stemmed from the same investigation—were heard in the Ninth Circuit Court as *United States v. Comprehensive Drug Testing, Inc.* (2010). The ruling stated that the information should have been redacted and the investigators had overstepped the warrant, resulting in other ball players' privacy being infringed on.

Using Legal Databases

The amount of case law is staggering, and even as early as the 1800s, it became apparent that a method for finding information quickly was needed. The two leaders in legal databases are Westlaw and LexisNexis. LexisNexis acquired several legal archivists and publishers over the years, including Butterworth's in 1818 and Martindale-Hubbell, founded in 1868 as a legal directory. By the early 1970s, this company had begun developing into the LexisNexis now familiar to those in the legal profession. The Ohio State Bar Association contracted Data Corp to create a text retrieval system, which was later purchased by the Mead Corporation as Lexis. Initially, Lexis contained statutes and cases for only Ohio and New York. By 1979, attorneys could access the database over 1200-baud modems. The Nexis portion was created for news media around the same time. In 1988, LexisNexis acquired the Michie Company, which had been recording state statutes since 1897, and in 1997, launched its first true Internet search engine for legal data (LexisNexis, 2013).

Westlaw grew along different lines. John West, a salesman who recognized lawyers' needs, founded a publishing company in 1872. His company created the American Digest System, which categorizes cases by topic and a key number, and started the *Federal Reporter* in 1880 to publish the decisions of federal district and circuit courts. The American Bar Association endorsed his method of sorting cases in 1897. Thomson Reuters Publishing purchased John West's company in 1996 and retained the name Westlaw (Duhaime, 2012). Like LexisNexis, the West database went online in the 1970s.

Most universities and many community colleges have access to Westlaw or other legal search engines, so students researching case law typically begin with Westlaw. Depending on the school, a subscription also enables you to search for appeals and other related cases. Using Westlaw is straightforward. Figure 8-2 shows a typical search screen. There are two types of searches: by a specific case or by topic. You use the pane on the left to search for cases when you know the document number or document title. The document number is the citation

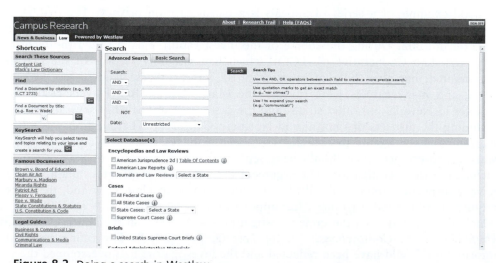

Figure 8-2 Doing a search in Westlaw

Source: *www.westlaw.com*

number assigned by courts, such as 134 F.3d 817 for a federal case or 246 App Div 2d 682 for a case at the state level. The document title includes the names of parties in the case, in the form *plaintiff* v. *defendant*.

You use the pane on the right to search by using keywords, such as "Enron," "cell phone," or "cost shifting." You must also select a database to search, such as one consisting of state-specific journals. You can also limit the search to federal cases, Supreme Court cases, or cases in a specific state. In the hands-on projects, you have an opportunity to use Westlaw or a similar database to look up cases.

If you don't have access to Westlaw, free legal research Web sites are available, such as FindLaw.com. You can search for attorneys and legal advice and find links to legal forms, blogs, and legal news. This site also offers information on criminal law, civil law, consumer rights, and other topics. You can find a wealth of articles by using search terms such as "computer crime" and "electronic discovery."

As mentioned in Chapter 4, other Web sites include *www.justia.com* and *www.plol.org*.

As the field of e-discovery expands, so do online resources for it. K&L Gates, LLP, maintains the Web site Electronic Discovery Law (*www.ediscoverylaw.com*). The site posts new cases specific to e-discovery regularly and includes a database that as of this writing has more than 2000 cases to review. Figure 8-3 shows that you can select which part of the FRCP you want to search, for example.

K&L | GATES

www.ediscoverylaw.com

Electronic Discovery Case Database

K&L Gates maintains and continually updates a database containing over 1,500 electronic discovery cases collected from state and federal jurisdictions around the United States. This database is searchable by keyword, as well as by any combination of 29 different case attributes, e.g., on-site inspection, allegations of spoliation, motion for a preservation order, etc. Each search will produce a list of relevant cases, including a brief description of the nature and disposition of each case, the electronic evidence involved and a link to a more detailed case summary if available. For an alphabetical list of all cases contained within the database, click the search button at the bottom of the page.

Please select one or more of the following case attributes and/or enter keyword search terms below:

E-Discovery Rules

☐ FRCP 26(b)(2)(B)   ☐ FCRP 34(b)   ☐ FRCP 26(b)(5)(B)
   "Not Reasonably Accessible"   Procedure or Format   or FRE 502

☐ FRCP 37(e) Safe Harbor   ☐ FRCP 26(b)(2)(C)   ☐ Local Court Rule, Form
                    Limitations   or Guideline

Figure 8-3 The K&L Electronic Discovery Law database

Source: *www.ediscoverylaw.com*

Figure 8-4 shows other items that can be used to narrow a search. In addition to searching only parts of the FRCP, you can search on metadata, cost shifting, backup tapes, privileged materials, and a host of other items, including searches on keywords you specify.

Context

☐ TRO or Preliminary
Injunction

☐ Motion to Compel

☐ Motion for Sanctions

☐ Motion for Preservation
Order

☐ Motion for Protective
Order

☐ Early Conference or
Discovery Plan

☐ Third-Party Discovery

Particular Issues

☐ Data Preservation

☐ Records Retention Policy

☐ Backup Media Recycling

☐ Backup Tapes

☐ Deleted Data Recovery

☐ Admissibility

☐ Mirror Images

☐ On-Site Inspection

☐ Keyword Searches

☐ Format of Production

☐ Metadata

☐ Adequacy of Search /
Identification or Collection (added
03/13)

☐ Cost Shifting

☐ Spoliation

☐ Court-Appointed Expert

☐ Privilege or Work Product

☐ Lack of Cooperation or
Inaccurate Representations

Enter keyword search terms:

[   ]

Figure 8-4 Search terms for the K&L database
Source: *www.ediscoverylaw.com*

American Lawyer Media (ALM) created Law.com to make better use of the Internet. This site has also added Law Technology News, with the subsection E-Discovery and Compliance. With the number of laws, regulations, and statutes that can affect e-discovery and digital governance, it's an excellent resource for new developments in the industry, such as cases that have been appealed or new legislation being proposed. In addition, free instructional webinars are offered on the latest topics, such as e-discovery of mobile devices or cloud storage (see *www.law.com/jsp/lawtechnologynews/e_discovery.jsp*).

You can find more information on the development of Law.com at *www.alm.com/about/history*.

TIP

Vendors such as Kroll Ontrack (*www.krollontrack.com/resource-library/case-law/*) have databases and documents with summaries of hundreds of cases, and you can easily get full copies via Westlaw or FindLaw. The rapid expansion of the e-discovery field means that more organizations will be adding resources. The sites discussed in this section aren't exhaustive, but they give you a start on finding established, reliable sources. Others are listed in Appendix A.

Examining U.S. Case Law

Case law on e-discovery is still emerging. The cases examined in this section are meant as examples of the challenges presented by changes in technology and their effect on organizations' policies and procedures. Ten years ago, cell phones were unwieldy, and not everyone had one. Today, smartphones and tablets are quickly replacing laptops. When companies provide these devices for employees, who actually owns the information on them: employees or employers? Because it's inevitable that a company will be involved in litigation at some point, developing policies to ensure that this information can be retrieved is essential. The ease with which ESI can be destroyed is of particular concern when a litigation hold has been issued.

Determining which laws or regulations apply is an important part of e-discovery. The case of *Donato Aponte-Navedo, et al, Plaintiffs v. Nalco Chemical Company, et al* (2010) involved a change of venue and discovery requests being unfilled, challenged, or declared too broad. The employees at a plant in Puerto Rico sued Nalco Chemical on the grounds of discrimination under the Americans with Disabilities Act (ADA), age discrimination, and Title VII (a section of the Civil Rights Act of 1964 that protects against discrimination on the basis of race, religion, and so forth in employment practices). The plaintiffs were charged with being overly broad in requests for personnel files and not complying with meet and confer requirements. The FRCP played a major role in this case, particularly Section 34(b)(2)(C). In the end, monetary damages for failure to deliver weren't imposed on the defendants because neither party was found to be at fault.

A particularly good example of the effect of ESI's fragility can be seen in the case *Landmark Legal Foundation v. Environmental Protection Agency* (2003). Landmark Legal Foundation made a request for EPA information under the Freedom of Information Act and feared the data would be "lost" during a change of administrations. The judge granted an injunction that effectively placed a litigation hold on the ESI. Nevertheless, the EPA destroyed backup tapes, reformatted hard drives, and deleted e-mails. Although the EPA was fined, the injunction had little effect. In May 2012, Landmark filed a similar suit about EPA records on greenhouse gases and accused the EPA of destroying evidence. In December 2012, the U.S. District Court ruled that the preliminary injunction wasn't necessary, and the EPA has stated it will preserve the records.

E-mail and Privacy

E-mail constitutes a large percentage of what's retrieved in e-discovery. In the past, business e-mail was stored on a company's e-mail server and nowhere else. With the advent of cloud storage and offsite storage, e-mail can be found in a variety of locations. In the case *Peskoff v. Faber* (2006), the defendant was charged with diverting company funds for his personal use, but the plaintiff's e-mails that could have been used as evidence were missing. These e-mails could have been in any of five locations: on a NextPoint account, on tape backups, on space sublet on a law firm's server, stored with other employees' e-mails, or in storage areas that would require a digital forensics examiner to find. The case was heard two more times in the U.S. District Court of the District of Columbia to determine whether the information was accessible and who should pay the estimated $33,000 in digital forensics costs. In the end, it was ruled that the defendant, Mr. Faber, would have to pay the vendor's costs to the court, and the court would reimburse the vendor.

E-mail also constitutes a substantial portion of the electronic data that can be presented in court, and for this reason, establishing policies on the use of business e-mail accounts is critical. If employees are using their company e-mail addresses for personal correspondence, for example, does the content belong to the employees or the employer? In an article in *Duke Law & Technology Review* (2001), Corey A. Ciocchetti addresses employees' rights for e-mail housed on company servers and the impact of the Electronic Communications Privacy Act. He also explores the issue of what a company can do when an employee signs a consent form acknowledging that e-mail can be monitored. Does this consent form entitle the company to read all e-mails, only those related to company business, or none at all? Ciocchetti explains that courts have used two approaches to evaluate how a company can monitor employees' e-mails: content and context. With the content approach, an employer is allowed to monitor any e-mails related to the regular course of business but can't monitor personal e-mails. For example, a monitoring system might check for malware and perhaps scan for particular words. With the context approach, the court tries to determine whether an employer had a legitimate cause to monitor employees' e-mail. For example, if an internal investigation of an employee had been started, the court might decide that reading personal e-mail in this employee's company account was warranted. However, if a supervisor decided to read all employees' e-mail without cause, the court would probably deny the case. For employers to access an employee's e-mails, policies that take individual rights into account yet protect corporate interests must be established.

The U.S. Electronic Communications Privacy Act (ECPA), created in 1986, addresses online privacy, specifically when data is in transit. In addition, Title II, the Stored Communications Act (SCA), applies to e-mail and what laws and statutes apply (U.S. Department of Justice, 2010). As seen in the recent scandal involving U.S. General Petraeus, changes to the ECPA have been recommended because of advances in technology since 1986. Because Petraeus was the head of the Central Intelligence Agency (CIA), allegations of blackmail are certainly a matter of national security. Therefore, the Federal Bureau of Investigations (FBI) was allowed to obtain his e-mails without a warrant; only a subpoena from a federal prosecutor was needed (Ngak, 2012). The FBI examined more than 30,000 documents, many of them e-mails. What this investigation really exposed were the ECPA's shortcomings, which also affect the e-mails of ordinary citizens who use services such as Yahoo! and Gmail.

In a WIRED article (Kravets, 2012), a Google Transparency Report showed how many user data requests the government makes annually. Warrants to see this information (including personal e-mail) aren't necessary; only a subpoena is needed. According to this article, the United States is not the only government requesting this data:

> *Of the 31 nations surveyed, the U.S. led the pack in requests for user data. India came in second, with 2319 requests for data on 3467 accounts. The United Kingdom, Brazil, France, and Germany each made roughly 1500 requests.*

This number is growing annually. At the end of 2009, the U.S. total was 12,539. From January to June 2012, more than 20,000 requests were made. When these requests are going to a company such as Google that hosts e-mail, cloud storage, Google+, and a host of other online storage, the ECPA's shortcomings are apparent. The ECPA was written when hard drives were 10 to 20 MB as opposed to the terabyte hard drives available now. The average file size was 10 to 15 KB, and storing e-mail for more than six months was unthinkable. Today's small flash drives can store 4 or more GB of data, and you can store e-mail online for years.

Chapter 9 covers the proposed Online Communications and Geolocation Protection Act (OCGPA), an amendment to the ECPA.

In another case involving e-mail privacy, the ECPA, and the SCA, Steven Warshak sued the U.S. government, claiming that paragraph 2703(d) of the Stored Communications Act was unconstitutional and a violation of his Fourth Amendment rights. Under the existing law, the government compelled his ISP to give them copies of his e-mail without a warrant and without notifying him. He was able to appeal his case to the Sixth Circuit Court (*United States v. Warshak*, 2010). The Sixth Circuit Court found in his favor and stated that his rights had been violated. The salient point in the case affecting General Petraeus (and average citizens) is that e-mails older than 180 days don't require a warrant to be searched. E-mails more recent than 180 days do, however, require a warrant. These laws were created when storage was costly and space was at a premium, so most e-mails were deleted shortly after receipt (Ngak, 2012). With advances in storage media, people can now retain e-mail for years and perhaps even decades in the future. If employees are using Gmail accounts, for example, to discuss business transactions, the government doesn't need a warrant to examine these e-mails for an investigation if they're more than 180 days old. Companies should train employees to be aware of these regulations to help safeguard their privacy and limit the possibility of confidential information being collected during an investigation.

Litigation Holds

As you've seen, litigation holds are becoming more common, and cases involving not complying with litigation holds are described in legal journals with increasing frequency. So far, noncompliance with litigation holds hasn't resulted in more than fines. Coming up with deterrents might have to be done on a case-by-case basis; other options include revoking business licenses.

A good example of violating a litigation hold is *Einstein and Boyd v. 357 LLC and the Corcoran Group, et al* (New York State Supreme Court, 2009). This pivotal case resulted in sanctions when it was proved the defendant had purposefully misled prosecutors and the plaintiff about the existence of certain e-mails. The case also involved intentional destruction of ESI, such as deleting e-mails. After a litigation hold has been issued, routine purges of e-mail, log files, and any other ESI should cease. This case upheld a company's obligation to retain electronic evidence, such as e-mails, when a litigation hold is in place.

Another example of violating a litigation hold happened when JPMorgan Chase, one of the largest banks in the United States, was charged with deliberately continuing scheduled purges, which included data needed in a pending Equal Employment Opportunity Commission (EEOC) case (*EEOC v. JPMorgan Chase Bank*, 2013). The judge stated that JPMorgan Chase is "not unlike the person who murders his parents and then throws himself on the mercy of the court because he is now an orphan." Formal document requests had been sent before an official litigation hold, yet 10 months' worth of data was destroyed as part of routine document deletion. The document requests should have been enough to put the company on notice that a lawsuit was pending.

 You can find the full case at *www.aceds.org/us-judge-lambastes-jpmorgan-chase-imposes-sanctions-for-deleting-data-after-it-knew-of-looming-litigation/*.

Sanctions in cases involving violations of litigation holds can range from $250 to $8 million (Willoughby, 2010). In the JPMorgan Chase case, the judge dismissed the case, so the sanctions were minimal. When a small fine is compared with a potentially high judgment, the choice from a monetary standpoint is simple: Destroy the ESI. This action, of course, isn't the ethical, moral, or even legal course, but it's the one that's often chosen, whether the choice is deliberate or just a result of neglect. Until penalties adequately address the consequences of their actions, many companies and people will continue ignoring litigation holds on ESI.

Effects of Criminal Case Law

When collecting ESI for a criminal case (or a civil case that becomes a criminal proceeding), Rule 41 of the Federal Rules of Criminal Procedures (FRCrP) comes into play as well as the Bill of Rights (namely, the Fourth Amendment). There are some important differences in the approach to collecting ESI between civil cases and criminal cases. In criminal e-discovery, the financial burden is on the government, so there's no cost shifting. If litigation is anticipated and ESI is destroyed, parties can be charged with obstruction of justice, which carries severe penalties, including fines and jail terms. Because of the extensive document shredding that happened during the Enron scandal (Murphy et al, 2012), the Sarbanes-Oxley Act was created to address failure to preserve evidence.

The requirement to retain ESI is applicable to government agencies, too. In the case *United States v. Suarez* (2010), the FBI failed to preserve text messages from a key witness. The defendant used the civil e-discovery standard that the text messages were critical and his case would suffer without them. As a result, the jury acquitted him (Murphy et al, 2012). In addition, the plain view doctrine must be considered in criminal cases, too, when evaluating the extent of a warrant, as you saw in the discussion of the BALCO case earlier in this chapter. Another case, *United States v. Stabile* (2011), resulted in a different interpretation. Salvatore Stabile was suspected of counterfeiting. A warrant was issued to search for evidence of financial records. The agents seized several computers and found child pornography in addition to evidence of counterfeiting. The case was appealed to the Third Circuit Court, which determined that because investigators had obtained search warrants legally during each phase of the investigation, the child pornography evidence fell under the provision of "inevitable discovery" and was deemed admissible.

In civil cases, the term **data dump** is used when opposing counsel sends more information or data than could be examined in a reasonable time. You've probably seen data dumps happen in movies: A truck drives up to an office, filled to the brim with boxes of paperwork. Apply this same example to ESI, and a data dump might consist of opposing counsel sending 20 TB of data that isn't organized at all. For example, in *United States v. O'Keefe* (2008), O'Keefe was charged with taking bribes to process immigrant visas. Over several trials, he demanded that the government produce the files of all visas and related documents issued during his employment term. The FRCrP has no procedure for discovery of this magnitude, so Rule 34 of the Federal Rules of Civil Procedure was applied. It requires putting information in an organized format.

The issue was so hotly debated that the Joint Electronic Technology Working Group (JETWG) published "Recommendations for ESI Discovery in Federal Criminal Cases" to address these issues (Murphy et al, 2012). This document explains how to plan for criminal e-discovery procedures and includes a checklist with items such as determining whether classified information or trade secrets are involved. It also addresses legacy data, wiretaps, paper documents, and other matters (JETWG, 2012). With these guidelines, e-discovery procedures for criminal cases will be more standardized.

International Law and Multijurisdictional Cases

Multinational companies have to be cognizant of the laws and regulations of each nation or jurisdiction in which they do business; not understanding other countries' laws can have serious consequences, particularly when dealing with privacy issues. For example, a U.S.-based company was investigating an employee who lived at a company branch in his native country in the EU. The company investigators used a VPN tunnel to examine his business computer and ascertain whether their suspicions were valid, and then sent an investigator to his country to retrieve the hard drive. The employee, meanwhile, had noticed the tunneling and reported it to the authorities. When the investigator stepped off the plane, he was arrested for violating the country's privacy laws. Although this case was settled later (Phillips, 2013), it illustrates how easily the laws of another country can be violated, even when following standard U.S. business practices.

When comparing U.S. law with the laws of other countries, rules on privacy vary the most (Phillips, 2013), such as the rights of individuals in business and personal e-mail and the contents of mobile devices. Most countries in the EU address privacy in their constitutions, as do many African nations. Privacy laws also have a major effect on what evidence can be collected during digital investigations.

The dot-com boom of the late 1990s thrust businesses onto the Internet, and e-commerce introduced a new layer to the already complex field of international business law and arbitration. The UN Model Law on International Commercial Arbitration was created to address commerce and, later, e-commerce (United Nations Commission on International Trade, 2006) and give some standardization to international business law. It deals mainly with civil matters, and one of its goals is to address differences in laws so that international cases aren't halted because of these legal differences. Domestic laws are well suited for situations that happen within a country's borders but often aren't suitable for handling cases involving lawyers or clients from other countries. The UN Model Law relies on member countries having domestic laws in place; however, many countries simply don't have laws established to deal with the overwhelmingly rapid progress of technology. Many nations use this law as a starting point when creating their own e-laws. The United Nations Economic Commission for Europe (UNECE) spells out the UN Model Law and establishes the requirements for electronic data interchange (EDI) between countries (*www.unece.org/cefact/edifact/welcome.html*).

In addition, civil litigation is a uniquely U.S. phenomenon. As a result, many countries haven't embraced e-discovery in the same manner as in the United States. In the EU, this result is caused partly by more restrictive privacy laws and a narrower focus in discovery orders (which can happen before litigation holds). For example, Yannella and Reid examine the adoption by Canada, Australia, and the UK of the kind of e-discovery as it's practiced in the United States and conclude that countries are looking toward the United States for guidance in handling the complexities of dealing with electronic evidence (Yannella and Reid, 2009). This article also points out issues in addressing varying privacy laws when multinational companies in particular are responding to discovery orders. For example, litigation holds, which are common in the United States, are now required in Nova Scotia, as is the "meet and confer" specified in the 2006 FRCP revisions, and discovery orders aren't common in countries such as France. In 2009, a French case demonstrated a privacy challenge in a civil proceeding. During pretrial discovery, a U.S. court requested information from a French company. French data protection is similar to EU law, so questions of cross-border litigation are examined, such as what constitutes a small amount of data, and what has been anonymized adequately. "The CNIL (the French Data Protection Agency) urged companies to ensure that American authorities comply with French data protection principles, even if the personal data of French residents is already located on U.S. territory, such as in a centralized human resources database of an American company with a French subsidiary" (VenBrux, 2009). This article also describes the safe harbor rule and corporate rules that must be in place when doing business with foreign subsidiaries. For example, a U.S. firm must have each client sign a waiver stating that its personal data can cross international borders daily when servers are backed up.

The safe harbor rule states the U.S. companies can move data from Europe as long as they have adequate data security safeguards.

When a case crosses borders, whether they're state or international lines, laws can vary enough to create problems when collecting and retaining ESI. Privacy is of utmost concern to users of e-mail and the Internet. In 2011, the Israeli National Labor Court established new principles in what employers could and could not do when monitoring employee e-mails (Mirchin, 2011). In one case, an employee, Tali Isakov, sued because her employer, Panaya Ltd., had read her business e-mail and found evidence to use against her in a civil proceeding. The Regional Labor Court in Israel ruled against Isakov because of the employment agreement she signed. However, in another case, the court ruled that an employee's rights had been violated when an employer, Afikei Mayim, examined this employee's personal e-mail that he had printed and discarded while at work. Mirchin points out in his article that these cases show an increase in employees' rights to privacy in e-mail. He also emphasizes that corporate e-mail policies need to be well crafted on an international level, too, to be enforceable. Should a company have the right to view personal e-mail if employees have printed and discarded it at work or used the company network to access it? Technically, these employees are using company property to conduct personal business. If their employment agreement states that anything on the network is subject to investigation, is personal e-mail included? These questions illustrate the need for clearly defined policies in all companies.

Multinational companies present challenges in more than just e-mail policies and discovery orders. As discussed, civil e-discovery procedures are usually more structured and established than criminal ESI procedures. The International Competition Network (*www.internationalcompetitionnetwork.org*) was formed with the goal of standardizing its members' investigation procedures. This organization published the Anti-Cartel

Enforcement Manual, which includes a chapter on gathering digital evidence. It assembled material for this chapter by sending out a questionnaire to members, who include 104 competition agencies from 92 jurisdictions, such as the U.S. Department of Justice and the U.S. Trade Commission.

The term "anti-cartel" is synonymous with the term "antitrust" in the United States.

Twenty-four agencies responded, including those in the United States, the United Kingdom, and Japan. The manual describes processes for gathering digital evidence in an organization, handling privileged and private data, training staff, handling data stored offsite, and other procedures. Chapter 1 of the manual focuses on search and seizure of company premises and explains when a search warrant is needed and how to prepare for a search, put together a team, conduct a search, and search arrested people. The manual is particularly thorough in coverage of the different countries involved and the requirements for investigating an antitrust complaint involving ESI.

Using the E-discovery Database

To help e-discovery students and practitioners research state/province and country laws that might apply to a case, a database with an easy-to-use interface has been created. This section describes the user interface and the database that's used in this chapter's hands-on projects. Figure 8-5 shows the Navigation Menu, which can be used to view or add data.

Figure 8-5 The Navigation Menu in the database interface
Source: ©Amelia Phillips, 2013

The purpose of this database is to create a resource that's detailed enough to help investigators and lawyers working on cases involving digital evidence. Figure 8-6 shows the database's original table design, which starts at the country level and works down to specific case law.

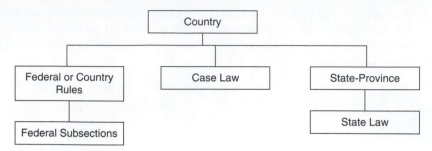

Figure 8-6 The original table design
Source: ©Amelia Phillips, 2013

The database is designed to compare state/province and country laws. It begins at the country level, where you enter a country name and code (based on ISO standard 3166, *www.iso.org/iso/country_codes*), and then you can browse each country's laws. Countries might have multiple jurisdictions, and to make research even more complex, in countries such as the United States and Canada, each state or province might have different civil laws. This information is essential when a case is tried at the state level or if an investigation begins in one state and moves to another. After entering provinces/states and their related laws, you can look up or enter applicable case law.

Tables in the Database

Figure 8-7 shows the entity-relationship diagram for the database, which gives you an overall view of the tables' final design. "PK" represents a table's primary key (a unique value, such as Social Security number). "FK" represents a table's foreign key, indicating that the field is a primary key in a linked table.

The Country table consists of two fields for country names and codes (shown previously in Figure 8-5). A state ID is typically made up of the country code and the state abbreviation. For example, California is represented by US-CA. This two-part ID prevents confusion if the same state/province name occurs in more than one country, as in the U.S. state Georgia and the province Georgia in the former Soviet Union. This table also contains the name and URL for province/state civil and criminal rules and rules of evidence if they differ from the country's laws.

Common law nations have laws at the federal level, so the next table is labeled Federal or Country Rules. This table consists of five fields: Rule Number ID (a standard abbreviation, such as "FRCP" for the Federal Rules of Civil Procedure), Rule Description (the rule's full name), Country, Rule Type ID, and Search Criteria ID. The Rule Type ID and Search Criteria ID fields are described later in this section.

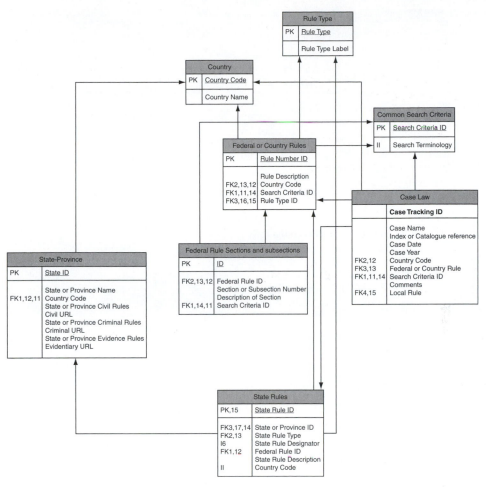

Figure 8-7 The database's entity-relationship diagram

Source: ©Amelia Phillips, 2013

The State-Province table (see Figure 8-8) reflects how laws can vary between states or provinces in a country. In addition to entering state names, you can enter related civil and criminal laws, and the state or province laws can be mapped to federal laws.

The Case Law table shows how cases are linked to a particular country, related laws, and key search terms (see Figure 8-9). Common law nations rely heavily on case law to address new technology, and you can use this table to look up cases that might be similar to the one you're investigating. The tracking ID is unique to the database. The case name and catalogue number follow the conventions of countries in the database. However, "*plaintiff* v. *defendant*" is used in the database instead of "vs." Depending on available sources, a ruling's exact date might be known, or you might be able to find only the year. As a result, both the year and exact date are included in the database.

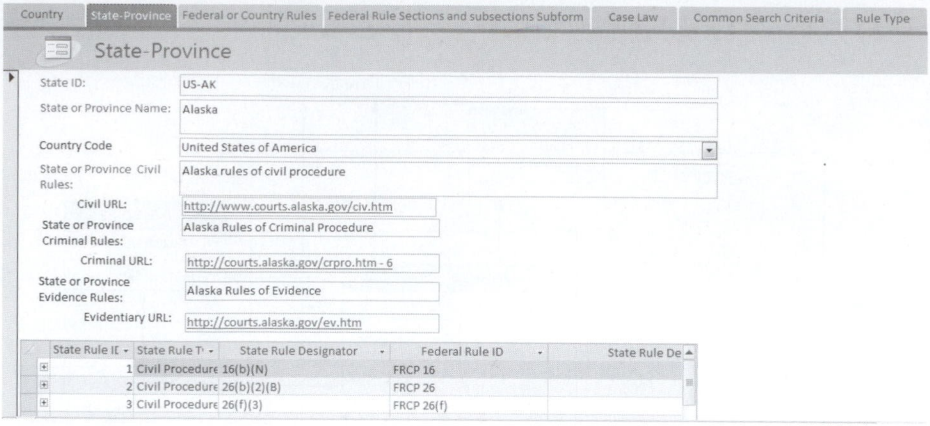

Figure 8-8 Using the State-Province table
Source: ©Amelia Phillips, 2013

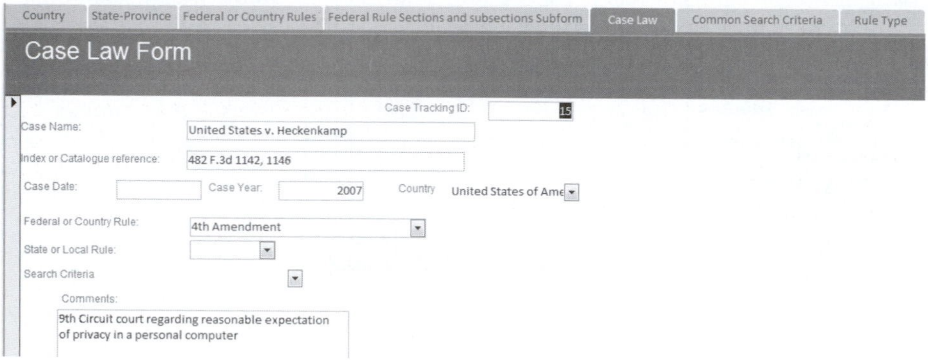

Figure 8-9 The Case Law Form window
Source: ©Amelia Phillips, 2013

As the database was developed, it became apparent that searching the database wasn't easy for someone unfamiliar with a specific country. To make this task easier, two tables were created: Common Search Criteria and Rule Type. As shown in Figure 8-10, you can use the Rule Type table to look up rules based on specific categories, such as constitutional. The Common Search Criteria table has two fields: Search Criteria ID (a simple auto-numbered field) and Search Terminology, which lists search terms that are common to different laws. Figure 8-11 shows some common search terms.

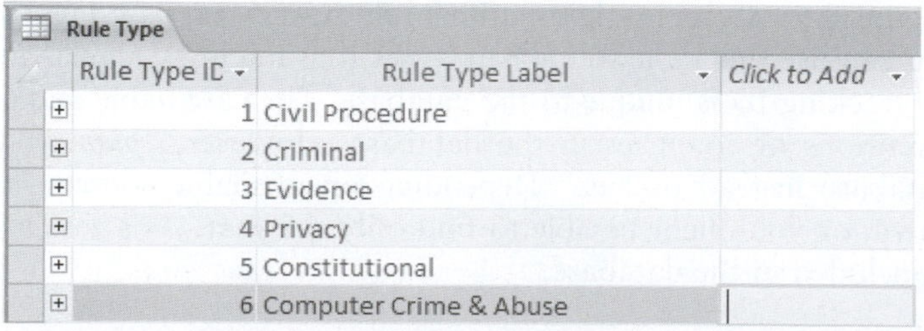

Figure 8-10 Using the Rule Type table
Source: ©Amelia Phillips, 2013

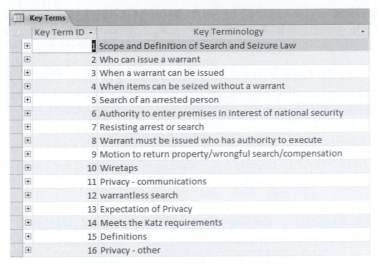

Figure 8-11 Reviewing key terms for searches
Source: ©Amelia Phillips, 2013

After these two supporting tables were populated, the Federal or Country Rules table (see Figure 8-12) was populated. Determining which search terms to link to a rule gives you a clearer understanding of how a country's laws are related. As you can see in this figure, several laws have no search terms listed yet.

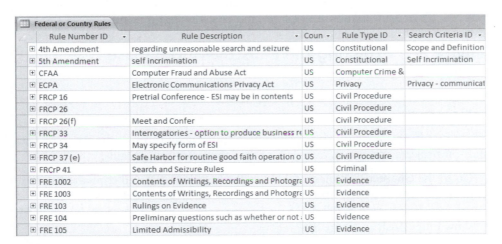

Figure 8-12 The Federal or Country Rules table
Source: ©Amelia Phillips, 2013

When populating the tables, items of interest appeared, such as Mississippi having rules of civil procedure for ESI that predate the 2006 changes to the FRCP. The database entries also show which states haven't amended their civil procedures as a result of the 2006 FRCP amendments. Many states rely on federal statutes and case law, so they don't have laws specific to their jurisdiction. For states with their own specific civil, criminal, and evidence rules, another table was added: State Rules. Because so many states have similar rule numbers, an auto number was used as the key field—State Rule ID—so that a one-to-many relationship to the State or Province table could be set up. The next field is used to distinguish between civil, criminal, and evidentiary rules. The data in the State Rule Designator field is the specific name a state or province uses for the rule. Mapping is enhanced with the next key that links to the Federal or Country Rules table. The State Rule field is used to describe a rule's function. Finally, a foreign key to the country is provided. After scripts and queries are developed to enhance the database, this foreign key might be redundant, but it's included for now.

After several cases had been entered, it was clear that more detail was needed, so a table for sections and subsections of federal or country laws was created. It shows, for example, different sections of FRCrP 41 that refer to warrants, arrests, and so forth (see Figure 8-13).

	Federal Rule Sections and subsections				
ID ▾	Federal Rule ID ▾	Section or Su ▾	Description of Section ▾	Search Criteria ID ▾
1	FRCrP 41	41(a)	Scope and definitions	Scope and Definition of Search and
2	FRCrP 41	41(b)	Who has the authority to issue a warrant	Who can issue a warrant
3	FRCrP 41	41 (c)	When a warrant may be issued	When a warrant can be issued
4	FRCrP 41	41(d)	The warrant must be issued to someone with author	Warrant must be issued who has au
5	FRCrP 41	41(g)	Motion to return property	Motion to return property/wrongfu

Figure 8-13 The revised table showing sections and subsections of federal rules
Source: ©Amelia Phillips, 2013

Understanding how applicable laws, rules, and statutes might affect a case you're working on can help you achieve a successful outcome at trials and other legal proceedings. As you've learned, the field of case law is changing even as you're reading these words, so having sources to help you organize and sort through information is essential.

Activity 8-1: Exploring the E-discovery Database

Time Required: 15 minutes

Objective: Learn to navigate through the database used in hands-on projects and become familiar with its contents.

Description: In this activity, you explore how to navigate through the database used later in hands-on projects and get an overview of the information it contains.

1. Go to the **Chapter08\Projects** folder on the book's DVD, and copy the Microsoft Access database **EDiscovery Database.accdb** to your work folder for this book's projects. If necessary, scroll down the left pane and double-click the **Navigation Menu** shown previously in Figure 8-5.

2. Notice the tabs along the top, which correspond to forms and tables in the database. When investigating these tabs, you might need to use the scrollbar on the right to see the record selection bar.

3. Click the **Federal or Country Rules** tab. Be sure to scroll to the bottom to see the record selector. A nested table shows subsections of the rules.

4. Scroll back to the top, and click the **State-Province** tab. As shown previously in Figure 8-8, it includes a nested table. Each state or province might have its own rules that might or might not map to federal rules.

5. Next, click the **Case Law** tab. You can use this tab to see cases are mapped to relevant laws or terms.

6. Click the **Common Search Criteria** and **Rule Type** tabs, and investigate what kind of information you can find.

7. Close the database.

Chapter Summary

- The judicial branch of the U.S. federal government is represented in all 50 states. Each state has its own hierarchy of courts ending in a state supreme court for appeals. Each state also has federal courts that address issues dealing with the U.S. Constitution, bankruptcies, treaties, and so forth. There are 94 federal district courts grouped into 12 circuit courts (also known as appellate courts). The final court of appeals is the U.S. Supreme Court. In a federal case, if plaintiffs or defendants disagree with the judge or jury's verdict, they can take it to a court of appeals or a district court. The appellant has to prove that a legal aspect of the case is incorrect, such as an error in the law or its interpretation.

- The number of online resources for e-discovery is growing. Traditional sources, such as Westlaw, LexisNexis, and FindLaw.com, supply the text of entire cases and their appeals, but other sources are specific to e-discovery. These sources, such as K&L Gates LLP's Electronic Discovery Law, the American Lawyer Media Web site Law.com, and Kroll Ontrack, have databases and PDF files that can be accessed online.

- The biggest challenge of e-discovery is litigation holds because they're often ignored, and as a result, ESI is deleted. A New York Supreme Court landmark case is *Einstein and Boyd v. 357 LLC and the Corcoran Group, et al*, in which a company blatantly and willfully ignored a litigation hold and deleted information, resulting in severe sanctions for the company.

- The issue of privacy in e-mail, whether it's business or personal, continues to be a concern when creating company policies in the United States and other countries.

- When civil cases become criminal cases, the rights of the individual and Rule 41 of the FRCrP (related to search and seizure) apply.

- The Electronic Communications Privacy Act (ECPA) doesn't adequately address issues related to the age of e-mail, data stored remotely, and other matters introduced as a result of cloud storage.

Key Terms

appellate courts   Courts where appeals to verdicts are heard. The United States has 12 circuit courts that hear appeals from the federal district courts in each state.

data dump   The process of sending the opposing party an inordinate amount of data or documents to process in an attempt to overwhelm and bog down the opposition.

Review Questions

1. The ECPA doesn't need to be updated because online privacy is less of a concern with the proliferation of social media sites. True or False?

2. Under the ECPA, if an e-mail is more than 180 days old, which of the following is needed to gather it for evidence?

    a. Warrant

    b. Subpoena

    c. Probable cause

    d. Affidavit

3. If a case has been tried in a lower state court and the defendant wants to appeal, typically the case goes to which of the following? (Choose all that apply.)

    a. An appellate court

    b. The U.S. Supreme Court

    c. A district court

    d. A circuit court

4. A company can do which of the following if a litigation hold is in place? (Choose all that apply.)

    a. Continue with normal file purges.

    b. Instruct employees to retain all e-mails.

    c. Retain all backups from the time the litigation hold is issued.

    d. Delete selected ESI.

5. The Stored Communications Act is part of which of the following?

    a. Rule 41

    b. FRCrP

    c. ECPA

    d. Fourth Amendment

6. UN Model Law applies to which of the following? (Choose all that apply.)

    a. Criminal issues

    b. Civil issues

    c. Commerce

    d. E-commerce

7. In general, a U.S. organization has the right to examine an employee's _____.

   a. Personal e-mail

   b. Company e-mail

   c. Twitter account

   d. Text messages

8. Which of the following is the penalty for deleting ESI after a litigation hold has been issued?

   a. 90 days in jail

   b. A fine

   c. Loss of revenue

   d. Loss of business license

9. If a company in the U.S. sends a discovery demand to a company in France, it must consider which of the following factors? (Choose all that apply.)

   a. Does any of the data fall under privacy laws?

   b. Has the data been anonymized?

   c. How much data is needed?

   d. How much will the discovery order cost?

10. The K&L Gates LLP database enables you to search on which of the following? (Choose all that apply.)

    a. State

    b. Specific laws

    c. Length of documents

    d. Metadata

11. Each U.S. state has its own rules of civil procedure that are separate from the federal rules. True or False?

12. To be heard in a district court, a case must:

    a. Have been judged unfavorable to the appealing party

    b. Involve an issue of interest to the public at large

    c. Have a legal issue that must be determined

    d. Be challenged in the lower courts first

13. To be heard in the U.S. Supreme Court, a case must:

    a. Have been lost in the lower courts

    b. Involve an issue related to the U.S. Constitution

    c. Have been rejected by the lower courts

    d. Be of interest to the media

Hands-On Projects

You can find data files for this chapter on the DVD in the Chapter08\Projects folder. If necessary, be sure to copy them to your working directory on your machine before starting the projects.

Hands-On Projects 8-1 and 8-2 require Microsoft Access 2007 or later. If you don't have this application, skip to Hands-On Project 8-3. Hands-On Project 8-4 requires access to Westlaw or LexisNexis or use of a similar legal search engine, such as FindLaw.com.

Hands-On Project 8-1

In this project, you conduct a search of two states and compare their laws.

1. Open the **EDiscovery Database.accdb** file you copied from the DVD. If necessary, scroll down the left pane, and double-click the **Navigation Menu** to open it.

2. Click the **State-Province** tab. On the Access HOME ribbon, click **Advanced** in the Sort & Filter section.

3. Click **Filter By Form**. A blank form is displayed. Type **US-WA** in the State ID text box. Notice that the other tabs on the Navigation Menu are grayed out.

4. Press the **Tab** key. The search term is displayed, enclosed in quotation marks.

5. Go back to the Sort & Filter section, click **Advanced** (if necessary), and click **Apply Filter/Sort.** If you scroll to the bottom with the scroll bar on the right, you can see that the view is filtered, and you have 1 of 1 records (see Figure 8-14).

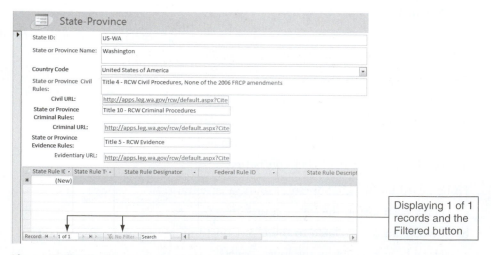

Figure 8-14 Filtering on the state or province
Source: ©Amelia Phillips, 2013

6. Do a screen capture of the form, paste it in a Word document, and save the file.

7. Click back in the form. Go back to the Sort & Filter section, click **Advanced** (if necessary), and click **Clear All Filters**. Repeat Steps 2 through 6, but this time, enter **US-FL**. Be sure to do a screen capture of the results.

8. If you aren't continuing to the next project, close the database. If you're prompted to save, click **No to All**.

9. Write a brief report (one to two pages) on your findings. Describe any major differences between what's in the database and what you found in these steps, and note whether you had any difficulty trying to verify the database contents. Include screen captures of your search results for Washington and Florida.

Hands-On Project 8-2

In this project, you enter data for the case *Einstein and Boyd v. 357 LLC and the Corcoran Group, et al.* This case, about willfully violating a litigation hold, was decided by the New York State Supreme Court in 2009.

1. If necessary, open the `EDiscovery Database.accdb` file. If necessary, scroll down the left pane, and double-click the **Navigation Menu** to open it.

2. Click the **Common Search Criteria** tab, and scroll through the contents to familiarize yourself with them. Then click the **New (blank) record** button (starburst icon in the status bar at the bottom) and add search keywords to the list.

3. Determine which federal or state rule this case falls under. Then scroll through both the Federal or Country Rules and State Rules tables to determine whether the rule is already listed. If not, add it in the correct category. For example, if the case involves a New York state statute, determine whether it's listed in the New York category.

4. Next, click the **Case Law** tab. At the bottom of the form, click the **New (blank) record** button (see Figure 8-15).

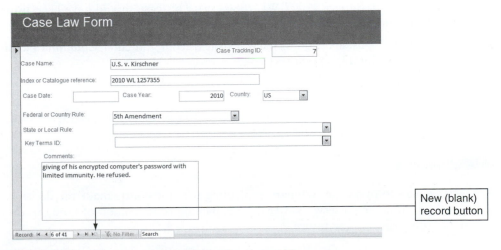

Figure 8-15 Adding a new record in the Case Law table

Source: ©Amelia Phillips, 2013

5. Enter the case name, catalogue number, year, key term (search criteria), applicable rule, and any comments. Do a screen capture of the form, and then close the database. If you're prompted to save, click **No to All**.

6. Write a two- to three-paragraph summary of the case, and explain why you made the choices you did about the rules that apply in this case. Include a screen capture of what you added.

Hands-On Project 8-3

In this project, you access the K&L Gates LLP online database.

1. Start a Web browser, and go to **www.ediscoverylaw.com**. In the left pane, click **E-Discovery Case Database**, and then click where instructed to access the free database.

At the time of this writing, the database was available at *https://extranet1.klgates.com/ediscovery/*.

2. To conduct the search, under E-Discovery Rules, click **FRCP 26(b)(2)(B) "Not Reasonably Accessible"** and under Context, click **Motion for Preservation Order**. Then scroll to the bottom and click **Search**.

3. Note the items listed in the results, such as nature of the case and attributes. Write a one- to two-page explanation of how this information could be useful when researching cases.

Hands-On Project 8-4

For this project, you need access to Westlaw, LexisNexis, or a standard search engine, such as FindLaw.com.

1. If you're using Westlaw, log on. At the left, enter information for the case *Columbia Pictures Indus. v. Bunnell* (2007 WL 2080419). This case should have been listed in the search results in Hands-On Project 8-3.

2. If you're using LexisNexis, go to **www.lexisnexis.com** and enter **Columbia Pictures Indus. v. Bunnell** in the search text box.

3. Read the case, using the FIRAC method introduced in Chapter 2.

Remember that FIRAC stands for facts, issues, rules and references, analysis, and conclusions.

4. Write a one- to two-page summary explaining why the courts made the decision they issued on preserving a server's RAM. Also, include your opinion of how this decision might affect cases in the future.

Case Projects

Case Project 8-1

An employee is using her company-supplied smartphone to text friends, family, and doctors and to access her social network. A lawsuit has been filed against the company, and she has received an e-mail from her supervisor saying she can't delete any data on the phone. What steps should be taken to ensure her privacy if the data is unrelated to the lawsuit?

Case Project 8-2

One objective of the database you used in this chapter's projects is to list the laws and rules of countries and their provinces. Using a Google search to find information, write a one- to two-page paper on what could be added to the database for Canada. Be sure to refer to Canadian provinces, rules of civil procedure, rules of evidence, rules of criminal procedure, and any rules on e-discovery or ESI.

References

Ciocchetti, Corey. "Monitoring Employee Email - Efficient Workplaces vs. Employee Privacy," *Duke Law & Technology Review*, Vol. 0026, 2001.

Degnan, David. "United States v. O'Keefe: Do the Federal Rules of Civil Procedure Provide the Proper Framework for 'Data Dumping' in a Criminal Case?," Degnan personal works, 2008.

Duhaime, Lloyd. "John Briggs West, 1852-1922, Founder of Westlaw," 2012, *www.duhaime.org/LawMuseum/LawArticle-1175/John-Briggs-West-1852-1922-Founder-of-Westlaw.aspx*.

International Competition Network. Anti-Cartel Enforcement Manual, 2010, *www.internationalcompetitionnetwork.org/working-groups/current/cartel/manual.aspx*.

Joint Electronic Technology Working Group. *Recommendations for ESI Discovery in Federal Criminal Cases*, 2012.

Kravets, David. "Post Petraeus Scandal Google Releases Stats Showing Uptick in Government Requests for Data," November 13, 2012, *www.wired.com/threatlevel/2012/11/google-user-data-report/*.

LexisNexis. "LexisNexis History," 2013, *www.lexisnexis.com/en-us/about-us/about-us.page*.

Mirchin, David. "Israeli Privacy Update: Landmark Case Establishes Guidelines for Monitoring Employee Online Activity," The Privacy Advisor - IAPP, 2011, *https://www.privacyassociation.org/publications/2011_12_05_israeli_privacy_update_landmark_case_establishes_guidelines_for*.

Murphy, Justin P., Matthew A. S. Esworthy, and Stephen M. Byers. "Chapter 8: E-discovery in Criminal Cases," *The State of Criminal Justice*, 2012 (ISBN 978-1-61438-552-3).

Ngak, Chenda. "Email Privacy: What Petraeus needed to know," 2012, *www.cbsnews.com/8301-205_162-57549755/email-privacy-what-petraeus-needed-to-know/*.

Phillips, Amelia. *An Investigation of Digital Forensics Concepts in an International Environment: The U.S., South Africa and Namibia*, 2013.

UNECE - United Nations Economic Commission for Europe. *www.unece.org/cefact/edifact/welcome.html*.

United Nations Commission on International Trade. *UNCITRAL - Model Law on International Commercial Arbitration*, 2006.

United States Courts.gov. "Federal Courts in American Government," *www.uscourts.gov/FederalCourts/UnderstandingtheFederalCourts/FederalCourtsInAmericanGovernment.aspx*.

United States Courts.gov. "The Appeals Process," *www.uscourts.gov/FederalCourts/UnderstandingtheFederalCourts/HowCourtsWork/TheAppealsProcess.aspx*.

U.S. Department of Justice. Electronic Communications Privacy Act of 1986, 2010, *http://it.ojp.gov/default.aspx?area=privacy&page=1285*.

VenBrux, Lisa. *French Data Protection Authority Issues Guidelines on Pre-Trial Discovery*, The Bureau of National Affairs, 2009.

Willoughby, Dan, Rose Jones, and Gregory Antine. "Sanctions for E-Discovery Violations by the Numbers," *Duke Law Journal*, November 2010.

Yannella, Philip and Abraham Reid. "Canada, Australia, and United Kingdom Adopt U.S. Style Electronic Discovery," *Privacy and Data Security Law Journal*, June 2009, pp. 538–544.

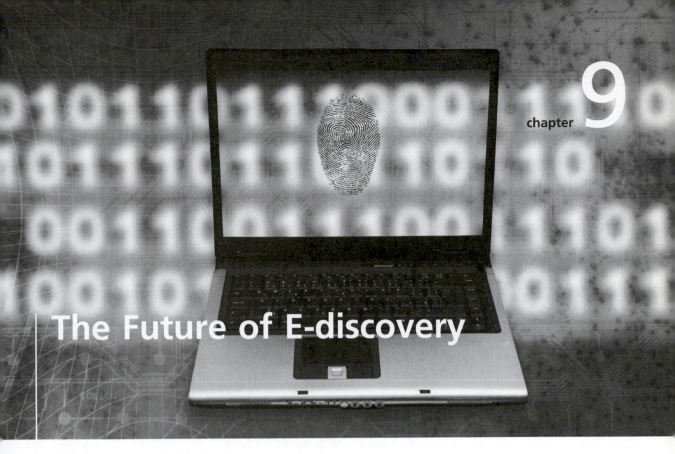

The Future of E-discovery

After reading this chapter and completing the exercises, you will be able to:

- Summarize new developments in national and international privacy laws
- Explain how new technology affects the rights of individuals and small businesses
- Describe the effect of anti-forensics on e-discovery procedures

E-discovery has become a multimillion-dollar industry and changed business processes and the way information is viewed. Privacy laws vary from state to state and from country to country and are made even more challenging by the development of multinational companies, cloud storage, and other factors. In addition, new technology, such as smaller and more pervasive mobile devices, mobile applications, social media, and black boxes, has been incorporated into standard business practices. As with all new technology, there are those who will find ways to circumvent it—hence this chapter's discussion on anti-forensics.

Privacy Revisited

Privacy of electronic data has become difficult to protect, and the laws aren't always able to keep pace with technology. Thirty years ago, privacy issues focused on wiretaps, eavesdropping, and personal mail. With the advent of the Internet and related technology, privacy concerns extended to places such as e-mail and voicemail. Now mobile devices, the cloud, GPS locators, and social media have added more layers where information is stored, and existing regulations and laws often don't address the issues created by new technology.

In the United States, most people think of the Fourth Amendment in relation to privacy issues, but the amendment actually covers unreasonable search and seizure without probable cause. The Electronic Communications and Privacy Act (ECPA) and the Stored Communications Act (SCA) do grant privacy of e-mail (both in transit and stored), but they aren't a true guarantee of privacy. As discussed in Chapter 8, the ECPA hasn't kept pace with technological advances, so collecting e-mails that owners haven't accessed in the past 180 days doesn't require a warrant; only a subpoena is needed.

As you've learned, each U.S. state has privacy laws (in addition to federal laws) that can affect what's allowed to be collected in an investigation. For example, Article 2, Section 10 of the Montana state constitution says, "The right of individual privacy is essential to the well-being of a free society and shall not be infringed without the showing of a compelling state interest" (Montana Legislature, 2011). California, which specifies privacy as an inalienable right, has the most detailed laws on digital investigations (Overly, 2004). In addition, California has started creating templates for use in e-discovery cases. The Northern District of California began with "Guidelines for the Discovery of Electronically Stored Information," which states that most discovery now involves electronic discovery and emphasizes the need for cooperation in preserving, collecting, and producing ESI (U.S. District Court, 2012). This district has also published a checklist, which specifies that parties aren't required to send a preservation letter, but if they do, they should make sure its scope isn't too broad. Other states will likely follow suit and create guidelines for e-discovery, particularly for both parties to agree on case issues early in the process.

As a result of the Petraeus scandal, the House of Representatives has proposed a new bill, the **Online Communications and Geolocation Protection Act (OCGPA)**, as an amendment to the ECPA that severely restricts tracking citizens by using GPS locators in mobile devices (Whittaker, 2013). Law enforcement officers would have to get a warrant for all electronic communications, regardless of the data's age. At the time of this writing, the U.S. Department of Justice is challenging these limitations because they could hamper criminal investigations.

The OCGPA was proposed by Representatives Ted Poe (R-TX), Zoe Lofgren (D-CA), and Suzan DelBene (D-WA).

Canada has the **Personal Information Protection and Electronic Documents Act (PIPEDA)**, which came into full effect in 2004. It requires organizations to notify people when personal information about them is collected or disclosed. It also gives people the right to see any of these records and make corrections. Canada still doesn't have a law specifically for e-mail privacy, however.

Multinational corporations need to be aware of the laws in countries where they operate. Penalties for privacy violations can vary widely. The investigation departments of these corporations sometimes have employees in each country who specialize in privacy laws because the ramifications of not following them can be severe. Keeping up with laws that affect ESI, whether it's e-mail, social media content, or Web sites visited, is critical.

New and Proposed ISO Standards

The law often lags behind new technology. However, at the end of 2012, a new ISO standard was created to help set more specific guidelines for digital evidence: ISO 27037:2012, Information technology – Security techniques – Guidelines for identification, collection, acquisition and preservation of digital evidence. Its objective is to help with "identifying, collecting and/or acquiring and preservation of potential digital evidence" (ISO, 2012). This standard isn't intended to address readiness for digital investigations; it was developed to describe how to respond to an investigation after the fact or in real time. Although it's geared toward forensic investigations, the collection methods it describes can be applied to some civil cases. Digital forensics as a profession has emerged only in the past two decades. Its procedures are fairly standard, although the courts' acceptance of them varies. In addition, laws on digital evidence vary from country to country. This new ISO standard sets guidelines for managing digital evidence in an attempt to standardize practices worldwide (ISO, 2012).

As of this writing, you can purchase a copy of this ISO standard at *www.iso.org/iso/catalogue_detail?csnumber=44381*.

Another challenge that has plagued the digital forensics community has been qualifications for digital forensics investigators, such as required education and years and type of experience. Several states, for example, require digital forensics investigators to be licensed private investigators. In states such as South Carolina, a digital investigator who takes the witness stand without a PI license can face a jail sentence and a fine. Barring vendor certifications, no standardized requirements were available. To address this problem, Annex A of the new ISO standard specifies skills needed for a digital evidence first responder (DEFR).

A digital evidence first responder is authorized and trained to collect and transport digital evidence at an investigation scene (ISO, 2012).

As a result of the ISO standard on digital forensics, a new proposal for an ISO standard on e-discovery has been approved: ISO/IEC 27050, Information technology – Security techniques – Electronic discovery. The close relationship between e-discovery and digital forensics is evident in this standard. One expert states, "So it comes as no surprise that the development of an e-discovery standard represents a convergence with computer forensics" (Teppler, 2013).

The Effects of New Technology

New technology and the interconnectedness it brings are introducing challenges no one could have foretold even a decade ago. With technological advances such as the cloud, social networking, tweets, and blogs, what will e-discovery encompass? What will its global impact be? What do legal and technical professions need to do to be ready for the challenges ahead? In this section, you see how past case law is applied to new technology and learn about potential effects of cloud storage, social media, and other new technologies and trends.

An example of how the law needs to keep pace with new technology can be seen in the use of global positioning system (GPS) devices. Using GPS devices to track suspects has become common, especially with built-in GPS tracking available on most mobile devices now. Two important U.S. Supreme Court cases involving tracking devices are *United States v. Knotts* (460 U.S. 276, 1983) and *United States v. Karo* (468 U.S. 795, 1984). In *United States v. Knotts*, a tracking device was placed in chloroform containers the defendant had purchased. The case was appealed to the U.S. Supreme Court on the grounds that information collected from the tracking device violated the defendant's Fourth Amendment rights. However, because the tracking device only augmented what officers could observe while following the defendant's car, there was no expectation of privacy, and the conviction was upheld.

The case of *United States v. Karo* is similar, in that law enforcement planted a tracking device in a container of ether. However, activating the tracking device after the container entered private property constituted a violation of the Fourth Amendment because an expectation of privacy inside the home is considered reasonable. On private property, a warrant is required to use a tracking device. Similarly, in the case *United States v. Antoine Jones* (615 F. 3d. 544, 2011), which involved suspected drug trafficking, the use of a GPS tracking device over a period of 28 days was challenged all the way to the U.S. Supreme Court. The verdict was split 5 to 4, and the ruling stated that extended use of the tracking device was a violation under the Fourth Amendment. However, the Supreme Court didn't rule that the search was unreasonable and cited the Katz test in its interpretations.

 As discussed in Chapter 8, the Katz test requires that the people in question expected privacy (such as being in their own home or closing the door to a phone booth) and that a reasonable person would expect privacy in this situation.

Chapter 7 introduced the term "bring your own device (BYOD)." What happens when mobile devices, such as smartphones and iPads, are included in a litigation hold? Do employees have the right to delete their personal information from these devices after a litigation hold is issued? Although the answer depends on the country's laws, many organizations have a policy stating that anything connected to their network can be searched. This policy can also apply to mobile devices, which fall into these categories:

- Issued by and paid for by the employer
- Purchased and paid for by an employee

In the United States, if the employer purchased the device and the employee signed an agreement for its use, the employer can search data on the phone. In other countries, the employee's privacy takes precedence. Whether the employer is allowed to search an employee's phone, however, there's always the risk of data being deleted inadvertently. Everyone has deleted a text message or voicemail by mistake.

How data can be retrieved from mobile devices depends on the type and age of the device and the service provider. A device's type and age affect whether data is stored on the device or with the service provider. Cheaper, basic, and older cell phones usually store text and SMS messages on the device, and voicemail is stored on the service provider's servers. Therefore, accessing voicemail requires a subpoena or a warrant. Service providers might save voicemail for only 15 days and then delete them (Wright, n.d.). With smartphones and other advanced mobile devices, storage of data such as time of a call, a message's sender, voicemail messages, and so forth is typically on the device (Zdziarski, 2008). How much the provider stores or keeps at a backup location varies according to the provider, the subscription type, and any third-party software the subscriber is using.

Unified messaging (also called "unified communications") is the capability to store audio, video, and text and SMS messages in the same inbox so that they're all subject to the same laws during investigations (Wright, n.d.). As this capability becomes the norm for mobile devices, its importance for e-discovery will increase.

The number and variety of mobile devices mean data formats vary widely. So where is data actually located? Depending on the service provider and type of device, it might be in one of these locations:

- Voicemails are stored on the provider's servers or in smartphones' memory.
- Text messages are saved on the device.
- E-mail is stored in a mobile device's memory or on an e-mail server (a Webmail or company server).
- File attachments can be stored on company servers, on cloud storage, or on a mobile device.

Mobile devices that access a company's wireless network show up in the network server logs, but some employees might use their own mobile hotspot, so their usernames may or may not show up in logs. The term **bring your own application (BYOA)** refers to the more than half a million third-party applications available to be installed on mobile devices. These applications can pose a security risk (in the form of embedded malware, for example) and might record usage data and other information. If mobile devices loaded with these applications are connected to a company network, confidential information stored on the network might be sent to third parties as a result of embedded malware.

Searching Data on Mobile Devices in Criminal Cases

The question of when a warrant is needed to search data on mobile devices is of interest in criminal cases. An officer is allowed to search an arrested person and his or her immediate surroundings, which means within the suspect's control or reach. In the case *Arizona v. Gant* (556 U.S. 332, 2009), Rodney Gant's car was searched after he had been handcuffed and placed in a police car, but the Supreme Court later threw out the products of the search because the car shouldn't have been searched (Starbuck, 2012). The police were arresting him for a suspended driver's license and he was already in the squad car, so they had no grounds to search his vehicle. In a related case, *Chimel v. California* (395 U.S. 752, 1969), the police had a warrant for Chimel's arrest and searched his home after his wife objected. This search was a Fourth Amendment violation of "search incident to arrest" (FindLaw.com, 1969). The term **search incident to arrest** means officers can search anything suspects or arrestees have in their possession and in their immediate control (clothing, purses, knapsacks, and so forth). The court ruled that anything in the suspect's immediate control could be searched, but searching the entire house required a warrant. Another related case is *United States v. Robinson* (414 U.S. 218, 1973). The police did a patdown, which revealed the suspect was carrying a packet of heroin, and the Supreme Court upheld this search as reasonable.

If a suspect or an arrested person has a cell phone or other mobile device, can a law enforcement officer search the phone's contents, such as contacts and text messages? To explore this question, two issues must be considered: inventory searches and closed containers. The case *Illinois v. Lafayette* (462 U.S. 640, 1983) is an example of the inventory search issue. Lafayette was arrested for getting into a fight at a local theater. The police searched the suspect's shoulder bag and inventoried the contents. When they found drugs in the bag, additional charges were filed. On appeal, it was ruled that "it is proper for police to remove and list or inventory" items in the possession of an arrested person about to be jailed. Another case, *South Dakota v. Opperman* (428 U.S. 364, 1976), addresses inventory searches—in this case, an impounded vehicle. Opperman's car had been impounded for being illegally parked. To minimize claims against the city, the police followed established policies and inventoried the contents. They found marijuana, so when Opperman came to claim his vehicle, he was arrested for possession. The U.S. Supreme Court ruled that this inventory search was reasonable.

For the second issue, computers have been treated as closed containers in a legal sense, much like a filing cabinet or a plastic container, and mobile devices fall into this category. In the case *California v. Acevedo* (500 U.S. 565, 1991), for example, police had probable cause to pull the defendant over and search a container they believed to contain marijuana. When the case was appealed, the warrantless search was upheld because of exigent circumstances—in this case, that the evidence would be compromised.

The term "exigent circumstances" means a person's life is in danger, as in a kidnapping or a bomb threat, or the threat of harm to property or destruction of evidence exists.

Because mobile devices can contain personal information, careful consideration must be given to searches. Based on the cases discussed in this section, a search incident to arrest is reasonable. In addition, because most people carry their mobile devices on them or in a bag of some type, taking a mobile device and listing it as part of inventory search is reasonable. However, does that mean searching the device's contents is reasonable?

Two state Supreme Courts have ruled on this question. The State Supreme Court of Ohio ruled in 2009 that police are obligated to obtain a warrant to search data on a cell phone "when the search is not necessary to protect the safety of law enforcement officers and there are no exigent circumstances" (Supreme Court of Ohio, 2009). In 2012, the Oregon Supreme Court made a similar ruling, stating that in the case *Schlossberg v. Solesbee* (2012 WL 141741 D.Or., January 18, 2012), "warrantless searches of such devices are not reasonable incident to a valid arrest absent a showing that the search was necessary to prevent the destruction of evidence, to ensure officer safety, or that other exigent circumstances exist" (Brown, 2012).

Figure 9-1 shows a decision structure to follow based on these cases, assuming a cell phone or mobile device has been seized during an arrest. The next decision is whether the device's contents can be searched without a warrant. As the Oregon Supreme Court suggested, one of three conditions must be met. First, is the officer is danger? If a cell phone is a bomb trigger, for example, a search of the physical device is warranted but not a search of the phone's contents. Second, does the device contain evidence that could be destroyed? This condition would be true if the suspect still had the device, but if it's already been seized, destroying the evidence isn't likely. Third, do exigent circumstances exist? If so, getting

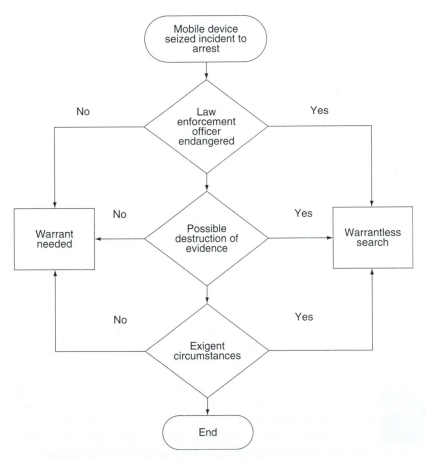

Figure 9-1 The decision flow for handling a warrant to seize a mobile device
Source: © Amelia Phillips, 2013

information quickly is critical, as in a kidnapping case. As technology advances, knowing which laws to apply to mobile devices will become more critical.

E-discovery and Social Media

In the EU and many other countries, such as Australia, personal privacy has precedence over corporate rights. Every country in the EU has a privacy law, and data retained by social media sites, such as Facebook, has become a privacy issue. For example, Max Schrem, an Austrian law student at the University of Vienna, launched a one-man crusade against Facebook for what he called "illegal practices." Schrem claimed that Facebook collects and markets users' data, often without their consent (O'Brien, 2012), and demanded his Facebook file. It was more than 1200 pages, and in addition to information he had entered, it contained locations he had visited but hadn't posted on his page as well as information he had deleted (Semgupta, 2012). As you probably know, if you log on to Facebook and other social media sites via the wireless connection at coffee shops and other public settings, your location is posted automatically. The media coverage of this case caused more than 40,000 EU citizens to demand their Facebook files, too.

To promote his cause, Schrem created the Web site EU versus Facebook (*www.europe-v-facebook.org/EN/en.htm*), which tracks the latest trends in this ongoing battle.

The director of Privacy International made the following statement about methods of tracking users, particularly on social media sites (Semgupta, 2012):

> *"Europe has come to the conclusion that none of the companies can be trusted," said Simon Davies, the director of the London-based nonprofit agency Privacy International. "The European Commission is responding to public demand. There is a growing mood of despondency about the privacy issue."*

Social networks are used to promote businesses, stay in touch with friends and family, and share photos, Web sites, and so forth. Facebook is free because it displays ads to users and uses tracking cookies. EU countries are trying to curtail the use of tracking cookies because they constitute a violation of privacy. A bill, nicknamed the "Cookie Law," proposed to the European Parliament would require companies to delete old information in a timely manner, mandate explicit consent to being tracked on Web sites, and require data breach notifications, among other provisions. It would also limit GPS tracking, similar to the OCGPA's provisions. In addition, companies transferring personal data across borders would be fined up to 2% of their gross revenue, which could be substantial for large companies (Marshall, 2012). If this bill passes, online tracking cookies and other types of tracking code would also be illegal. Unless a reasonable compromise is reached, this change could substantially change free enterprise online.

Facebook has announced the development of its own phone that will have the Facebook home page and contain all Facebook contacts, messages, pictures, and so forth. This development will likely make applying privacy laws even more complex, particularly when deciding whether a warrant is needed for criminal investigations.

Because many companies use Twitter, Facebook, and other social media as part of doing business, policies on their use should be developed. These policies need to take employees' privacy into account as well as the laws of other countries where the company does business. Companies have already been censured for requiring employees to "friend" them so that they could determine whether employees had criminal acquaintances. In addition, students are cautioned that posting their social exploits online (or even their friends posting about them) could ruin their careers before they even graduate from school. One of Max Schrem's concerns, for example, was that if social media sites retain information indefinitely, postings can come back to haunt people years later when they might no longer hold the same views.

The government also uses Facebook to investigate people. One woman bragged on Facebook about being a "tax fraud pioneer." She was later charged with 57 counts of tax fraud. She claimed her Facebook account was hacked, but the IRS, which uses Facebook as a standard investigation tool, gathered enough evidence to convict her (Lou, 2010). In addition, federal investigations of gang members have resulted in convictions based on information placed on Facebook or MySpace. Although these investigative uses have positive results, they illustrate the wide-ranging effects of social media sites.

How much discussion of work occurs on social networks? Google+ is another social media site being marketed to people and businesses. It can be used for business meetings as well as virtual customer "drop-ins" and what are called "hangouts." Would these meetings be considered discoverable ESI, however? Would recordings of them be covered under the Wiretap Act? Google+ might be a handy tool for companies, but they should educate employees on how to use it and develop policies for conducting meetings via this tool.

"Discoverable," in the legal sense, can include notes, diaries, and so forth pertaining to a case. So if meetings are recorded in these locations, they could fall into this category and be subject to discovery.

Twitter feeds are another example of the far-reaching effects of social media. When the Egyptian comedian Bassem Youssef made fun of the Egyptian president in his monologue, a link to it was placed on the U.S. Embassy Cairo's Twitter feed. It sparked a controversy when the Egyptian government took offense, and the embassy's Twitter feed was shut down until the offending tweet was removed (CBS News, 2013). This example brings up other questions about postings and comments on social media sites. For example, if employees post tweets about their supervisors or customers, does retrieving this material in an investigation violate privacy rights? Or is it a standard part of ESI that must be produced in response to a litigation hold? Answers to these questions are still to be determined.

Another issue related to social media sites is how long government agencies should retain records of content posted on these sites. Different laws can affect retention periods. For example, the Freedom of Information Act (FOIA) applies to most content a government agency posts on a social media site. When an FOIA request is filed, government agencies must produce this information in a reasonable amount of time. For this reason, a new industry has emerged that handles archiving social media content for government and corporate clients. ArchiveSocial, a leader in this new field, was recently granted a contract to store North Carolina's state archives, including tweets, Facebook and LinkedIn posts, and other online information along with metadata in these files. The ArchiveSocial Web site (*http://archivesocial.com*) states that its software is compliant with many rules and regulations, including the following:

- Financial Industry Regulatory Authority (FINRA)
- Securities and Exchange Commission (SEC)
- Freedom of Information Act (FOIA)
- Federal Rules of Civil Procedure (FRCP)
- Sarbanes-Oxley Act

TIP Other vendors in the social-media archiving field include Actiance, XI Discovery, Patrina Corporation, and Reed Archives. To learn more about them and other archiving tools for social media content, visit *http://ediscoveryjournal.com/2013/03/a-real-experience-with-social-media-archiving/*.

In developing policies on the use of social media, companies should determine what files need to be stored and for how long. As shown in the example of Max Schrem requesting his Facebook file, Facebook keeps information for years, but this storage time isn't likely to be practical for companies with thousands of employees who use Facebook as a way to interact with clients and customers. However, to comply with laws such as the FOIA, companies might be required to keep posts and comments for at least three to five years because this information could be considered discoverable ESI.

Storage in the Cloud

Cloud storage offers easy access to files and makes it possible to work on a lightweight smartphone or tablet, instead of lugging around a laptop while you're traveling. Google Docs was the one of the first cloud storage applications. With it, users could share and modify documents easily from anywhere in the world, although limitations on files and storage space were problems. Other cloud storage applications followed, including DropBox, SkyDrive, and iCloud.

These applications ease concerns about transporting proprietary information across borders. Business travelers no longer have to carry confidential files with them and risk the possibility of theft or loss because the files are stored in the cloud. Another benefit is being able to synch with any computer you use. You don't have to remember to copy a file to a flash drive or e-mail to yourself before you head home because it's available in the cloud. If you access the file on your home computer, however, it's then stored on that machine, which could complicate timeline details (such as determining the most recent access date and time) in a criminal case.

Privacy can be an issue with cloud storage, too. If an employee needs to access a personal file stored in DropBox while she's at work, the file is copied to her company system. If all files on her system have to be examined in an investigation, her personal files might be intermingled with company files. Therefore, companies should create clear policies explaining the need to store personal files in folders labeled to indicate their private nature, for example. Many companies allow some personal use of office computers because they realize that employees might need to send an e-mail during lunch, for instance, but don't have their personal computers or mobile devices with them. As a matter of fact, Australian privacy laws assume that some personal data will exist on company systems. Companies should make an effort to preserve their employees' privacy if stored information isn't related to litigation or an investigation.

Small business owners need to exercise caution when using cloud storage, too. Although advice about not commingling business and personal files abounds, following this advice isn't always easy because of the interconnectedness of mobile devices and desktop computers. A small business owner might be able to afford only one smartphone account and one computer, instead of having separate accounts and equipment for home and business. If one device is compromised, both are, and so is the data stored on them. In addition, any litigation holds would apply to both devices.

Emerging Trends

New technology can often affect people's rights to privacy. For example, the same technology used for airplane black boxes to determine how plane crashes occur is being used in passenger vehicles. These **event data recorders (EDRs)** are now used to record information such as seatbelt use, airbag deployment, use of brakes, and so forth. The National Highway Transportation Safety Commission (NHTSC) has proposed legislation that makes them mandatory for all new cars and allows accessing the information stored in them after a crash. According to the NHTSC, this access isn't intended to be an invasion of privacy, and the devices don't make use of a tracking device. However, many are concerned that accessing this information could be an invasion of privacy. For example, car manufacturers might be able to access it after a recall without notifying owners. If these devices become standard, would they be used in civil suits to prove who caused an accident? In spite of the safety improvements EDRs offer and the lives they could save, they do introduce legal issues.

Technological advances can have other consequences. For example, airplane parts and other products that can't be made easily with traditional machinery can be produced with 3D printers. Because of the ease in going from an idea to an actual prototype with a 3D printer, intellectual property rights can become clouded. Privacy might be an issue, too, if the memory of 3D printers is considered discoverable ESI. What was once considered mere science fiction is now possible.

For an interesting article on how guns have been created from 3D printers, go to *www.foxnews.com/us/2013/05/23/govt-memo-warns-3d-printed-guns-may-be-impossible-to-stop/*.

Another trend is the development of new ways to tackle sifting through the huge amounts of data in many litigations. One new product is Recommind (*www.recommind.com/business-solutions/seamless-ediscovery*), which uses predictive coding (discussed in Chapter 8) to sort through thousands of terabytes of data. In 2013, the SEC's Enforcement Division began using Recommind to accelerate coding and sorting documents. As these new techniques and tools become more widely available, e-discovery will continue to grow and develop.

Anti-forensics in E-discovery

As you've seen, e-discovery tools and collection methods focus on information embedded in native files, such as e-mail and Office documents. Can they be used to find information that's been hidden deliberately, however? Ask most civil attorneys whether they're concerned the opposition would deliberately conceal or delete information to be produced in response to a formal discovery request, and they usually respond, "No, we trust they're giving us everything we ask for." Ask a criminal prosecutor or law enforcement officer the same question, and the answer is a resounding "Yes! Are you kidding?" These different responses are based on their past experiences, as problems with evidence being destroyed or hidden happen far more often in criminal cases. However, these problems are starting to crop up in civil cases, too.

Many civil attorneys still think of evidence in terms of paper documents and aren't aware of how easy it is to delete or obscure digital information. Furthermore, they might not think to examine the actions of employees who could remove evidence of inappropriate computer use during work hours, such as watching pornography, shopping online, and downloading music files. While deleting this evidence, employees could accidentally or deliberately remove relevant discovery without management or counsel's knowledge.

Civil attorneys should become as informed about digital forensics as criminal prosecutors are and learn about methods used to delete or hide evidence, to circumvent a forensics examination, and similar actions. These methods are commonly known as **anti-forensics**, described as any measure used to defeat or obstruct a forensics examination. Craig Ball, a trial lawyer and e-discovery/computer forensics special master, defines anti-forensics as "efforts to frustrate the tools and methods of computer forensics and encompasses deliberate efforts to hide data, destroy or alter artifacts, and cast doubt on forensic examinations" (ARMA, 2011). During civil litigation, evidence of anti-forensics activity is usually deemed spoliation by the courts, so these acts are subject to court sanctions. In criminal cases, evidence of anti-forensics is usually used to support the prosecutor's claims of criminal activity.

For example, *Du Pont De Nemours & Co. v. Kolon Indus., Inc.* (No. 3:09cv58, 2011 WL 2966862) and the subsequent criminal case *United States v. Kolon Indus., Inc.* (No. 3:12-Cr-137, 2012) involved corporate espionage. Kolon Industries, Inc. and several high-ranking Kolon employees were charged with violating Title 18 of the U.S. Code, which applies to tampering with a witness and imposes criminal penalties for document destruction done to obstruct a federal proceeding. These charges are common when defendants have deleted ESI in an attempt to thwart a criminal investigation, but the federal proceeding against Kolon was for theft of trade secrets. Just like Enron, civil cases can and do become criminal cases. Despite the requirements of proportionality in discovery, civil cases involving evidence destroyed during forensics examinations are on the rise.

Anti-forensics Methods

There are numerous methods for hiding or destroying digital information and interfering with a forensics examination. They range from simple, such as emptying the Recycle Bin, to more complex techniques that require in-depth knowledge of OSs or hard drive configuration. These methods typically use command-line scripts or specialized software, with varying degrees of success.

The Remove Hidden Data feature in Microsoft Office and Adobe Acrobat could be considered an anti-forensics method if it's done outside the course of normal business activities.

Traces of most anti-forensics activities are stored in the Registry or other areas of the OS. However, if the original hard drive or a bit-by-bit copy of it isn't available, you can examine only the data or metadata that remains embedded in native files. So if you suspect discovery material has been deleted or altered, you should try to get forensic images of the hard drive. A skilled digital forensics examiner can inspect these drive images to search for evidence of deletions and alterations.

Reviewing how a file is deleted in Windows can be helpful in understanding anti-forensics. Emptying a computer's Recycle Bin doesn't destroy the information stored in it; it just changes markers in the File Allocation Table (FAT) that reference file locations on the hard drive. These files aren't actually deleted until the computer determines that the space for storing them is needed for another task. The File Allocation Table (FAT) in older Windows OSs or the Master File Table (MFT) in newer Windows versions is a database of information about files and is stored in a part of the hard drive users don't typically see.

PST and OST e-mail files have a similar structure. The act of deleting an e-mail changes only the e-mail markers stored in the database; it doesn't delete the e-mail itself. You can think of this process in the context of an index card cabinet in a library. Deleting an index card removes just the reference to the book's location in the library; the actual book is still on the shelf. To see how this process works, take a look at *http://windowsitpro.com/outlook/recovering-deleted-items-pst-files*, where you can see an e-mail file (PST format) at the binary level. The process of deleting changes the file's first 8 bits to FF, which signals to the OS that the space this file occupied can now be used for other data. The body of the e-mail is still intact elsewhere on the drive until new data overwrites it. You can recover a deleted e-mail by restoring these altered bits. Reviewing these concepts with employees who aren't well versed in forensics or IT is important to make sure the correct files are being produced in response to discovery orders.

Chapter Summary

- Privacy laws vary from state to state and country to country. Laws covering privacy of electronic communications haven't kept pace with technology, and modifications to regulations such as the ECPA and SCA are needed.

- Multinational corporations need to plan for differences in privacy laws and how they affect employees, corporate policies, and internal investigations.

- ISO 27037:2012, Information technology – Security techniques – Guidelines for identification, collection, acquisition and preservation of digital evidence, has been approved for guidelines on digital forensics investigations, and ISO/IEC 27050, Information technology – Security techniques – Electronic discovery, has been proposed for e-discovery guidelines.

- Smartphones and other mobile devices pose a challenge when litigation holds have been issued. The issue of whether information stored on them is personal or business might be clouded, and stored information on mobile devices is more likely to be deleted inadvertently. Whether data can be retrieved from mobile devices usually depends on the type and age of the device and the service provider.

- When determining whether law enforcement can search the contents of a suspect's cell phone, two issues must be considered: inventory searches and closed containers.

- Data retained by social media sites, such as Facebook, has become a privacy issue, particularly in EU countries. For example, a bill, nicknamed the "Cookie Law," proposed to the European Parliament would mandate explicit consent to being tracked on Web sites. Because many companies use Twitter, Facebook, and other social media as part of doing business, policies on their use should be developed that take employees' privacy into account as well as the laws of other countries where the company does business.

- Cloud storage could complicate timeline details (such as determining the most recent access date and time) in a criminal case and can result in privacy issues, particularly when personal and company files are intermingled on office computers.

- Anti-forensics are methods of destroying or altering ESI in an attempt to obstruct a digital forensics examination. Traces of most anti-forensics activities are stored in the Registry or other areas of the OS, but having a digital forensics examiner inspect forensic drive images is the best way to detect evidence of alterations and deletions.

Key Terms

anti-forensics   Methods of deleting, altering, or hiding evidence to obstruct a digital forensics investigation.

bring your own application (BYOA)   A term encompassing the more than half a million third-party applications available to be installed on mobile devices. These applications can pose a security risk and might record usage data and other information.

event data recorders (EDRs)   Devices that record the use of airbags, brakes, safety belts, and so forth. The National Highway Transportation Safety Commission describes them as a contribution to safe roads; others consider them a violation of privacy.

Online Communications and Geolocation Protection Act (OCGPA)   A bill proposed to amend the ECPA that would limit access to e-mail and GPS location information without a warrant.

Personal Information Protection and Electronic Documents Act (PIPEDA)   Canada's privacy act.

search incident to arrest   A term used to specify that law enforcement can search an arrested person and anything in the immediate vicinity, including clothes, purses, briefcases, and so forth.

unified messaging   The capability to store audio, video, text, SMS, and other data formats in the same mailbox in a mobile device.

Review Questions

1. The Online Communications and Geolocation Protection Act severely restricts tracking citizens by using event data recorders. True or False?

2. The proposed EU bill called the "Cookie Law" would require which of the following? (Choose all that apply.)

   a. Deleting old information in a timely manner

   b. Using cookies to track users' preferences for tracking

   c. Limiting the use of GPS tracking

   d. Mandating users' explicit consent to being tracked on Web sites

3. The Personal Information Protection and Electronic Documents Act addresses privacy of which of the following? (Choose all that apply.)

   a. E-mail

   b. Health information

   c. Stored ESI

   d. Twitter and Facebook posts

4. In the United States, if employees sign an agreement for using cell phones their employer supplies for them, their right to privacy takes precedence over the employer's right to search the phones' content. True or False?

5. Name two of the three conditions the Oregon Supreme Court suggested for determining whether a cell phone's contents could be searched without a warrant.

6. In civil litigation, evidence of anti-forensics activity is usually judged as spoliation. True or False?

7. Explain why the use of GPS tracking devices in the case *United States v. Knotts* was deemed reasonable.

8. ISO Standard 27037:2012 was created to set guidelines for assessing readiness for digital investigations. True or False?

9. Cloud applications such as Google Docs can result in commingling personal and business data. True or False?

10. Which of the following actions might be considered an anti-forensics method? (Choose all that apply.)

    a. Copying the Master File Table

    b. Emptying the Recycle Bin

    c. Using the Remove Hidden Data feature

    d. Shredding documents

Hands-On Projects

HANDS-ON PROJECTS

Hands-On Project 9-1

In this project, you use the Access database you used in Chapter 8. If you haven't done so already, copy it from the DVD folder Chapter08\Projects to your computer.

1. Double-click the **Ediscovery Database.accdb** file to open the database in Access. If necessary, scroll down the left pane and double-click **Navigation Menu**.

2. Click the **Country** tab if it is not visible. At the bottom of the form, click the **New (blank) record** button (with a starburst icon).

3. In the Country Code text box, type **CA** (for Canada), and press **Tab** to move to the next field. Enter the full country name, and press **Tab** again to go to a blank form.

4. Click the **Federal or Country Rules** tab and click the **New (blank) record** button.

5. In the Rule Number ID text box, type **PIPEDA**, and then press **Tab**. In the Rule Description text box, type **Personal Information Protection and Electronic Documents Act**.

6. Click the **Country Code** list arrow, and then click **Canada** in the list of options.

7. Click the **Search Criteria** list arrow, and then click **Privacy - other**. Your form should look like Figure 9-2.

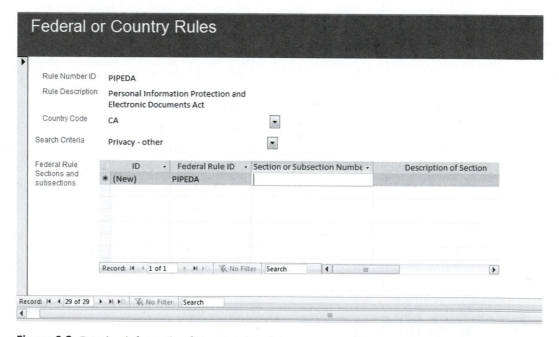

Figure 9-2 Entering information for a new record
Source: © Amelia Phillips, 2013

8. Go online and find two more Canadian laws that might apply to e-discovery, using keywords such as computer crime, meet and confer, and so forth. Follow Steps 4 through 7 to enter these laws, and do a screen capture after adding each one.

9. Write a brief description of each law. Explain why you chose it and why you associated it with the keyword you selected. When you're finished, exit the database and your Web browser.

Case Projects

Case Project 9-1

Research the Online Communications and Geolocation Protection Act. What are the arguments for and against this amendment to the ECPA? Which ones do you agree with and why? Write a one- to two-page paper summarizing your findings and conclusions.

Case Project 9-2

Research the arguments for and against the EU privacy legislation nicknamed the "Cookie Law." If it passes and limits the use of tracking cookies, what would the ramifications be for online marketing? Write a one- to two-page paper summarizing your findings and opinions.

References

ARMA International Newswire. "A-N-T-I-F-O-R-E-N-S-I-C-S Spells Trouble for Companies," 2011, *www.arma.org/r1/news/newswire/2011/04/26/a-n-t-i-f-o-r-e-n-s-i-c-s-spells-trouble-for-companies*.

CBS News. "Daily Show Triggers U.S.-Egypt Twitter Kerfuffle," 2013, *www.cbsnews.com/8301-505263_162-57577894/daily-show-triggers-u.s.-egypt-twitter-kerfuffle*.

ISO. ISO 27037:2012, Information technology – Security techniques – Guidelines for identification, collection, acquisition and preservation of digital evidence, 2012, *www.iso.org/iso/catalogue_detail?csnumber=44381*.

ISO 27001 Security. "ISO/IEC 27037," 2012, *www.iso27001security.com/html/27037.html*.

Lou, Kim. "Is Your Facebook Friend a Spy or IRS Agent?," *Money and Risk*, 2010, *www.moneyandrisk.com/living-well-on-less/philosophy/is-your-facebook-friend-a-spy-or-irs-agent/*.

Marshall, Tracy et al. "Sweeping EU Privacy Proposal Unveiled," January 30, 2012, *www.martindale.com/corporate-law/article_Keller-Heckman-LLP_1428446.htm*.

Montana Legislature. Montana Code Annotated, 2011.

Murphy, Barry. "Social media and your eDiscovery strategies," November 21, 2012, *www.techrepublic.com/blog/tech-manager/social-media-and-your-ediscovery-strategies/8051*.

O'Brien, Kevin. "Austrian Law Student Faces Down Facebook," *New York Times*, 2012, *www.nytimes.com/2012/02/06/technology/06iht-rawdata06.html?pagewanted=all&_r=0*.

Overly, Michael. *Overly on Electronic Evidence in California*, West Publishing, 2004, ISBN 40169478.

Semgupta, Semini. "Should Personal Data Be Personal?," *New York Times*, February 4, 2012, *www.nytimes.com/2012/02/05/sunday-review/europe-moves-to-protect-online-privacy.html?pagewanted=all&_r=0*.

Silvistreni, Elaine. "IRS Says Woman Bragged About Tax Fraud on Facebook," March 13, 2013, *www.cpapracticeadvisor.com/news/10876997/irs-says-woman-bragged-about-tax-fraud-on-facebook*.

Supreme Court of Ohio. "Warrantless Search of Cell Phone Data Barred Unless Necessary for Officer's Safety or to Preserve Evidence," 2009.

Teppler, Steven. "International Standard for Project for E-Discovery Approved," 2013, *www.law.com/jsp/lawtechnologynews/PubArticleLTN.jsp?id=1202597948357&kw=International%20Standard%20Project%20for%20E-Discovery%20Approved&slreturn=20130402013645*.

U.S. District Court, Northern District of California. "Checklist for Rule 26(f) Meet and Confer for Electronically Stored Information," 2012.

U.S. District Court, Northern District of California. "Guidelines for the Discovery of Electronically Stored Information," 2012.

Whittaker, Zak. "Justice Department to Congress: We want greater email, Facebook, Twitter snooping powers," ZDNet, 2013, *www.zdnet.com/justice-dept-to-congress-we-want-greater-email-facebook-twitter-snooping-powers-7000012786/*.

Wright, Benjamin. "Voicemail and Other Audio Legal Records, Forensics and Retention Policy: Preservation, Authentication and Evidence of Cell Phone Records and Unified Messages," *http://hack-igations.blogspot.com/2008/06/voicemail-other-audio-legal-records.html*.

Zdziarski, Jonathan. *iPhone Forensics: Recovering Evidence, Personal Data, and Corporate Assets*, O'Reilly, 2008, ISBN 978-0-596-15358-8.

Resources

The following resources are helpful in navigating the fields of e-discovery and computer forensics. Lists are divided into laws/legal, technical/software, miscellaneous (publications, organizations, and so forth), and training categories. At most organizations' Web sites, you can enter "e-discovery" as a search term to find more information.

This appendix is not an endorsement of any resources. Students are encouraged to evaluate any training or certification courses carefully.

Laws/Legal

- *www.uscourts.gov*—Federal court rules and other information
- *www.fjc.gov*—A branch of the federal courts dedicated to education and research
- *www.justice.gov/usao/eousa/foia_reading_room/usab5903.pdf*—The May 2011 Department of Justice bulletin on e-discovery issues in criminal cases
- *www.justice.gov/usao/eousa/foia_reading_room/usab5601.pdf*—The January 2008 Department of Justice bulletin on issues related to digital forensics in criminal cases
- *www.justice.gov/criminal/cybercrime/documents.html*—Department of Justice manuals on cybercrime
- *www.justice.gov/atr/public/electronic_discovery/*—The Department of Justice's guidelines for e-discovery
- *www.ediscoverylaw.com*—K&L Gates summaries of notable e-discovery case law

Technical/Software

- National Institute of Standards and Technology (NIST, *www.nist.gov/index.html* and *http://trec.nist.gov/tracks.html*)—A useful Web site for many technology-related topics
- TREC Legal Track (*http://trec-legal.umiacs.umd.edu/*)—An offshoot of NIST that focuses on research related to information retrieval used in civil litigation

- International Legal Technology Association (*www.iltanet.org*)—Offers international and local groups that focus on technology-related topics in the legal industry, including e-discovery
- EMC² (*www.kazeon.com/products2/data_center.php*)—An e-discovery software package with a variety of features

Miscellaneous/General

- Law.com (*www.law.com*)—A helpful Web site offering publications on technologies used in the legal industry, including e-discovery
- Association of Records Managers and Administrators (ARMA, *www.arma.org*)— Now offers a wide variety of information on records management, including e-discovery
- Digital Government Institute (*www.digitalgovernment.com*)—Focuses on technology used in government, including e-discovery
- National Archives (*www.archives.gov*)—Manages electronic information from federal agencies and includes topics related to e-discovery
- PinPoint Labs (*www.pinpointlabs.com/trialgraphics.html*)—Offers e-discovery and forensics software as well as trial graphics, which can also be helpful in the classroom
- Association of Certified Fraud Examiners (*www.acfe.com*)—Has courses and conferences on fraud prevention and investigation, including digital forensics and e-discovery
- The Sedona Conference (*www.thesedonaconference.org*)—Numerous e-discovery resources, including articles such as *https://thesedonaconference.org/publication/ sedona-conference%25C2%25AE-commentary-achieving-quality-e-discovery-process*
- Women in E-discovery (*www.womeninediscovery.org*)—A nonprofit organization for women in e-discovery
- Georgetown University (*www.law.georgetown.edu/continuing-legal-education/ programs/cle/ediscovery-institute/*)—Continuing education classes in legal fields

Training

- Association of Certified E-discovery Specialists (*www.aceds.org* and *www.aceds.org/ certification/eligibility/*)
- Kroll Ontrack (*www.krollontrack.com/events/education/certification-workshops/*)— A two-day e-discovery certification course
- LitWorks Certified Litigation Support Professional Training (CLSP; *http://litworks.net/ consulting-training/training-classes/professional-training/*)—A four-day certification class
- Organization of Legal Professionals (*www.theolp.org*)—Certification for nonattorneys

Glossary

alternative dispute resolution A method of settling disputes outside a court setting by using mediation or arbitration.

anti-forensics Methods of deleting, altering, or hiding evidence to obstruct a digital forensics investigation.

appellate courts Courts where appeals to verdicts are heard. The United States has 12 circuit courts that hear appeals from the federal district courts in each state.

attorney-client privilege (ACP) This privilege protects any communication between an attorney and a client, which can include written material as well as speech and actions.

authority lists Lists created for use in databases to improve accuracy and consistency of document coding.

bill of particulars A request to prosecution for details and evidence of an alleged crime. *For civil cases, see* interrogatories.

Boolean operators The AND, OR, and NOT operators used when performing keyword searches on documents and other ESI. These values return true or false values that specify whether a keyword meets the search criteria.

bring your own application (BYOA) A term encompassing the more than half a million third-party applications available to be installed on mobile devices. These applications can pose a security risk and might record usage data and other information.

bring your own device (BYOD) The use of personal mobile devices on a corporate network.

broad e-discovery scope An e-discovery method that attempts to capture as much data as possible, on the premise that relevant data will be found.

business process management (BPM) A practice that aims to improve the effectiveness and efficiency of processes by being more flexible than traditional hierarchical management approaches.

central document repository A network location for storing all documents related to a case or project so that searching and sorting files are more efficient.

chain of custody The path evidence takes from the time the investigator obtains it until the case goes to court or is dismissed.

Children's Online Privacy Protection Act (COPPA) A U.S. federal law intended to protect children's privacy; it sets guidelines for collecting information via a Web site from people under the age of 13.

clawback agreements Agreements negotiated during an initial meeting that allow the opposition to identify and exclude materials from use in the case.

cloud computing On-demand access to remote servers, software, applications, and other computing resources; generally categorized as software as a service (SaaS), platform as a service (PaaS), and infrastructure as a service (IaaS).

coding The process (automatic or manual) of examining documents to identify names, dates, and relevant terms or phrases so that information can be entered in database fields.

computer abuse Gaining illegal access to a computer or the information stored on it.

Computer Fraud and Abuse Act (CFAA) A federal law passed in 1986 to address the ongoing problem of computer abuse, fraud, and illegal access to government and financial computers.

consultant A person or company offering services or professional advice; consultants can testify as experts if they meet the same qualifying standards.

cost sharing The process of plaintiffs and defendants sharing resources voluntarily to reduce case costs; can also apply to third parties. It's the opposite of cost shifting, which is usually involuntary.

Cross-Matter Management Created by Daegis eDiscovery, it's a procedure for handling multiple litigations that involves identifying and collecting custodian data, processing it, hosting it in a single repository, and then reusing the data and resulting work product for subsequent cases.

custodians People in an organization with the responsibility of granting access to data or e-mail and protecting the organization's assets.

data Numbers, documents, files, and other information (such as e-mail) stored on digital devices.

data dump The process of sending the opposing party an inordinate amount of data or documents to process in an attempt to overwhelm and bog down the opposition.

data mining A method used to gather information about customers or vendors by monitoring what they purchase, examining where they go on a Web site, and culling other ESI. *See also* electronically stored information (ESI).

demonstratives Evidence other than testimony intended to clarify case facts, usually presented during a civil or criminal trial; can include animated videos, charts, timelines, and models.

deposition Giving testimony under oath outside court; a key form of discovery.

digital evidence Any evidence that's stored or transmitted electronically or in a digital format.

digital forensics The application of traditional forensics procedures to acquiring computer evidence; used to retrieve existing files, deleted files, hidden data, and metadata on digital devices. *See also* metadata.

digital forensics consultants A person or company offering digital forensics services or advice; can subcontract some or all of the work.

digital forensics examiners People who perform the actual forensics examination of digital hardware or software. They can give testimony on their findings or other related matters.

digital hash A value created by using a mathematical formula (a hashing algorithm) that translates a file into a unique hexadecimal code value; used to determine whether data in a file has changed or been altered.

discovery The process of identifying, locating, securing, and producing information and materials for use in litigation.

document management system (DMS) A system that uses a central repository to help sort documents according to their relevance and applicable regulations. *See also* central document repository.

duty to preserve A provision of the FRCP that states a company involved in a case must retain all documents and data pertaining to the case.

e-discovery Gathering ESI for use in litigation. *See also* electronically stored information (ESI).

e-discovery consultants People or companies providing a broad range of e-discovery services or advice, from digital forensics and data collection to file conversions, database administration, and hosting; these services sometimes include trial consulting.

electronic data interchange (EDI) A system for automating business transactions and transmitting documents electronically; widely used before the Internet was available.

Electronic Discovery Reference Model (EDRM) A model developed as a guideline for handling electronic evidence and culling what's relevant. It includes these stages: information management, identification, preservation, collection, processing, review, analysis, production, and presentation.

electronically stored information (ESI) Any information stored electronically or in a digital format.

event data recorders (EDRs) Devices that record the use of airbags, brakes, safety belts, and so forth. The National Highway Transportation Safety Commission describes them as a contribution to safe roads; others consider them a violation of privacy.

evidence The testimony of witnesses and the introduction of records, documents, exhibits, objects, or any other probative matter offered for the purpose of convincing a judge, jury, or other litigation party of a fact or belief.

expert Under FRE 702, a person with special knowledge, experience, training, education, or skills; can also function as a consultant.

fact-finding The process of reviewing discovery to find evidence related to case issues.

Family Educational Rights and Privacy Act (FERPA) An act created to protect students' educational records. It allows parents or students to examine records and request corrections and prevents this information from being shared without their written permission.

Federal Rules of Civil Procedure (FRCP) Rules created by the U.S. Supreme Court that govern the way evidence and procedures are applied in civil cases.

Federal Rules of Criminal Procedure (FRCrP) Rules created by the U.S. Supreme Court to ensure that defendants' constitutionally guaranteed rights are protected in federal court cases.

Federal Rules of Evidence (FRE) Rules that spell out how evidence can be gathered and used in both civil and criminal cases in U.S. federal courts. Created by the U.S. Supreme Court and signed into law in 1975, the FRE have been updated and amended by both Congress and the Supreme Court.

fielded searching Searching for words or data that might not be in the document contents but are important descriptors; they're entered in database fields during the coding process.

FIRAC A method used to analyze cases; stands for facts, issues, rules and references, analysis, and conclusions.

forensic linguistics A new method that relies on a person's unique use of language to determine who wrote a particular document or e-mail.

forensics mediator A forensics expert who is neutral to the case and functions as a mediator between parties.

Freedom of Information Act (FOIA) An act that allows requesting information stored by the U.S. federal government. Exceptions to this rule include items of national security, trade secrets, medical records, and cases in the process of being litigated.

full-text searching Searching document contents that have been converted to OCR.

fuzzy searching A sophisticated search method that finds even misspelled words.

Gramm-Leach-Bliley Act An act that restricts the disclosure of nonpublic personal information stored by financial institutions. *See also* nonpublic personal information (NPI).

Health Information Technology for Economic and Clinical Health Act (HITECH) An act created to allow placing patients' healthcare records online to improve the efficiency of physicians accessing their records.

Health Insurance Portability and Accountability Act (HIPAA) A federal law that protects patients' privacy and requires notifying them when third parties are given access to their medical records.

information governance A method for ensuring that data is managed correctly from the top down.

Information Governance Reference Model (IGRM) A model created during development of the EDRM that targets information management. It illustrates the processes of information management and the effects on these processes of communication and collaboration between three groups: legal, risk-management, and regulatory departments; business users; and IT support staff. *See also* Electronic Discovery Reference Model (EDRM).

interrogatories Under FRCP 33, written lists of questions served by one party to another. *For criminal cases, see* bill of particulars.

key field A database field used to hold a unique record identifier.

legal hold An order to preserve data in anticipation of litigation, an audit, a government investigation, or another matter; it prohibits people from destroying or processing records. *See also* preservation letter.

load file A set of scanned images or electronically processed files containing pages and attachments to documents, e-mails, or files. A load file can also contain data related to documents it contains, such as selected metadata, coded data, and extracted text.

MAC times Metadata that specifies dates and times that a file was modified, accessed, and created. *See also* metadata.

meet and confer A meeting required by FRCP 26(f) that takes place between opposing counsel and unrepresented parties to address potential problems of discovery, scheduling, and other case matters.

metadata Information about data that can be used to determine when a file was created, modified, accessed, or destroyed.

Metadata Encoding and Transmission Standard (METS) The standard used for objects in a digital library; developed by the Digital Library Association and maintained by the Library of Congress.

motion for protective order This motion is filed to prevent records (such as those involving a company's trade secrets) from becoming part of the public domain.

motion to compel A form of legal pleading used to force the opposition to produce evidence previously requested but not delivered.

motion to quash A legal procedure used to reject, invalidate, or suppress evidence.

native file A file in the originating application's format, such as a Microsoft Word document in `.doc` or `.docx` format.

nonpublic personal information (NPI) Data that can specify an individual, such as Social Security numbers.

normalization The process of standardizing data formats.

objective coding Automated or manual coding done to search for bibliographic data (such as names and dates). *See also* coding.

Online Communications and Geolocation Protection Act (OCGPA) A bill proposed to amend the Electronic Communications and Privacy Act that would limit access to e-mail and GPS location information without a warrant.

optical character recognition (OCR) A software method of scanning a picture (or a scanned picture of a document) and converting the characters to text.

pattern search A search method used to find items that follow a specific pattern of letters or numbers, such as phone numbers, credit cards, and IP addresses.

personal health information (PHI) Confidential information collected by a medical practitioner for the purposes of treatment; includes medical tests, lab results, insurance data, and so forth. This information is protected under HIPAA.

Personal Information Protection and Electronic Documents Act (PIPEDA) Canada's privacy act.

predictive coding A new search method that combines computer speed with human reasoning in a form of artificial intelligence, used to sort and index files. It's useful in dealing with large volumes of data efficiently. *See also* coding.

preservation letter Same as a legal hold but typically used between opposing counsel. *See also* legal hold.

proportionality Under FRCP 26(b)(2), the process of limiting the burden of discovery by weighing it against its likely benefits. This concept can also be applied to criminal cases.

protected computer A computer used exclusively by a financial institution or government entity or used in interstate or foreign commerce.

protected discovery Any case material that must be shielded during the review process, such as trade secrets or witness identities.

redaction Obscuring or removing privileged or proprietary information from a file or document before it's produced.

request for admission Under FRCP 36, a form of discovery that asks the opposing party to accept or deny certain facts of the case in writing and under oath.

request for production Under FRCP 34, a form of discovery, usually in writing, that requests documents, electronically stored information, or other tangible items; can also be used in criminal cases.

reverse funnel method An analogy describing how discovery can begin with small, targeted data collections and expand in scope based on parsing and reviewing data in the initial collection.

Sarbanes-Oxley Act A law passed in the wake of the bankruptcies of Enron and WorldCom that requires retaining documentation for up to seven years.

search incident to arrest A term used to specify that law enforcement can search an arrested person and anything in the immediate vicinity, including clothes, purses, briefcases, and so forth.

special master Under FRCP 53, someone appointed by the court to perform a certain role or duties; can also be used in criminal cases.

stemming A search method that finds all variations of a word.

subpoena duces tecum A written command issued by the court (or a lawyer as an agent of the court) to appear with certain evidence or to permit some action, such as inspecting property.

summary judgment A decision rendered by the court, usually before trial, that eliminates an issue in dispute.

synonym search A search method used to find words with similar meanings. Typically requires uploading a thesaurus.

targeted e-discovery scope An e-discovery method that focuses on small data collections, usually from specified data locations or custodians; typically, the data collection is expanded as relevant data is identified.

under seal This policy allows keeping protected discovery away from public access and review. *See also* protected discovery.

unified messaging The capability to store audio, video, text, SMS, and other data formats in the same mailbox in a mobile device.

Uniform Task-Based Management System (UTBMS) A task-based billing system that assigns a code to each legal task.

unitization The process of organizing documents and attachments. Physical unitization uses physical features (date, title, staples, folders, and so on) of pages to identify a complete document. Logical unitization uses human interpretation of page content to identify a complete document.

value-added networks (VANs) Third-party service providers for transferring EDI documents. *See also* electronic data interchange (EDI).

waiver of privilege Usually an involuntary surrender of a right to attorney-client privilege under FRE 502; typically includes documents produced but not noted in a privilege log.

wildcard search A search method that uses a question mark (?) to search for a single-character variation or an asterisk (*) to match a combination of characters.

witness impeachment The process of attacking the accuracy of a witness's testimony or showing that a witness isn't credible.

work-product privilege This privilege protects any work an attorney has done in representing a client, including writings, statements, and testimony; also includes an attorney's impressions, tactics, opinions, and thoughts.

Index